The Holy Way

the Holy Way

Practices for a simple life

PAULA HUSTON

LOYOLAPRESS.

CHICAGO

LOYOLAPRESS.

3441 N. ASHLAND AVENUE
CHICAGO, ILLINOIS 60657
(800) 621-1008
WWW.LOYOLABOOKS.ORG

Cover and interior design by Megan Duffy Rostan
Cover photo: © Shaun Egan/Getty Images

Library of Congress Cataloging-in-Publication Data
Huston, Paula.
  The holy way : practices for a simple life / Paula Huston.
    p. cm.
Includes bibliographical references and index.
  ISBN 0-8294-1441-X
  1. Spiritual life—Catholic Church. 2. Simplicity—Religious aspects—Catholic Church. I. Title.
  BX2350.3.H87 2003
  248.4'82—dc22

                                        2003018764

Printed in the United States of America
03 04 05 06 07 08 09 10 Versa 10 9 8 7 6 5 4 3 2 1

devoted much time and energy to this project, and their care and concern are much appreciated.

Other people not directly involved in the writing of this book but crucial to my being able to write at all are, first and always, my beloved husband, Mike, without whose support I would not be able to think about such projects; my dear friends and fellow oblates, particularly Hunter and Janet; my four kids—Andrea, Johnny, Kelly, and Greta; my clan of siblings—Gail, Ron, Gretchen, and Tina (Hi, Mom!); my longtime breakfast partner, Ken; our local Merton expert, Larry; my extended family of in-laws and nieces and nephews; the early Mass crowd at St. Pat's in Arroyo Grande; and the international Camaldolese kinship group, particularly the monks of Big Sur, Berkeley, Rome, Umbria, and Tuscany.

Acknowledgments

I am grateful to many people for helping make this book possible. First and foremost, to my friend and agent Tom Grady, who not only proposed the idea—a book about the Christian simple life—but also suggested that I tie each chapter to a particular saint. Then, he rolled up his sleeves and went to work on the first draft of chapter 1 and didn't quit till we were both happy with it. Fr. Raniero Hoffman, present prior of New Camaldoli Hermitage, graciously allowed me to use the community's library, which saved me months of research time. My local oblate group provided a sounding board as I was working out various chapters. I owe a special debt of gratitude to Donna Stone, who read both the first and second drafts of the entire manuscript and caught all sorts of embarrassing glitches. I am also grateful to Fr. Bruno Barnhart, former prior of New Camaldoli, who took on the role of "technical advisor" in the areas of spirituality and monasticism, thereby helping to steer me through dangerous waters. Many additional thanks to Fr. Michael Fish, oblate master extraordinaire, Fr. Romuald Duscher, shepherd of our local group, and Fr. Isaiah Teichert, intrepid spiritual guide. My editors at Loyola Press— Vinita Wright, Matthew Diener, and Jim Manney—

CONTENTS

I recommend to you holy simplicity.

St. Francis de Sales

For Gail, who lives in the spirit of St. Francis

Introduction

How narrow the gate and constricted
the road that leads to life. And those
who find it are few.

Jesus, in Matthew 7:14

We were walking down a dirt lane, pretending hard
not to be what we actually were: tourists from
California, out gawking at the Amish. It was still quite
early—the dawn sky was a sober pearl gray—and we were
hoping to do some undetected snooping before the world
woke up and caught us in the act. Mike was there to
check out the classic Pennsylvania Dutch barns (he'd just
spent two years building a modern version on our four
acres at home), while I greedily inspected tomato after fat
heirloom tomato.

We both come from farming backgrounds—Minnesota
Norwegians on my side and Kansas Scotch-Irish on his—
but that doesn't quite explain our ongoing fascination
with this closed-off and seemingly antiquated culture.
The capacious white farmhouses, the horse-drawn plows
sitting idle on this Sabbath morning, the wooden water
mills, the flower gardens spilling over with sweet peas
and hollyhocks: these were strangely powerful images,

symbols, perhaps, of a better way of life, one that seemed hauntingly familiar yet completely out of our reach.

Then from behind us came the measured clop-clopping of hooves on pavement, and we realized to our dismay that the Amish get up very early indeed and that we were about to be engulfed by black buggies on their way to church. "Don't turn around," I whispered, embarrassed that these very private people had caught us on their private road.

Mike, equally uncomfortable, nodded, and we picked up the pace, just an innocent couple out for some morning exercise. Then the first horse, a sleek healthy bay with white stockings, trotted past. We allowed ourselves a single sideways glance; there sat the driver, a big man with a wide black hat and a beard that began at the edges of his jaw. Beside him was his wife. They did not look at us, nor did they smile, but as they passed by, each of them lifted a hand as though in benediction.

Framed in the back window of the buggy were two small blonds, perfect replicas of their parents, staring out at the strangers on their isolated lane. What were they thinking, these farm children of a bygone era? How must we have appeared to them? I longed to run after them and ask—yet at the same time I wished that we could vanish on the spot. No matter how I wanted to deny it, the modern world trailed along behind us, noxious and invisible and inevitably mucking up whatever it touched. Our innocent desire to momentarily join them in their seventeenth-century lives could only do damage in the long run. We needed to leave.

This, at least, was the easy way to explain the oddly wrenching impact of that Sunday morning scene. I couldn't seem to forget about it; years later, the image was still rising in me, poignant and compelling. I finally decided that we'd been born in the wrong era; we were not meant to live in a society of blinking computer screens and jammed freeways. And certainly this discouragement with contemporary life was not entirely misplaced. Indeed, we do live in an anxious culture, a "culture of despair," as some have called it. In many ways, we seem to have lost our moorings, while people like the Amish apparently still know who and what they are. Thus, my yearning for the simple beauty and order of their lives could not be dismissed as mere romantic fantasy.

But my sense of longing that morning could not have been generated solely by the problems of modernism. For centuries, people of widely varying cultures and times—some just as rural as the Amish—have struggled to get clear, to find a less cluttered kind of life. For the majority, it has been enough to simply read about and admire those (such as Buddha and Socrates) who actually managed to live this way. Others—"extremists" like Gandhi—could not rest until they put it into practice for themselves. Catholic history is literally crowded with this kind of saint.

For Mike and me, the Amish seemed to be guardians of a treasure long since forgotten by our own society: the secret to a simple, integrated life. I've slowly come to believe, however, that what was lost can be found again, that no matter what the existing circumstances, a decision for simplicity can be made. When this decision is taken seriously, it can provide a powerful alternative to the status quo.

Simplicity can provide that alternative because, first of all, it generates hope. In a consumerist society like ours, people who wish to live simply must make a series of intentional choices *against* what is habitual, like the unrestrained use of credit cards, driving when walking is possible, and the unchallenged notion that faster or bigger or newer is always better. In the process of saying no, they will discover that they can successfully resist manipulation by faceless commercial or political forces. They can retain their own power and dignity in the face of immense pressure to become objects instead of human beings.

Second, simplicity leads to greater unity, both within an individual and in society at large. When people control or entirely set aside materialistic desires, when they let go of raging ambition, and when they challenge media-generated paranoia, they no longer feel torn in a hundred directions. Interior chaos subsides; the psychic battlefield goes calm and silent. People can experience themselves as whole and at peace, at one instead of fragmented. They begin to see others as compatriots ("My joy!" as St. Seraphim of Sarov used to greet every stranger he met) instead of as competitors or, worse, wolves masquerading as sheep.[1]

Finally, when adopted with a whole heart and for a lifetime, simplicity leads to an often striking tranquility. This, in spite of the fact that such a life is not necessarily easy—many times, in fact, it is quite difficult. Certainly, convenience and comfort are not its core values. Hard work, both manual and mental, has traditionally accompanied intentional living. Security issues inevitably arise. Freed up from *needless* worry, however, people can think more clearly about what they do and how they do it. Thus, a genuinely simple life is one in which actions are more often rooted in principles than in the demands of the emotions.

At least some of the "good news" that Jesus brought had to do with this kind of liberation. The New Testament is filled with reassurances that this world is a safe place for us to be. Time and again, Jesus reminds us that God loves us and will provide what we need. "Therefore I tell you, do not worry about your life and what you will eat, or about your body and what you will wear," he says. "For life is more than food and the body more than clothing" (Luke 12:22–23). He continues, "Can any of you by worrying add a moment to your lifespan? If even the smallest things are beyond your control, why are you anxious about the rest?" (Luke 12:25–26).

Jesus doesn't promise that we will find this a comfortable way to live, but he does assure us that even when human life seems to be a terrible struggle, we are not alone. He says, "Do not be afraid any longer, little flock, for your Father is pleased to give you the kingdom" (Luke 12:32). In other words: Calm yourselves. Be still. Listen.

In my own life, the yearning for simplicity preceded my first attempts to make any actual changes by many years. Like most contemporary women, I worked full-time. We had four children to support, a mortgage to pay, cars to fuel, groceries to buy, insurance to maintain, tax bills with which to deal. We had siblings (eight of them between us), elderly parents, friends, students, and social responsibilities. Along with my university teaching job, I was also a writer.

The hours were so jammed with activity that I often lay awake half the night prioritizing my responsibilities for the following day. The apparently serene and focused life of the Amish seemed miles and eons away from the one *I* was living. You can't do this, I told myself, unless you walk away completely and become a cloistered nun or join a religious commune. The modern reality is that we can't slow down for a minute, much less go back to milking cows. It's hopeless.

Then, in Mass, I would hear it again, the call of the Gospels to a simpler, purer life:

> "Notice how the flowers grow. They do not toil or spin. But I tell you, not even Solomon in all his splendor was dressed like one of them. If God so clothes the grass in the field that grows today and is thrown into the oven tomorrow, will he not much more provide for you, O you of little faith?" (Luke 12:27–28)
>
> "Provide money bags for yourselves that do not wear out, an inexhaustible treasure in heaven that no thief can reach nor moth destroy. For where your treasure is, there also will your heart be." (Luke 12:33–34)
>
> "Do not work for food that perishes but for the food that endures for eternal life, which the Son of Man will give you." (John 6:27)

"Peace I leave with you; my peace I give to
you. Not as the world gives do I give it to you.
Do not let your hearts be troubled or afraid."
(John 14:27)

Over and over, I heard that gentle, insistent urging to
rethink my direction, to stop my anxious striving.

Eventually, thanks to a friend who invited me to come
along with her, I was introduced to a simple-living community much closer at hand than the Amish: the monks of
New Camaldoli Hermitage on the central coast of
California. The white-cowled Camaldolese of Big Sur live
in many ways as they lived a thousand years ago in Italy,
where the order first began. Their day is ordered around
the ringing of the bells, the multiple calls to worship and
prayer that take precedence over whatever work they might
be doing. I'd never seen anything remotely equivalent.
Even during my first brief visit, I sensed that this, perhaps,
was the place I'd been looking for, the place that might
teach me what I'd been trying so long to grasp on my own.

A two-hour drive from my home near San Luis
Obispo, the hermitage was close enough for frequent day
trips—sometimes just for Mass followed by a picnic overlooking the sea, and sometimes, despite the winding road
and evening fog, for a whole precious morning and afternoon. On occasion, I talked with whichever monk was on
duty in the bookstore, asking as many questions as I
thought he could bear, but most often I simply walked or
sat watching from a bench. Eventually, I began to make
retreats of several days, learning a little more each time

about the disciplines of monastic simplicity. Inevitably, I tried to carry some of these home with me, down the mountain and back into what I called the real world.

The reasons I might have set out on this course of simplicity are myriad: it is better for the environment; it is "fairer" to the rest of the world if I adopt a simpler lifestyle; the original Americans intended for us to live this way; it is healthier; it is infinitely more enjoyable; I am a nicer person when I let go of things. Certainly any of these are a compelling enough reason to give it a try. I've found, however, that to sustain the experiment, I've had to take my cue from the Camaldolese monks and the Amish farmers: I've had to anchor myself in a single, central reality—my longing for God—and allow everything else to arrange itself accordingly.

In doing so, I've made an interesting, if painful, discovery: the path to simplicity runs right through the middle of *me*. In other words, the world may be a complicated and confusing place, but even if it were as serene as a Japanese garden, I'd manage to stir things up for myself. I've developed a large collection of habitual attitudes over the years, and these hold me in complicated thrall no matter what the setting. Most of the clutter, in fact, has turned out to be internal rather than external, a result of the kind of person I am rather than the time and place in which I live.

It is extremely difficult to let go of these longtime habits of thinking, emotional response, and reaction. When Jesus reminds Peter that the spirit is willing but the flesh is weak, this is in part what he means. Too often we are tripped up not by serious temptation or dramatic sin but by ingrained patterns, some of which are so much a part of us that we can no longer even recognize a different approach. It is far easier, far more comfortable, to do what we've always done than to change our ways.

One of the first tricks I tried to play on myself was to pretend that some parts of me were exempt from this difficult transformative process, for example, my tendency to exaggerate. *This* trait, I told myself, comes with a writer's personality—and there's absolutely nothing I can do about it if I want to keep on being a writer. God made me a writer, so who am I to change what he put in me in the first place? Besides, exaggerating has nothing to do with my spiritual life.

It did not take long to figure out that the quest for a simpler, holier life eventually must touch on every aspect of our nature, and that Jesus refers to the spiritual path as the "narrow way" for a good reason. It is sometimes wrenching to see just what a complicated muddle we've made of ourselves, and why it is we have allowed that to happen. It's even more painful to realize that there are no "spiritual holidays"—that there is no division at all between the secular and the spiritual—when we truly understand what St. Paul means when he says, "So whoever is in Christ is a new creation: the old things have passed away; behold, new things have come" (2 Cor. 5:17). We put off the old version of ourselves so as to make way for the new.

For this reason I found myself leaning heavily and gratefully through the years on exemplars: particular people

who had actually *done* what I was trying (so often unsuccessfully) to do. Christianity is a gold mine of such individuals. From the Desert Fathers to the medieval
mendicants to Mother Teresa's Missionaries of Charity, the
tradition overflows with proof that a simpler, holier life is
indeed possible, and that this quest begins in pretty much
the same way for all of us: in a sincere desire to change.

In addition to the powerful examples of the lives of the
saints, one of which is discussed in each chapter of this
book, there are the legacies that they left behind, often in
the form of a new or reformed order: the Benedictines,
the Cistercians, the Franciscans, the Jesuits. Taken
chronologically, the histories of these various foundations
and reforms become to a large degree the history of
Catholicism. I approached them here in a different way—
thematically rather than chronologically—but found in
the course of writing this book that they fell into a certain
historical order after all. I have extracted from each
order's Rule that which best supports and explains the
principle of simplicity I discuss in each chapter.

The word *rule,* as Thomas More points out, comes
from the Latin term *regula,* which in Roman times meant
"pattern" or "model." Such models, I've found, can be just
as helpful in their own way as the examples of saintly lives.
The rules of each order were written in response to the
reality of lived community experience. They were not the-
oretical, but practical, the result of much trial and error.

When I finally took oblate vows at New Camaldoli
Hermitage—vows that formalized my by then long-
standing relationship with the community—I promised to

incorporate into my nonmonastic life, in whatever way I might best do this, the Brief Rule of St. Romuald: "Sit in your cell as in a paradise. Put the whole world behind you, and forget it. Watch your thoughts like a good fisherman watching for fish. . . ."[2] His little rule might be more appropriately called "Some Advice from St. Romuald for Struggling Neophyte Contemplatives," and it is not the kind of monastic rule that communities actually adopt. Still, it has helped me redirect the flow of my days, as it no doubt also helped those eleventh-century Benedictines who became the Camaldolese, those long-ago monks who yearned for more solitude and silent prayer.

The more I've immersed myself in the Christian way of simplicity, the more I've come to see how much of that path we share with *all* the major world religions, for the simple life is most often taken up by those on a quest for holiness. Each religion adds or subtracts certain tenets, but the overall pattern is startlingly similar, whether the doctrine is Hindu, Buddhist, Taoist, Jewish, or Muslim, or whether one is looking at one of the major strains of Christianity: Protestant, Orthodox, or Catholic.

People of all faiths have long taken note of a "perennial philosophy," a common wisdom that grows naturally out of the practice of various age-old disciplines. Unfortunately, contemporary Christians—unless they happen to be monastics—do not hear much about this anymore. Those who wish to find out what these practices are often have to do some serious digging. I certainly did, and this in spite of the fact that so many people these days seem to be searching for the same lost treasure.

The bedrock of this perennial philosophy is lived experience in such areas as solitude, silence, asceticism (fasting, for example), chastity, poverty, and meditation. The principles of simplicity discussed in each chapter of this book are rooted in these disciplines. Some of them—solitude, for example, or right livelihood—will no doubt seem more or less compatible with contemporary values. Others, such as the ancient forms of asceticism or chastity, can seem antithetical to modern notions about self-fulfillment.

Taken together, these disciplines reveal an integrated picture of human nature, a sort of anthropology that is both very old and surprisingly current. First, they help bring into focus our common identity, the fact that we are, every one of us, made in the image of God. Bombarded as we are with examples of human evil, it is very easy to forget or even deny this central spiritual truth. The quest for holy simplicity, however, is *founded* on the notion that there is something better—something actually divine—at our core. We have lost sight of this wonderful fact because we are often hopelessly distracted by needless anxiety and tyrannous desire.

When we experience ourselves in the light of these age-old practices, we understand who we are as individuals. We recognize—and even cherish—that heavy bundle of attributes and defects that will bend our backs throughout a lifetime. Orthodox theologian Paul Evdokimov calls this burden of individuality our "personal cross," defining it as a "combination of what is given and what is desired." The disciplines of simplicity, rooted as they are in the larger spiritual disciplines, have the uncanny ability to reveal that cross and hence "the facts of our destiny."[3]

Though at times this can be painful, the alternative—not to know who we are, why we are here, and what we are meant to do—is more agonizing by far. Only in retrospect can I see that my wistful yearning for a simpler life held this at the center: I could not rest until the vast clutter of shoulds and oughts and want-tos, fears and angers and addictions, had been cleared away long enough to glimpse what I am in relationship to God. Though I'm starting to grasp that this will be a lifelong process and that we humans always see through a glass darkly, when it comes to the most important truths, the path itself provides me with enough meaning to keep at it.

As Evdokimov says, the spiritual journey "introduces order, reveals the rhythm of its own growth, and requires a progressive march."[4] It keeps us moving *toward* instead of *away from*. Even when it drags into view our deepest and most shameful wounds, our most fiercely guarded secrets, it does so in service of that forward movement, that progress toward the light. Without seeing ourselves as we are, we can never see ourselves as we were meant to be.

The seventh-century ascetic St. Isaac the Syrian, steeped in the hard-won wisdom of this same spiritual path, reminds us that there is nothing more important that we can do with our time here on earth. The willingness to look at what we have become in the world and then do our best, in partnership with God, to change that borders on the miraculous for St. Isaac. If we can only stay with it, this lifetime struggle ultimately teaches us that it is the "simplicity of God [that] unites" while it is the "complexity of evil [that] disperses."[5] This is why he insists so strongly that "[he] who sees himself as he is, is greater than one who raises the dead."[6]

St. Paul urges the same quest upon us in his letter to the Ephesians, the quest so clearly taken up by the Amish, the monks of New Camaldoli, and everyone throughout the ages who has ever heard and responded to the thrilling challenge of the Gospels: "Awake, O sleeper, / and arise from the dead, / and Christ will give you light" (Eph. 5:14). My hope is that in these complicated times of ours we can rediscover the joy and peace that accompany this difficult journey; and that somewhere along the way we can reclaim our lost simplicity.

PART I

WITHDRAWING AND TAKING STOCK

A genuine life change is often a dramatic life change because of the uproar that ensues. The great tectonic shift in human character that we call "conversion" leaves everyone exhausted. The realization that we are unnecessarily complicating our lives—that there is a better way to live and that we must ourselves undergo transformation in order to find it—can hit with all the force of a full-scale conversion experience. This makes sense when we realize that a whole set of values, some of them never before questioned, is being relinquished in favor of a new way of thinking—a way that those closest to us may unfortunately find irresponsible or even irrational.

For a while, nothing in our changing lives seems to fit. Family relationships are put to the test. Friendships either accommodate the transformation or quietly fade away. Sometimes anger predominates (if I'd known you were going to do *this,* I never would have married you). A more likely response is grief (what's come over you? you didn't use to think this way). We are leaving something—a certain kind of relationship based on a certain set of shared beliefs—behind forever. In a very real sense, something is dying.

Our natural response is self-protective withdrawal. It is too much to cope with such monumental changes in ourselves while dealing with the adverse reaction of others. We feel hurt (nobody understands!) and even abused (he promised to love me for better or for worse!). Self-doubt sets in (maybe I'm crazy after all) coupled with loneliness (am I ever going to find someone who thinks like I do?).

All of this is to be expected. It is confirmation that the transformation, so long felt as a kind of vague but insistent subterranean rumbling, has actually begun to manifest itself publicly. It is proof that the change is not imaginary; other people are noticing it, too. This is exciting, and some of the bleakness lifts a bit. A new thought comes: Okay, if I'm going to have to go it alone for a while, I might as well see what's up ahead without worrying about all my usual distractions. Suddenly the withdrawal, at first so self-protective, becomes an opportunity to grow.

The two chapters in this section, "Solitude: The Way of the Hermit" and "Silence: The Way of the Cenobite," are about this first stage on the path of holy simplicity. They are about what happens to us when we realize we must simplify our lives, regardless of the cost. They are about that cost, which can sometimes cause considerable pain. They are also about the dawning of a new realization about life and its purpose, and this dawning can come to us only when we are alone and quiet. Such insight is the unexpected reward of those who allow themselves—often with great guilt and trepidation—to temporarily disconnect from the rush and whirl of the world.

These chapters also deal with one of the earliest movements in Christianity, that of withdrawal to the desert in order to find God. St. Anthony (A.D. 251–356) is considered to be the first important Christian hermit; St. Pachomius (A.D. 292–346) founded the first Christian monasteries. Between them, they laid the foundations for a path that is still being followed today.

CHAPTER I

Solitude:
The Way of the Hermit

> Just as fish die if they stay too long out
> of water, so the monks who loiter
> outside their cells or pass their time
> with men of the world lose the
> intensity of inner peace. So like a fish
> going towards the sea, we must hurry
> to reach our cell, for fear that if we
> delay outside we will lose our inner
> watchfulness.[1]
>
> *St. Anthony the Great (A.D. 251–356)*

Henry David Thoreau believed that the only way he could simplify his life—to live "deliberately," as he put it—was to leave society and build himself a tiny, rough-hewn cabin in the woods surrounding Walden Pond. Long ago, I saw a replica of that cabin, and it intrigued me. What would it be like to seek out the path that leads to solitary purity as Thoreau did?

Later, as an overburdened adult, I sometimes yearned for solitude with such intensity that it frightened me.

This longing was potentially disruptive, even dangerous; the price for abandoning my responsibilities to go off on a Walden-quest would have been far too steep, and of course I *knew* that. Yet in the midst of my bustling life, I could not help dreaming of peaceful silence, and Thoreau's little cabin in the woods hung in my mind as the very image of sanctuary.

It was this impulse toward solitude that first attracted me to the community of hermit monks at Big Sur. I'd read about such people—people who deliberately withdrew from the normal hustle of life in order to focus on God—but I thought they were long-vanished historical anomalies, admirable though certainly half crazy. Perhaps they were so eccentric that they'd had no *choice* but to live a solitary life. At New Camaldoli, however, I found a surprisingly varied group of twenty-seven men united by, among other things, their obvious ability to get by in the world quite well, had this been what they had chosen to do. Painters and craftsmen, poets and scholars, gardeners and mechanics, carpenters and cooks, they were a multitalented bunch with charisma to spare.

Which is probably why so many people seek them out. Their 860 acres of wilderness, five hours north of Los Angeles and four hours south of San Francisco, attract a constant stream of visitors and retreatants; the nine-room guesthouse and three private hermitages are booked six months to a year in advance. People come for a multitude of reasons—for the peace and beauty of the landscape, for the well-stocked bookstore, for the Benedictine liturgies throughout the day, for spiritual guidance—and once they come, they are often drawn back again and again.

In the midst of this little beehive live the monks themselves, doing their best to fulfill their roles as hosts at the same time that they are living out their vocations as hermits. Each of them has his own cell within the monastic compound, a simple apartment of 1950s' yellow stucco attached to a small garden that is screened off by slat-wood fences. Each has his duties within the community—booking reservations for the guesthouse, for example, or keeping the bookstore running. Not exactly solitude as Thoreau knew it. Yet ultimately, the focus at the Hermitage is on contemplative prayer, both communal and individual, which means that a lot of time is spent alone.

The Greek root for *hermit* is *eremites,* which in turn comes from *eremia* ("desert"). The word came into Christian usage in the third century, when hundreds of men and women from Palestine and Egypt fled to the barren, rocky caves of the Negev and the Sinai. Here they often stayed for decades, preferring their isolated and austere existences to anything civilization could offer. It is from this group that the so-called Desert Fathers arose. Eight hundred years later, the Camaldolese—Benedictine monks with a strong need for more silence and solitude than was possible in the large monasteries of the day—made central to their practice the withdrawal to a symbolic desert or wilderness.

The Big Sur hermitage is thus appropriately situated. Perched as it is on the steep shoulder of a mountain overlooking the Pacific, it demands a certain hardiness and chutzpah from those visitors it attracts—particularly during the winter rainy season when Highway 1 is regularly blocked by landslides, some of which take months for highway workers to bulldoze aside. Worse, every few years the ridge is cut off entirely by mounds of soupy mud and boulders—then, the only way out is to hike over the top of these mounds to a vehicle waiting on the other side.

The hot fall season brings a new danger. Multistory thunderheads, charged with dry lightning, pile up over the mountains. A single rainless storm can bring fire, a whirlwind of exploding pine trees and crackling sage, and animals scurrying for their lives. The monks have been evacuated more than once, but they have never been burned out. It's a dangerous, incandescently beautiful world that they inhabit.

By their deliberate choice of this isolated and often harsh setting, the Camaldolese of Big Sur are helping to keep alive the long tradition of Christian solitude. During my Protestant childhood, I never heard much about this tradition except through its relatively recent transcendental offspring—Thoreau, for example. Later, as a Catholic adult, I picked up oblique references to the Desert Fathers, but very little solid information, except what I happened to read on my own. During one of my early retreats at the hermitage, however, I came across an excerpt from St. Athanasius's *Vita St. Antonii,* where I first read about St. Anthony the Great, one of the earliest of those third-century solitaries we know anything about. This discovery led me to realize that, from the beginning, solitude has been an integral aspect of Christianity.

St. Anthony in the Desert

Anthony was born about A.D. 251 in the village Koma, approximately sixty miles south of Cairo, Egypt. His parents were prosperous farmers who owned more than 250 acres of fertile Nile valley cropland, and he was their heir. The family were devout Christians during an era of intense persecution launched by official edict of the Roman emperor Decius. Like all Egyptian believers, they faced the prospect of being forced to sign a *libellus*—a written statement of their loyalty to the old divinities— and to make public sacrifice to these gods. If they refused to sign the *libellus,* they could be tortured or killed.

Their small Christian community would have certainly urged them not to recant, no matter what the consequences. This was partly because of the strong belief in parousia, or the imminent Second Coming, which was very much in the air. Equally influential was the growing phenomenon of martyrdom: the crumbling Roman Empire seemed to be a seedbed for religious heroism. Chrisitians of that time were willing to die rather than renounce their faith, a position that might seem extreme to many of us today.

When Anthony was about twenty, both his parents died. Suddenly, he was put in charge of their land, their wealth, and his younger sister; suddenly, he was a rich young man. This is perhaps why, some months later, a sermon about Jesus' conversation with the rich young man of the Gospels struck him with such overwhelming force: "If you wish to be perfect, go, sell what you have and give to [the] poor, and you will have treasure in heaven. Then come, follow me" (Matt. 19:21).

Like St. Francis of Assisi almost a thousand years later, Anthony left church that day, went home, and began giving away all that he had, starting with the 250 acres of prime farmland. In less than eight hours, he divested himself of all the property his parents had accumulated over the years. Afterward, he sold the family furniture and gave most of the money to the poor, retaining only a small portion for the support of his young sister. He then apprenticed himself to one of the "old men," an experienced hermit, who eventually deemed Anthony ready to go off by himself.

He first spent thirteen years in an empty tomb near the village. After that, he walled himself up for two more decades in a decaying fortress at Pispir, where he no doubt would have stayed for the rest of his long life had not would-be disciples finally broken down the door and forced him back into the world.[2]

I didn't quite know what to do with this story. On the one hand, I admired the single-mindedness of a twenty year old who could walk away from money and social status that way. The image was so compelling that for a while I found myself brooding on it in the midst of my daily rounds. On the other hand, Anthony's repudiation of "normal" life seemed terribly irresponsible—whatever happened, for instance, to that poor little sister who, thanks to him, became a brotherless orphan in a village convent? What would Anthony's hardworking parents have thought about the great land giveaway?

I had been raised to believe that our real purpose in life lies in activity, not withdrawal. We are to fight injustice, alleviate pain and suffering, protect the weak and defenseless, and work for the good. Though I'd never even come close to living up to such ideals, they were part and parcel of my nature, the standard against which I measured my life. For me, the significant question was whether solitude could be defended as a valuable enterprise when there was so much out there waiting to be *done.*

I turned from Anthony's story to the Bible, hoping to find there something that would justify or at least explain this strange and seemingly antisocial impulse in both lives, his and my own. To my relief, I discovered that an important part of Christ's teaching did indeed focus on the necessity for extended periods of aloneness. In fact, Jesus required these solitary times himself.

In the book of Mark, for example, Jesus rose "very early before dawn" to go "off to a deserted place, where he prayed" (Mark 1:35). After the feeding of the five thousand, a miracle of stupendous drama, he "made his disciples get into the boat and precede him to the other side toward Bethsaida, while he dismissed the crowd. And when he had taken leave of them, he went off to the mountain to pray" (Mark 6:45–46).

Likewise, when the first apostles went out on their own to preach and heal, they were full of good news on their return and could not quiet down. He listened for a while, then said, "Come away by yourselves to a deserted place and rest a while" (Mark 6:31). This was in part because of the crowd that surrounded them ("they had no opportunity even to eat" [Mark 6:31]), but also because this was how it worked in Jesus' own life: the power he expended teaching and healing could be renewed only in solitude and prayer.

In the books of Mark and Luke particularly, there seems to be a pendulum-like swing between the times of pouring out and the times of taking in. Where had I gotten the notion that *I* was exempt from this spiritual law?

My longing for solitude did not lead to an actual retreat for quite some time, however. The first step was simply sitting alone for fifteen minutes each morning. This, I quickly discovered, was surprisingly difficult for a busy person like me, no matter how much I liked to think about Thoreau's little cabin.

How Solitude Sifted My Soul

We live on a few acres in the country, so I didn't have to seek out a quiet spot in which to do my sitting. Over the years, I'd discovered a number of these potential lairs to which I could escape when life in our sometimes chaotic stepfamily became too much for me. Off I'd trudge into the pines, where I would hide out until I'd calmed down enough to return to the fray. Sometimes Mike and I, the two parents, would find ourselves on either side of a yawning gulf, and back to the pines I'd go, sniffling and waiting for him to hunt me down.

Never before had I gone out just to sit, however. Since I worked full time, I would have to conduct my experiment early in the day. That first morning, I rose to our alarm, which I had set for 5:00 A.M., put on a hooded sweatshirt, folded up a lawn chair, and hiked a hundred yards along the faint trail that snakes across the hillside. There's a huge jack pine out there that towers over all the others, and this is where I set up my solitary outpost.

Within two and a half minutes, however, the dogs, all three of them, had stumbled out of their houses, expectant noses lifted to the dawn breeze, and converged upon me. Next came the cats. After ten minutes or so, they all finally figured out I wasn't moving and wasn't going to move, grew bored, and either returned home or sacked out in the pine needles around my lawn chair. This was not exactly what I had in mind.

Interestingly enough, it was the disappointing or even "failed" attempts, rather than the "successful" ones, that proved most educational in the long run. The daily interruption by those attention-hungry pets, for example, helped highlight at least one disconcerting fact about me and my unsimple life: I often took on unnecessary responsibilities. Evidence of this was the permanent to-do list emblazoned across my brain (the pets were on it, along with many other foolish commitments), and every morning this list had to be deliberately set aside if I was going to sit without squirming.

I soon figured out that the reason I'd been oversleeping for so many years (which meant I had to live the rest of each day at anxious top speed) was embarrassingly straightforward: I was exhausted by the effort of keeping up with my to-do list. I'd always been so indignant at the malicious wizardry of time; instead, I should have long ago taken a look at the impossible number of tasks I was trying to complete each day.

Christ compares faith to a mustard seed, a tiny fleck of botanical matter that nevertheless becomes the tallest and most billowy and yellowest of shrubs. My small, daily, and often failed start at solitude was like the mustard seed. One discovery led to another and then to another, until suddenly I was stumbling over what had previously been well and safely buried: my *real* motivations for doing most of what I did. I was starting to understand that a simple life begins in solitude because this is the only way we can see, as from a sudden distance, the crowd of unnecessary responsibilities threatening to trample us underfoot.

When I actually *did* manage to get out of bed at 5:00 A.M. and sit in that predawn light beneath the jack pine, sometimes shivering, sometimes half asleep, sometimes sipping a cup of steaming coffee, there was a powerful effect on the rest of my day all out of proportion to the time spent in my lawn chair. It was as though I'd centered my day somehow, sighted it and lined it up against reliable quadrants, and everything that followed was much steadier.

Memories of God's Presence

The black pines against the salmon pink sky, the black V of ducks that quacked overhead each morning, the peat-mossy damp smell of night giving way to the rising sun: it all reminded me of something, though it took me a while to figure out what. One morning, I realized that the last time I'd had such pure experiences of the moment was as a child. I'm pretty sure that children are *born* solitaries. By this I mean that most of them seem capable of being in their own company without anxiety or loneliness—that is, if they have not yet learned to think that liking aloneness is a symptom of some serious deficiency.

During those morning sits under the jack pine, my own childhood experiences of solitude, which happened to me between the ages of about eight and ten, slowly resurfaced: all the hours of lying flat in long grass, watching the sky; my beloved limb in the backyard maple, that peaceful cloister of green leaves. The natural world—sunlight, thunderheads, warm grass, birdsong—was more than just beautiful then; it was in some way a comrade, a better friend than I'd ever had before.

I believe that this had been my first taste of God's presence. When I read Psalm 104, I seemed to catch a glimpse of what had been going on in my child's mind:

> Bless the LORD, my soul!
>> LORD, my God, you are great indeed!
> You are clothed with majesty and glory,
>> robed in light as with a cloak.
> You spread out the heavens like a tent;
>> you raised your palace upon the waters.
> You make the clouds your chariot;
>> you travel on the wings of the wind.
> You make the winds your messengers;
>> flaming fire, your ministers. (verses 1–4)

Eventually, Mike built me a wooden bench out there in the pines, a permanent locale for my solitary sitting. I added fifteen minutes of alone time to the end of the day as well. Now the sky flared pink behind me, the same **V** of ducks retraced their morning flight path, the air grew chill, and I began to get a sense, which I hadn't had in years, of being part of all this: the sun's rising and its setting, the day's beginning and ending cupped in two palms far larger than my own.

As Ps. 19:2 reads: "The heavens declare the glory of God; / the sky proclaims its builder's craft." I began to feel in a visceral, deep down way that indeed and of course

> One day to the next conveys that message;
>   one night to the next imparts that
>   knowledge.
> There is no word or sound;
>   no voice is heard;
> Yet their report goes forth through all the earth,
>   their message, to the ends of the world.
>   (Ps. 19:3–5)

I saw for myself that

> God has pitched there a tent for the sun;
>   it comes forth like a bridegroom from his
>   chamber,
>   and like an athlete joyfully runs its course.
> From one end of the heavens it comes forth;
>   its course runs through to the other;
>   nothing escapes its heat. (Ps. 19:5–7)

I asked myself how I had so entirely lost this knowl-edge for so many years. How had I lost my membership in the great creation?

Those quiet moments at the beginning and the end of each day proved to be the heralds of a new era in my life. Once solitude had a grip on me, once I experienced the clarity it brought, I couldn't get enough of it. My long-time ache for Thoreau's little cabin now had a name; my secret yearning for aloneness had an explanation. Perhaps I was not such an oddball after all; perhaps there were many others like me who craved solitude without know-ing exactly what it was we were craving.

I decided to add forty-five minutes of solitary walking to my day. Again, I was fortunate: our property has a horse pasture, and around the horse pasture is a dirt road fringed with ryegrass and wildflowers. There, I could walk without seeing anybody. There, I could go as slowly and meditatively as I wanted.

Perhaps it was the bodily activity, so different from those quiet times on the bench, but walking brought something new into the picture. I tended to think more while I was walking, and my thoughts were both more complex and more logically coherent than usual. Something about putting one foot in front of the other allowed me to take an idea to its natural conclusion in a way that had always been hard for me. Sometimes while struggling to understand what I was learning during these silent, cogitative walks, I'd ask God to send me the spirit of wisdom.

I was aware that my country setting was an unusual blessing in our modern day and age, and every so often I wondered whether one could find solitude in a city. I thought back to the busy suburbs in which I'd grown up, the cars passing ceaselessly up and down the streets, the kids on the sidewalks, shouting and calling to one another, the dogs barking from one backyard to the next. What if I lived in a real city, like New York, where every time I turned my head I saw at least a thousand people coming my direction?

If the desire for solitude was as widespread as I thought, then people must figure out how to find it, even in the urban press. I remembered being in Kathmandu and going up to the rooftop of the my hotel at dawn so that I could write in my journal and perhaps catch a glimpse of the Himalayas in the light of the rising sun. This quiet time, however, was soon invaded by wheeling pigeons landing in clouds on the roofs of buildings all over the city.

It took me a while to realize what the pigeons were waiting for: women carrying shallow plates of uncooked rice and marigold petals. I watched, fascinated, as these sari-clad worshippers bowed and prayed—morning puja—then tossed their offerings to the wind and the birds. They did not look at one another or speak: this time was sacrosanct, their time of solitude at the beginning of otherwise work-filled, noisy urban days.

Is there anything, I wondered, that absolutely precludes a big-city prayer walk? Certainly that kind of environment would be potentially more distracting than the one I took around the horse pasture each day. Yet, birds sing in the city, flowers bloom there, trees flourish. In Portland, I once saw a mother raccoon and her three babies amble across a boulevard in the early morning on their way to the basement of a nearby school. Coyotes lope across parks in Los Angeles, and falcons dive from skyscrapers in New York City. If the natural world can penetrate so deeply within an environment that seems utterly man-made, then surely the spiritual can, too.

Even the man-made can be holy—cities have thousands of churches, mosques, temples, synagogues, and cathedrals that horse pastures can't provide. One can duck inside a heavy wooden door, as I've done in Florence and Athens and Jerusalem, for a long sit in cool darkness among flickering tapers. One's eyes can feast on silver icons, gold crucifixes, and stained-glass windows, or one can kneel in a back pew while somebody practices Bach on a pipe organ.

Even in the most overcrowded conditions, people manage to find ways to be alone. I saw this in India, where for the vast majority of the population privacy as we Americans know it does not exist. Instead, solitude among many has been developed to a high art. Loin-clothed sadhus, or holy men, crawl on their hands and knees along downtown sidewalks. The big-city life swirling around them appears to make no impact at all. Families on their morning visits to street-side shrines seem equally unaffected by the fact that their private worship can be observed by anybody and everybody.

On the banks of holy rivers, cremations are performed on open burning ghats, or broad steps to the river, while the prayers of grieving loved ones rise like incense in the smog-laden air. Spiritual life is lived under the public eye, yet somehow people manage to withdraw into the private chamber of the heart in order to meet God.

There was something else I'd learned in India, something I'd tried not to think about too much over the years but which had now come back to haunt me: The Hindus believe that we must also have times of *genuine* aloneness, times without a single other human being in sight. For centuries, an important later stage of Hindu life has been that of the "forest dweller," one who retreats to a literal wilderness for purposes of spiritual discovery and growth.

As I pondered all this, I realized that something important was still missing from my own practice. Fifteen minutes twice a day and one solitary walk were simply not enough. It was time for me to take the next step: a real retreat.

To Become Like a Child, Alone with God

As I entered the austere little room in the Camaldolese guesthouse where I was to live alone and silently for the next three days, I was grappling with a whole range of emotions: curiosity, anticipation, nervousness, and, maybe most of all, guilt. I'd left my whole family behind, after all, and who knew if this retreat would do me any "good" in the long run.

Perhaps I was still acting on that old Thoreau's-cabin fantasy. Perhaps my powerful intuition about a general human craving for solitude was merely self-serving.

Perhaps I was simply antisocial after all. Maybe I should just turn around and go home.

In the midst of battling these doubts, I realized that I was also experiencing an odd sense of kinship with the countless generations from every religious tradition who've come alone to small bare rooms to think and pray and meditate. St. Anthony turned his impulse toward solitude into a lifetime commitment, but how many others over the centuries had been more like me, people who knew from the start that they'd spend most of their days in "the world" rather than in a hermit's cell, yet still scheduled for themselves regular times of deliberate aloneness?

It was true that my own frenetically bustling culture no longer saw these solitary pursuits as productive or worthwhile, but that sad fact could not take precedence over the wisdom of the ages. No matter how difficult it had been to arrive at this point, and no matter what obstacles lay ahead, I knew I could not stop now.

Heartened, I took a look around. There wasn't much in the room, by contemporary standards: a twin bed, a long plank desk, a wooden kitchen chair, and a recliner of shabby gold velveteen. Beside the recliner sat a floor lamp and a small table on which sat a brown plastic cafeteria tray. On the tray was a plate, a bowl, a fork, a spoon, a coffee cup, a water glass, and a burgundy napkin.

Then I noticed the kneeler sitting beside the single large window. Of simple design and made from blond wood, it was easily the loveliest item in the room. Over the bed hung a small crucifix; over the gold velveteen chair, an icon—the Theotokos, Holy Mother and Child. Near the door was a dish for holy water, now dry. On the wall beside that were the last lines of the Brief Rule of St. Romuald: "Empty yourself completely and sit waiting, content with the grace of God, like the chick who tastes nothing and eats nothing but what his mother gives him."

Now I was flooded again with emotion, this time relief coupled with mild panic. Here I was in a place where nobody knew me. Nobody would knock on my door, nobody could call me. What I did for the next three days was entirely up to me. I could sleep the whole time if I wanted to; I could attend the daily offices with the monks; I could walk up and down the mountain for hours. Or I could read. I never had enough time to read at home. What a gift, I thought. This is *wonderful.*

Then why was I wavering on the edge of tears?

It took the rest of the retreat to figure this out. Meanwhile, there was my bag to unpack, my jacket to hang in the closet, my laptop to set up—duties that took surprisingly little time. I picked up the schedule of services lying on the desk. The earliest—vigils—began at 5:45 A.M. No problem, I thought. That's later than my morning bench session.

Then came lauds at 7:00 A.M. (these two seemed awfully close together) and Eucharist at 11:30. At 6:00 P.M., it was time for vespers, followed by a half hour of meditation in the chapel. I added up all these times and came up with four hours, which was quite a few *more* hours than I'd ever spent in church on a single day. Maybe I should pick two services and leave it at that. I had no idea what was proper, what I could skip without inadvertently violating some monastic convention. Maybe I should stay away from the chapel completely. That way they'd never know I was missing.

This was an unexpected dilemma. I'd thought there would be no decisions to make, that an entirely open landscape (no Mike, no kids, no classes to teach, no pets to feed) meant no choices, either. Instead, the three days that stretched ahead of me seemed to demand a whole *series* of decisions, and this was feeling increasingly strange. What would I do, for example, in the next hour? What about the next ten minutes? Without deadlines, without my routine, I was suddenly floating free, and this was not an entirely pleasant sensation.

I looked again at the kneeler and thought about calling for help, but felt self-conscious for some reason, as though somebody were watching my every move and passing judgment. Surely I could figure out on my own how to fill up an hour. An active, disciplined person like myself could do this.

I wandered to the window, which looked out into a tiny yard. Somebody had planted dry purple flowers and arranged some round stones at the base of what looked like a small fig tree. I thought of Jesus cursing the unproductive fig and was suffused with guilty empathy. With it, I experienced a redoubling of the familiar doubts: Shouldn't I be home doing something useful?

The far edge of the little yard was open to the sea, which from my vantage point looked infinite. I'd never had such a view of the ocean before: a 180-degree sweep of dark blue with glittering silver lines running through it. The midafternoon sun was starting to drop toward the horizon, and I guessed that the silver lines came from sunlight striking the water at a slant. They were all running in roughly the same direction, as though the ocean had rivers in it.

I took the kitchen chair under my arm and went out into the yard with it, setting it as close as I could to the edge, which marked a steep drop down the mountainside. The sun was warm on my shoulders, the light bright against my eyelids, and a faint breeze stirred the dry purple flowers around the base of the fig. I stood for a while letting the sun sink into me, then sat down in the chair to do some serious looking at the ocean rivers. I could sense things beginning to calm down inside me.

Later that afternoon, I read some of Mark, looking for those passages about Jesus going off to pray by himself. Instead, I stumbled upon a scene in which he blesses the children. There are two of these scenes, in successive chapters. In the first, the disciples have been arguing about who among them is the greatest. Jesus calls them to sit down and listen. "Taking a child he placed it in their midst, and putting his arms around it he said to them, 'Whoever receives one child such as this in my name, receives me; and whoever receives me, receives not me but the One who sent me'" (Mark 9:36–37).

In the second scene, the disciples are caught rebuking a crowd of parents who want Jesus to pray over their children. He tells them, "Let the children come to me; do not prevent them, for the kingdom of God belongs to such as these. Amen, I say to you, whoever does not accept the kingdom of God like a child will not enter it" (Mark 10:14–15).

I was particularly struck by that last line: Whoever does not accept the kingdom of God like a child will not enter it. I'd heard this passage all my life, had read it myself a hundred times before, but suddenly I wondered, What does he mean? Does he mean that we cannot see the kingdom—which, he says over and over again, is already "among" us—unless we see it as a child would?

I thought back to my remembrance of childhood solitude during those first dawns on the bench in the pines. I thought about what it had been like to see creation through that particular lens. I thought about those days in which there'd been no barrier between nature and myself. That was a time in which God seemed to be everywhere—no worries about duties and responsibilities then, no to-do list, no guilt about whole days spent watching clouds sail the sky. It was the very essence of simplicity. This pure joy coupled with wonderment had taken me years to recapture, and then it only occurred in brief flashes during my fifteen-minute sits.

Here I now was with nothing before me but the great blue ocean. Perhaps this was my sole task for the next three days: to become like a child, alone with God.

I decided to let go of my niggling worry about how many services to attend—who would know or care? In the same spirit, I deliberately set aside all thoughts of my family; they would be fine, and if not, Mike would call the hermitage and a monk would relay the message to me. Finally, I made a vow to stop the internal debate about whether or not this retreat was going to "do me any good."

I read Psalm 139, one of my longtime favorites, and this time—after my conscious choice to proceed with the retreat—the words seemed fraught with new meaning:

> You formed my inmost being;
>> you knit me in my mother's womb.
> . . . .
> My very self you knew;
>> my bones were not hidden from you,
> When I was being made in secret,
>> fashioned as in the depths of the earth.
> Your eyes foresaw my actions;
>> in your book all are written down;
>> my days were shaped, before one came to be.
> (Ps. 139:13–16)

If this were true, then God knew me better than I knew myself, surely better than a parent, no matter how loving, knows his or her own child. It was safe for me to spend the next three days inside my child-mind—if that were even possible for a full-fledged adult to do. Perhaps it was not, but this was all I had to go on: walking, sitting, reading, chanting the psalms during vigils and lauds—everything as a trusting child.

In the long run, sad to say, this was not a very successful enterprise. Twice in the middle of the night, when the absolute darkness and silence of my little room made it feel more like Anthony's empty tomb than a refuge, I was struck by such a painful dart of longing for Mike's reassuring warmth that I lay awake until dawn. At other times, I found myself dwelling nostalgically on the kids to the point of distraction. On the second morning, a red fox came to my small yard and eyed me through the window, and I mooned around half the morning, wishing the kids could have seen her. Worst of all was the ever lurking to-do list, which on the third day began quietly reasserting itself.

One thing, however, did come clear: by the end of the retreat, I was pretty sure I understood the impulse to shed panicked tears that had come over me so strongly in the beginning.

The prospect of genuine solitude had jarred me out of my identity in a way that no amount of quiet time within the safe environs of home could possibly do. I was shaken by the temporary loss of my spousal, maternal, and teaching roles, my activities, and even my familiar anxieties. Without a family to cook for, how was I to know myself as a loving being? Without the stress of deadlines, how was I to know myself as important? What, in that anonymous little room, could possibly validate my existence?

I was beginning to get an inkling of what Anthony must have faced in the desert.

Simple Does Not Mean Easy

Strangely enough, I cried when I had to leave. I'm not *ready* yet, I kept thinking as I nosed the Volvo down the precarious mountain road. And the ocean—I was losing it with each drop in elevation. That broad vista of blue laced with its glittery silver rivers was shrinking, turning back into cold, salty water, becoming particularized, even mundane.

I felt extremely vulnerable, as though I'd just undergone interrupted surgery and had been released from the hospital against my will, only partially sewn up. Later, when I'd finally stopped sniffling, I thought about this awful image and what it might mean.

One clue, it seemed, lay in the lives of those early Christian hermits, who were convinced that by giving up the company of humans they had opened themselves to powerful and potentially transformative experiences. St. Anthony provides a good example of that for which they were striving: When those who wanted to follow him finally broke down his door twenty years after he entered the fort at Pispir, he showed every sign of a transformed life. Despite not speaking a word for two decades, his conversational skill level was reportedly normal, his memory perfect. He'd neither gained nor lost weight. He was in good health, and he was serene and confident. Even more impressive, a quiet, unmistakable power radiated from him. The people who had come to witness his disinternment began, almost immediately, to call him "Master."

I could only imagine what Anthony's long and lonely work must have been like. How often had he been distracted by worry about his young sister? How often during those long dark nights had he doubted his purpose? Had he dreamed at times of the wife and children he'd never had?

Whatever he'd gone through, it was clear that something both profoundly mysterious and mysteriously good followed those years of solitude. Like many of the original Desert Fathers, he became famous for healings, clairvoyance, and other seemingly supernatural abilities. It was as though, during his decades of focused attention on the voice of God, he'd become more spirit than man.

He was also described as being "tall, strong, healthy," even "robust" on the day that he emerged from his seclusion—he was a mentally and physically powerful person—as if what had really happened to him was an enhancement, rather than a diminishment, of his humanity. It seemed that he'd undergone a kind of divine "surgery" in which the unnecessary and the extraneous aspects of his being were carved or burned away, leaving only the good.

I'd experienced but the smallest taste of solitude, but even after three short days, I could feel the effects. I knew that from now on my life was going to be subtly different in some important way. No matter how incomplete the whole experience felt, this would have to be enough for now; enough until the next time.

When I was back in the swirl of my family, something else came to me: *Simple* does not mean *easy.* Anthony's life was an extremely simple one, a life unified around a single principle, yet how difficult it must have been—as it no doubt is at times for the hermit-monks of Big Sur. In much the same way that the Amish have chosen to "live by the sweat of their brow" in a land overstocked with air-conditioned John Deere tractors, the men of New Camaldoli have chosen their struggles with the wilderness—snapped water pipes, broken generators, crumbling roads—over the comforts and securities of big-city efficiency.

In so doing, they've been able to build a life for themselves that includes regular and ongoing periods of solitude. Every monk in the community is allowed, if he chooses to take it, his monthly "desert day"—a whole twenty-four hours away from all responsibilities, including that of attending services, in order to sit alone in his cell or to walk alone on the mountain. By committing and recommitting themselves to the "desert" in this way, they ensure that St. Romuald's original eremitical vision remains viable nearly a thousand years later. Given the pressures of the modern world to compete, produce, and conform, this is a remarkable accomplishment indeed.

Most of us will never know what it means to live a truly solitary life. Most of us, including me, would not be willing to give up family and friends and career and all the other joys and pleasures of "the world" in order to do so. Yet in a way, St. Anthony and the hermit-monks of New Camaldoli, and even Thoreau, have done it in our stead. They are there for us, exemplars of the powerful and life-changing effect that solitude can have on human beings.

They are icons of faith who give us courage—courage to make room for the blessed and transformative experience of being alone with God. Around this key experience, we can begin to build a unified life.

CHAPTER 2

Silence:
The Way of the Cenobite

Sitting in their houses, they shall
not speak.[1]

from the Rules of St. Pachomius
(A.D. *292–346*)

My first experience of total silence came two hundred
feet below ground level in Kentucky's Mammoth
Cave. A group of us stood in the middle of the great
cavern, listening for ghostly echoes of the concerts that
were once performed there by nineteenth-century musicians. The ranger said, "I'm going to hit the lights now. I
want you to stand perfectly still and not make a sound."

Suddenly we were plunged into a soundless darkness so
deep and black it was disorienting. The silence seemed to
batter me, pounding at my ears until I realized that what
I was hearing was not complete silence, but the sound of
my own blood pumping. Still, it was closer to being both
deaf and blind than I'd ever been before. The effect was
startling; I felt myself swaying, wanting to reach out and
grab something—an elbow, a shoulder—for balance. I'd

entirely lost control of my surroundings, and even of my own body. Without the input of my senses, I was cast adrift in a strange new world.

The ranger, thank heaven, seemed to know that few of us could handle more than thirty seconds of such oblivion and kindly snapped on the lights once again, laughing at our discomfort. I never forgot the experience, and there were times, when the noise of the modern world seemed to batter at me in a different and far more destructive way, that I actually wished to be in that cave once again, alone with the sound of my own coursing blood.

This may be because silence that deep reminds us of our primal condition, when we floated in a realm nearly soundless but for the muted sloshings of the amniotic fluid and the faint thud-thud of our mothers' heartbeats. Perhaps it takes us back to the quiet womb in which we grew—simple, not-yet-individualized creatures, utterly helpless yet curiously free in spite of being dependent for our very lives on mother love we could do nothing to control. Perhaps it takes us back to a time that seems the antithesis of self-responsible adulthood in a bustling, garrulous world.

The Old Testament writers seem to imply that something akin to this original mute and helpless state—as opposed to the "mature" adult one—is the state in which we come closest to God. In response to the question of evil, for example, one psalmist simply says, "Be still before the LORD; / wait for God" (Ps. 37:7). Similarly, when the composer of Psalm 46 begins to give in to a sense of insecurity during wartime, he is told, "Be still and confess that I am God!" (Ps. 46:11). The prophet Habakkuk teaches that the only proper response to the presence of the divine majesty is to fall mute: "The LORD is in his holy temple; / silence before him, all the earth!" (Hab. 2:20). Conversely, unless we go silent, we cannot hear his voice within us, which is (as anybody who has tried to do this can attest) so very still and small that it can be muffled by a stray thought.

No matter how many times I visited the hermitage in those early days, whenever I pulled into the parking lot at the top of the mountain, I was always startled, then delighted, by the stillness of the place. I still am. The transition from busy Highway 1 two miles below to the quiet of the hermitage is more than symbolic: suddenly the whir and buzz of normal human activity is gone. Though the monks are busy—and they work hard—their work is carried out with a minimum of unnecessary clatter or conversation.

Instead of voices or engine noises or the sounds of radio and TV, peace lies over the mountain. Guests invariably comment on this—where else can one find, in this modern world, a community free of noise?—and wild animals affirm this Edenic quality in their own way. Red foxes drift past, intent on their hunting and unaffected by the quiet presence of humans. White-tailed deer lead their fawns casually near guesthouse screen doors. Bunnies nibble grass beside the road, cocking their heads at passersby, then flicking off into the underbrush at the last possible moment.

St. Pachomius and the Search for Silence

It was only after numerous visits—and after I tried to duplicate this peaceful silence in my own home—that I realized how much deliberate effort goes into the creation of such a quiet environment and how easily it can be undone. Silence comes much more naturally in solitude than it does in community, as the desert hermits discovered when the third-century eremitical movement began to give way to the cenobitic way of life. Cenobitic monks lived in a *coenobium* or *koinobion*—a monastery—as members of an organized community. St. Pachomius, founder of the most famous of these early Christian monasteries, struggled unsuccessfully for nearly five years to establish his brotherhood before he realized that a set of rules was imperative—and that these guidelines must include specific precepts about silence.

His subsequent Chronicles and Rules provided the structure for what eventually became the famous *Koinonia*. The word *koinonia* refers to a loving community in which all goods are shared equally and all members submit to a common rule under a single holy father, chosen by God. Those monks who recorded Pachomius's life said of this spiritual experiment, which was never again duplicated to such a vast degree in the Western church, that "among the brothers there was no clashing voice in their midst; but their way of life was conformable to the holy laws. With them there was no care for this world; on the contrary, they were as if transported from earth to heaven as a result of the quiet and of the way of life they persevered in."[2]

Pachomius learned about the necessity of silence in the same way Anthony did—under the tutelage of one of the "old men," or spiritual fathers, who trained him in all the skills of hermit life. Like Anthony, he was born in Egypt at a time when the culture was still being transformed by the stories of the early Christian martyrs. Religious heroism was in the air, and the child Pachomius was apparently deeply affected by this Egyptian phenomenon, despite the fact that his own family was not Christian.

His pagan parents instead did their best to bring him up as a proper young man, teaching him neither Greek nor Latin, but taking him along to the river to make a "sacrifice to the [creatures] that [were] in the waters." However—and this was the first indication that they had a special child on their hands—when these river gods "raised their eyes in the water, they saw the boy, took fright, and fled away."[3]

A decade or so later, the Roman Empire was attacked by the Persians, and the emperor Constantine put out orders that the sturdy young men of the cities and villages were to be conscripted for war. The twenty-year-old Pachomius was rounded up with other youth in his town and herded onto a boat for the long sail north. When they reached the ancient city of Ne, or Thebes, they were taken ashore and locked up in prison to prevent any of them from deserting. That night, a group of kindhearted locals brought food to their cells and "compelled the recruits to eat, because they saw them sunk in great affliction."[4]

Pachomius, though just as frightened and despondent as the rest, was in spite of this deeply moved by the gesture and asked, "Why are these people so good to us when they do not know us?" He was told, "They are Christians, and they treat us with love for the sake of the God of heaven." At this, we are told by his biographers in *The Bohairic Life of Pachomius,* "he withdrew to one side and spent the whole night praying" before this amazing God, promising, among other things, that if he were delivered from prison he would "serve humankind all the days of [his] life."[5]

Soon after, the Roman army repelled the Persians and then released the conscripts. Pachomius traveled south until he came to a deserted village called Seneset, "scorched by the intensity of the heat." Something powerful drew him to the harsh isolation of the place. He went down to the river to pray in an ancient temple called Pmampiserapis, where he was told to "struggle and settle down here."[6] Obediently, he planted some palm trees and vegetables, and began his years of feeding the village poor and the occasional hungry traveler.

On the night he was finally baptized into the Christian faith, he had what proved to be a prophetic dream: "He saw the dew of heaven descend on his head, then condense in his right hand and turn into a honeycomb; and while he was considering it, it dropped onto the earth and spread out over the face of all the earth."[7] Though it took him years to begin living out the vision—first he would undertake the purely eremitical life, undergoing rigorous ascetical training at the hands of the legendary Apa Palamon—eventually it became clear that his vocation was to lead a community, a community that would grow to encompass twelve gigantic monasteries that housed thousands of monks.

The *First Sahidic Life of Pachomius,* which has come down to us only in fragmentary form, records his original, failed attempt to establish a real monastery. Following the well-established pattern of the great spiritual fathers, he tried to teach his would-be monks by example alone. But "seeing his humility and obligingness, they treated him with contempt and great irreverence because of the lack of integrity of their hearts toward God."[8] He endured their insolence and pranks for a long time, but as Adalbert de Vogüé says in his foreword to the *Pachomian Koinonia,* he finally saw that "if he [were] to direct souls, to form monks, to accomplish his mission, his desire for self-effacement and service had to be coupled with a frank acknowledgement of his own role as legislator and master."[9]

In this new role, one of his first tasks was to establish a peaceful atmosphere within the community, which meant the cherishing of silence. He accomplished this in two ways: through precepts that dealt with preserving environmental quiet and additional rules that dealt with control of the tongue. "If it happens," he declared, "that during the psalmody or the prayer or in the midst of a reading anyone speaks or laughs, . . . with neck bowed down and hands hanging down he shall stand before the altar and be rebuked by the superior."[10] He thought that people needed to be able to eat in peace, so, "If anything is needed at table no one shall dare to speak, but he shall make a sign to the ministers by a sound."[11]

Nothing could be more disruptive to a peaceful environment than gossip. Therefore, when monks returned to the monastery after being outside the boundaries of the community on errands, they could not, "in any circumstance, talk in the monastery about what they [had] done or heard outside." [12] In the fields or "at work, they [should] talk of no worldly matter, but either recite holy things or else keep silent." [13] By these methods, which at first sounded painfully severe to me, Pachomius was convinced he could re-create for his monks, in spite of their crowded communal life, the blessed silence of Anthony's solitary fort.

Creating Real Silence in Real Life

When I looked at my own life and asked myself whether I could make it more peaceful, I was not at all hopeful. Yet by now I'd reached a stage that required it; it was simply too jarring to keep going back and forth between two entirely different worlds. My efforts to turn our home into a quiet sanctuary seemed flatly doomed, however, until the day I had a miniversion of Pachomius's earlier revelation: the establishment of genuine silence requires that everyone in the community make a deliberate commitment to it—which means they agree to follow some rules.

First, however, I had to learn how to seek out and refresh myself in the pools of silence that lay hidden along the pathway of my noisy daily round. One obvious spot was my bench in the pines, where I'd already learned to open my eyes in a new, childlike way to ducks in flight, clouds, and acorns half-buried in oak mulch. Now I focused on what was happening with my ears. The first thing I noticed was that the wing feathers of flying ducks make a hushed but definite squeaking noise, like the stiff rustling of hurrying petticoats. This, of course, was not silence—but it *required* some measure of silence for me to even notice it.

Next, I heard the dawn wind stirring the tops of the pines. This reminded me of the verse in John in which Jesus is telling his disciples an important fact: "The wind blows where it wills, and you can hear the sound it makes, but you do not know where it comes from or where it goes; so it is with everyone who is born of the Spirit" (John 3:8). I realized that a person who did not regularly listen to the wind would miss entirely the point of Christ's metaphor—and would miss a fairly significant theological statement about how things work in the spiritual realm. This was a sobering thought. I wondered what else I'd failed to hear because I'd never learned, the way the monastery bunnies had, to cock my ears and listen hard; or maybe I'd just learned too well to shut out noise.

It was thus with some trepidation that I opened my senses for the first time in years to the roaring cataracts of activity in our teenager-driven house. What a revelation: the Indigo Girls on the living-room stereo, Garrison Keillor on the transistor in the garage, Van Morrison wailing upstairs, the dishwasher washing, the power saw sawing, the phone ringing, sinks running, dryers drying, dogs barking, kids calling, cats whining . . . and all this in a house without a TV. In addition, the neighbor up the hill was pruning his oak trees with a chain saw, the man down the road was testing the ignition system of his car, a motorcycle was screaming past, the UPS delivery person was grinding his brakes on the corner, and 37,000 feet in the sky jets were tearing holes in the clouds.

Ambrose Wathen says in his book *Silence*, "The present age is recognized by many as an age of noise. . . . There has been a rise in the incidence of deafness, and some are even afraid that man as a species will lose his sense of hearing due to the constant bombardment of sound. It has been observed that noise has an influence on blood pressure, circulation and nervous disorders." [14] I could agree with that. When I opened my ears fully to this flood of sound, it was a traumatizing experience, but what could I do about it?

Meanwhile, my search for silence went on. I discovered that my occasional, frustrating insomnia was actually a blessing, for it provided me with the only nonnoisy inside-the-house time I could get. Where in the past I lay between the sheets with clenched fists and anxious, hopeless thoughts, now I slipped out of bed almost gleefully, knowing that my noisy herd was sleeping like the dead. I padded downstairs and made myself a cup of tea, then sat cross-legged on a patch of moonlit carpet, reveling in the quiet. So it *could* really happen, I kept thinking. This house could be a peaceful sanctuary.

I found another pool of silence one morning on my twenty-minute drive to work. It was, surprisingly enough, inside the car. Naturally, there was the noise of the car engine and other traffic, but if I pulled a little trick on myself, I could make this sound like a heavy wind. The real challenge was to turn off National Public Radio, which at first felt like a sin. How was I going to stay in touch with world events without my daily dose of *Morning Edition?* How was I to keep up with my culture? After a couple of dead-air minutes, I grew nervous and turned it back on again. Suddenly, however, the radio voices seemed clamorous, invasive. I was no longer able to focus on what the reporters were saying—now it was simply more noise.

At that time I was teaching on a campus with about 18,000 students. My office had a big window that faced the corridor sidewalk. This meant that anybody walking past, even if they weren't planning to pay me a visit, could catch a glimpse of me at my desk and think of something they needed to tell me—which they regularly stopped and did. I also had an office mate, a lovely human being who liked to chat and knew that I shared this weakness. Up and down the hallway went my fellow faculty, often with a few minutes to kill before class. Was there, could there be, a campus pool of silence? It didn't seem possible.

To my surprise, it was. There was a tiny herb garden I'd spotted once and forgotten all about, a memorial garden for a deceased engineering professor. Having an hour between classes, I went to track it down. I found a circle of five benches amid clouds of rosemary, sage, oregano, and thyme. White butterflies rose and settled, and a couple of chickadees darted after insects. Two of the benches were occupied: one by a slender girl stretched full length with an open calculus book over her sleeping face, and the other by a young man in rusty black who was writing in his journal. I sat down, facing the sun, and closed my eyes, listening. Not yet silence—how could there be on such a crowded campus?—but the usual sounds (chatter, laughter, engines) seemed curiously muted. I focused instead on the faint ratcheting of a hummingbird, and, of course, the wind.

Morton Kelsey, Jungian psychologist and Episcopalian priest, says this about silence:

> The first step in finding . . . contact with God is learning to be alone and quiet. This is the beginning of silence, the process of introversion. There is just one aim to start with, to still the tumult of activity in mind and body and center down in a state of recollection. And this means shutting out the invading noises from both the outside world and the inner psychic one.[15]

Later he adds, "Silence can be a mini-experience of death and resurrection. It is a temporary cessation of one's doing and planning and desires."[16]

I felt something of this on my first day in the campus herb garden. Just as I'd made a deliberate (though mostly unsuccessful) search for silence at home, I was now making a concerted effort to find it during my workday. What a change this made in my focus. Now, instead of anxiously brooding over the everlasting deadlines of academic life, I thought about my beautiful secret: the quiet herb garden with its bees. After a long, tiring lecture, that is where I headed, sometimes bypassing my office entirely. As it turned out, fifteen minutes of purposeful silence—no speaking, no music, no reading (for reading is silent talk)—renewed me.

Clearly, something still had to be done about the chaos at home. First, however, there was another crucial stage for me to complete.

Taming of the Tongue

Pachomius was not the only one to notice that the single biggest threat to a quiet and peaceful environment is the human tongue. Most of his precepts having to do with silence are designed to rein in uncontrolled talking. It was easy for me to fall in love with silence—but it was far harder for me to think about shutting my own mouth in service of that goal.

I've always been a talker. My mother probably would have said "a chatterbox." The moment I got home from school each afternoon, I'd track her down and force her to listen to a detailed recounting of every hour I'd spent in class. This had to be an incredible bore, but because she was my mother, she couldn't wiggle out of it. Besides, if she looked away for a single moment, her poor mind beginning to drift, I pounced indignantly: "You're not *listening* to me!"

By the time I was eight or nine, I'd stumbled onto the fine art of storytelling—had in fact learned how to lie adeptly in service of a stronger punch line. People *reacted* to my stories: they laughed, they raised their eyebrows, they shook their heads. Talk had become my way to shine, that which set me apart from the average dullard who wouldn't recognize a good line if it were staring him in the face. I became smug about my gift of gab. I even practiced accompanying facial expressions in the bathroom mirror.

None of this, except for the *conscious* lying, went away in adulthood (small semiconscious lies still peppered much of my conversation). I was drawn to other talkers, verbal acrobats who knew how to break up a room. The college English department was thus my natural habitat: a veritable colony of high-toned gabblers. I felt right at home, especially in the campus writing group where people *really* knew how to spin a sentence. Once a month we'd meet in someone's living room to drink good wine and howl at each other's stories. At 10:30 or so, we'd finally haul out that evening's manuscript and begin our "real" work.

This love of speech permeated every aspect of my life. Among my siblings I had only one rival—the family "baby," who'd developed into a wickedly humorous raconteur. I could even hold my own with teenagers, both around the dinner table and in the classroom. If my students even hinted at growing supercilious or bored, *whammo,* I'd drop the perfect line and cut the ground out from under them.

I didn't only use humor. I could make people gasp at the suspenseful recounting of what would not have been an impressive adventure at all without my added hype. I could convince them, through intense eye contact and a voice that vibrated with confidence, that I knew *exactly* what I was talking about, even if, as was often the case, I didn't. In short, I knew how to "win friends and influence people"; I was (though of course this never entered my mind) a highly accomplished, fast-talking salesperson.

One day I was complaining to a colleague about the ghastly noise level in my house. He raised his eyebrow, then said, not unkindly, "Have you ever thought about trying to silence your*self*?" I stared at him, embarrassed beyond belief, but at the same time amazed at the profundity of his insight. How *obvious,* though I'd never seen it until that moment. Here I was, upset with everybody and everything for making too much noise, but when I was in the presence of other people, I never stopped talking. I was a babbling brook—the *mother* of all babbling brooks. On and on I went, assuming that as long as people were enjoying themselves, I was doing my job.

Chastened, I slunk off to the herb garden to think. I'd learned to listen for silence when I was alone, but among people I was still my old social self. One of the qualities of the Camaldolese community that I most appreciated was their care with words. I always felt welcome when I arrived—a raised hand here, a brief smile there—but nobody felt obliged to seek me out and sit me down for a good long chat. Any words exchanged were for a purpose: the words of the liturgy, of prayer, of the psalms. If something important came up—say, the fact that all the water had been shut of because of a broken pipe—a monk would appear at my door, a smiling but laconic young man who never stuck around to talk about the weather. In fact, the sense I had at the hermitage was that words were precious and not something one should waste.

Ambrose Wathen says, "Every word is born in silence and returns to silence. The word is born in silence, lives in silence, culminates in silence. . . . Language is a union

/ords and silence." [17] Until my colleague's not-so-offhand remark, I hadn't thought of this before—that silence is like the white space in a picture, that which gives objects their shape. When there are too many words, we can no longer hear what is really being said.

Perhaps this is why Jesus taught in parables—brief, pungent tales that left one feeling quizzical and interested and wanting to hear more. This is why, perhaps, he rarely *explained* anything. "Whoever has ears to hear ought to hear," he often said. [18] Given the impact of his brief preaching years on the following twenty centuries, it is amazing how few actual words are attributed to him. Clearly, he knew the power of silence: that it can sometimes communicate as well as, or better than, words.

His healings, for example, often concluded with a warning to the healed: "See that you tell no one anything," he told the grateful leper (Mark 1:44), and, "Do not even go into the village," he said to the newly sighted blind men (Mark 8:26). This held even for exorcisms, where "he drove out many demons, not permitting them to speak because they knew him" (Mark 1:34). He seemed fully aware of the wildfire nature of news—and the fact that stories of his works would generate crowds of thrill seekers who would impede his mission.

Sometimes, Jesus spoke directly about the awful power of speech: "I tell you, on the day of judgment people will render an account for every careless word they speak. By your words you will be acquitted, and by your words you will be condemned" (Matt. 12:36–37). He said to the complaining Pharisees: "You brood of vipers, how can you say good things when you are evil? For from the fullness of the heart the mouth speaks" (Matt. 12:34). He told the recent converts who were nervous about breaking ritual law: "Hear and understand. It is not what enters one's mouth that defiles that person; but what comes out of the mouth is what defiles one" (Matt. 15:10–11).

At certain moments, he fell completely silent, and his silence was far more profound than any words he might have spoken. For example, when the woman caught in adultery was dragged before him and the shouting of her accusers prevented anyone from hearing him even if he'd tried to speak, he simply took a stick and began to draw in the sand. Only when the crowd had uneasily quieted down did he look up calmly and say, "Let the one among you who is without sin be the first to throw a stone at her" (John 8:7).

Probably the most dramatic moment of silence in Jesus' short life came near the end. He was taken to King Herod, who, according to Luke, "questioned him at length." Jesus, however, "gave him no answer," in spite of the chief priests and the scribes who "stood by accusing him harshly" (Luke 23:9–10). At the end of this one-sided interview, they dressed him in resplendent garb and sent him back to his execution.

The Crucifixion itself was carried out in stunning silence. This was as predicted seven hundred years before by the prophet Isaiah: "Like a lamb led to the slaughter / or a sheep before the shearers, / he was silent and opened not his mouth" (Isa. 53:7). For silence in the face of terrible and unfair suffering was part of the message—and thus, when Jesus spoke his few short sentences on the cross, they reverberated through the millennia. He said about his executioners: "Father, forgive them, they know not what they do" (Luke 23:34). He said to the thief beside him: "Amen, I say to you, today you will be with me in Paradise" (Luke 23:43). His final words upon the cross were uttered to his beloved Abba: "Father, into your hands I commend my spirit" (Luke 23:46).

These examples from the life of Christ were far too compelling for me to take lightly. I decided to give up talking, or, at least, most talking, and see what happened next.

My first experiment took place in the writers' group, in the den of the scintillating conversationalists. I sipped at my wine, smiled at the right places in their stories, but stayed mum. Instead of talking, I *listened* in a way I never had before to what they were saying. I was astonished— not because I hadn't heard it all before (in fact, I'd said most of it myself), but because I'd never let it *sink in* exactly what it was we thought was so funny.

Two things immediately came clear: I often laughed at people who were not present to defend themselves, and the reason I laughed was because they were in some way or another *not measuring up. In*teresting, I thought. It must be a very big deal for me to measure up—otherwise, why would I get such a kick out of other people's failures? Was I inflating my self-esteem by pointing out others' weaknesses? I pondered this, still smiling and sipping but not talking . . . and then I realized I'd been noticed. My dear friends who'd known me for years were getting puzzled looks, then annoyed ones, on their faces. It was my turn, after all, to tell a great story of my own, and I wasn't stepping up to the plate.

I started to explain, then stopped myself. How much good would it do to stop talking if I then launched into a long, self-justifying explanation of the reasons for my silence? All I could do was continue to smile dumbly at them while the conversation lurched, nearly halted, and then recovered, though not very gracefully, when somebody else finally picked up the ball intended for me.

I felt ashamed—these were my longtime compatriots, after all, and who was I to run private experiments in the group without their permission? I felt that I should apologize for failing to play my position, for letting down the team. I felt guilty for causing them irritation, for they were irritated—I could feel it, though it was at first a very subtle sensation, hardly noticeable except to someone who'd been teaching herself to hear the rustle of duck wings.

I tried a more obvious version of the experiment on my raucous group of siblings, and their response was swift and not nearly so subtle: "What's wrong with *you?* You're not getting ready to join a *monastery* or something, are you?" Again, I felt a confused sense of shame—my silence in the group felt like a judgment, though I didn't mean it to be—and more than a little sorrow. If I proceeded with this, if I quit talking so much, I might lose people, folks I cared about deeply. Without talk, how was I going to have relationships?

During my bench time over the next few weeks, I thought hard about this problem. Talking was an integral part of my character, more so than for most people. The simple act of going silent cut into my very identity; I was starting to seem weird to others and myself—weird, unfriendly, antisocial. I tried to think of other people, people outside the hermitage, who didn't talk much. This was hard, too, because if someone didn't talk, I didn't notice them—or at least did not pay them much attention. Giving up speech meant giving up my place at the center of activity, retreating to the periphery like those other close-mouthed types I'd always labeled "shy" without ever bothering to find out if it was so.

Yet there was also something stabilizing about talking less—stabilizing and simplifying (and this conviction was quietly growing right alongside all my doubts). Telling fewer stories meant that I was less tempted to embellish. Getting fewer laughs meant that I was less tempted to perform. Talking less about others meant I was less likely to hand on destructive gossip. It was safer to take speech seriously when I was not overindulging in it.

The very earliest Christians, struggling to build their communities in the face of deadly persecution, dealt head-on with this issue. James spent much of one letter discussing unrestrained talk:

> If we put bits into the mouths of horses to
> make them obey us, we also guide their whole
> bodies. It is the same with ships: even though
> they are so large and driven by fierce winds,
> they are steered by a very small rudder wherever
> the pilot's inclination wishes. In the same way

the tongue is a small member and yet has great
pretensions.

Consider how small a fire can set a huge
forest ablaze. The tongue is also a fire. It exists
among our members as a world of malice, defil-
ing the whole body and setting the entire course
of our lives on fire, itself set on fire by
Gehenna. (James 3:3–6)

Paul says in his epistle to the Colossians, "Let your
speech always be gracious, seasoned with salt, so that you
know how you should respond to each one" (Col. 4:6).
More sternly, he writes: "But now you must put them all
away: anger, fury, malice, slander, and obscene language
out of your mouths. Stop lying to one another, since you
have taken off the old self with its practices and have put
on the new self, which is being renewed, for knowledge,
in the image of its creator" (Col. 3:8–10).

In 2 Timothy, Paul advises, "Avoid foolish and ignorant debates, for you know that they breed quarrels"
(2 Tim. 2:23). Three hundred years later, Pachomius tells
the brothers of his enormous *Koinonia,* "For this I war-
rant you: every idle word . . . , or unbecoming remark, or
foolish word or stupid saying, is a defilement of the
human soul before God." [19]

The truth was that I could not trust my tongue. For
too many years, it had been my instrument of self-
aggrandizement; it had developed its own destructive
habits, nearly impossible to break. I thought of how

complicated my relationships had always seemed, how easy it was for me to wound and betray others without meaning to do so. I realized that behind almost every ruined relationship in my life lay words—words spoken in anger, in haste, in high and unthinking good spirits, in deception. I knew that if I were ever to become a simpler being, single-minded in my dealings with others, I would have to permanently curb my tongue.

A sadder, quieter person, I returned to my original problem: the noisy chaos that reigned in my would-be domestic sanctuary. First I would have to lay down a few simple rules, ones that were easy to remember: For example, no one can play private music in the living room. If you happen to be addicted to the Indigo Girls, I visualized myself saying calmly at the dinner table that night, then play them in the privacy of your own bedroom, softly, with the door closed, or with earphones.

Second, too many people are doing too much laundry at all hours. We're getting rid of the dryer, and from now on (I could imagine their shock at what came next), we're going to *hang* the laundry—as in "from a clothesline." *That* should slow things down a bit around here.

Third, we're going to wash our own dishes at the sink the minute we're done using them. Why should those dishes get stacked a mile high on the counter, waiting for some unlucky person to get stuck with them? Why should they then be stuffed in a noisy dishwasher? The *monks* (I could hear their groans at the mention of those familiar paragons) do it this way. If it's good enough for the *monks,* it's good enough for us.

Finally, dear children, this phone is ringing off the hook. Your friends are going to have to be told that nobody's picking up the receiver after, shall we say 9:00 in the evening? That seems perfectly reasonable, doesn't it? (Of course it didn't, but I was fully prepared to go to 10:00.)

Suffice it to say, the reign of silence was short. The community's spirit was at least grudgingly willing, but their flesh was woefully weak. They were, after all, teenagers. I would have to wait a few more years for the natural silence of the empty nest to set in.

Facing of the Quiet

In our new quiet, how much we'd endured in terms of the audio assault came forcefully home to me. At the same time, that cacophonous clatter had been strangely re-assuring, which was perhaps the real reason we hadn't been able to give it up. No one was ever lonely in that long-ago house of ours. There were people stuffed in every nook and cranny, and you could hear them all. Life seemed very full then; the calendar that hung beside the ever-ringing phone was covered with a blurry mess of soccer practices, dentist appointments, choir rehearsals, and swim meets. Everybody, including me, was always on the go; you could hear us, like a monstrous hive of bees in full swarm. Our noise was a natural by-product of our (often unexamined) activity.

In this new, far quieter house, I was at first tempted to keep music on in the living room—not Van Morrison, of course, but music nobody else would ever listen to—

worthwhile, grown-up music. Sometimes I even cranked it up—Mozart's *Requiem,* say, at full volume. But this temptation faded as I became used to the new solitude and its accompanying silence. Every so often during a quiet evening of reading, Mike and I would give each other long looks that had the words "We survived!" stamped all over them. We'd smile a mite sentimentally, though without the slightest desire to go back to that clamorous, if lovable, time.

In our new peaceful sanctuary, it also became far easier to identify intrusive sounds. The telephone, for example, had slowed down a bit since the kids left, but not nearly enough, considering there were only two of us left in the house. As I traveled deeper into the realm of silence and began to feel its effects, that jangling instrument seemed more and more an unnecessary interruption. I did a little study; how many times, for example, was the person on the other end of the line one of our children? Now that they were all living in other states, it was not that often. How many times was it another relative, a close friend, or an urgent situation? Again, relatively speaking, not many.

One night when we'd had yet another quiet dinner broken up by a telemarketer, I said to Mike, "Why don't we disarm that thing? Why don't we just turn it off and let the machine pick it up? We can check it as often as we want to—if it's important, we can call right back." Though dubious at first, he finally agreed to try it out. Within a week, he was as convinced as I that we could live without the ringing of the phone.

It is a small thing, perhaps, but significant. What it symbolizes for me is the ongoing death of that old attention-hungry self, and also of that person who had to be in the midst of a beehive in full swarm to feel safe. In her place, someone new is slowly coming into focus. I don't know her well yet—the babbling brook is far more familiar to me—but if the practice of silence has taught me anything, it's to pay closer attention to those who move quietly through this world. So, I am listening carefully, hoping to learn.

On a recent retreat, I happened to be at the hermitage for Sunday Eucharist. This is always a special pleasure because it is when the singers and musicians of the community sometimes perform solos. The chapel was particularly full that day—in fact, it looked as though a whole vanload of people had just arrived. When the liturgy began, it quickly became evident that these visitors had not yet made the transition from Highway 1 to the mountain.

The services at the hermitage, whether they be vigils or lauds or Eucharist or vespers, move at a deliberate pace, each piece of the liturgy set off by long periods of sometimes profound silence. I say profound because more than once I've seen the experience bring people to tears.

This poor vanload, however, was not listening yet. All two pews of them were still moving along at the usual parish clip, snapping out their responses like schoolkids taking a flash-card test. Each time, the cantor waited patiently for them to finish and then led the rest of the congregation through the same response. Clearly, he was hoping, as Pachomius had for so many frustrating years, that they would watch and listen and learn by example. Finally, however, the presiding priest had to raise his right hand, turn to the speedsters, and explain what was going on and why.

Abashed but eager to make amends, they slowed down, listening carefully for their cues. Suddenly beautiful silence, into which "every word is born . . . and returns," [20] could make itself heard. I understood, then, why the old Latin texts have so many terms for it: *silere* (to be noiseless, still or silent); *silentium* (the state of being still or silent, a noiselessness or stillness); *tacere* (not to speak); *tacite* (silently); *taciturnitas* (restraint of the tongue, refraining from speech).[21] I saw why Eastern Orthodox Christians so treasure their hesychasts, solitaries who devote themselves to silent prayer.

One of the most famous of these, St. Isaac, says, "But if you embrace this life [of silence], I cannot tell you how much light it will bring you. When you put on one side of the scales all the works of this life . . . and on the other silence, you will find that the latter outweighs the former." [22] St. Gregory of Sinai adds, "The first requirements of silence are to have faith and patience, and, with one's whole heart, strength and power, to love and to hope." [23]

I've not been back to Mammoth Cave, though I'd like to return one day. I'd like to see, assuming I could talk the ranger into snapping off those lights again, if the experience of absolute silence is still so disorienting. I'd like to hear, once again, the lifeblood coursing—and perhaps, intermingled with that faint sound, the still small voice of God, audible at last.

PART II

CLEANSING AND FINDING STRENGTH

The natural result of solitude and silence is a far clearer picture of ourselves, whether or not we really want to see it. Longtime habits come into glaring focus; formerly innocuous-seeming quirks now appear embarrassing or even ominous. We can't simply enjoy our idiosyncrasies anymore; we've become aware of what sits behind them. The longer we look into the mirror of solitude and silence, the more we see: So *this* is what keeps me tied to that job I hate—my shopping habit. And this is what causes my irritable snapping—I always feel like I'm being cheated out of my fair share.

In time, we become restless. It's no longer enough to keep having revelations about our habits and proclivities; we want to change them. This notion fills us with energy; it's time to do something! We roll up our sleeves and prepare for the struggle . . . then realize that we don't know where to start. How *do* we give up lifetime habits? Where do we even begin?

The next chapters, "Awareness: The Way of the Ascetic" and "Purity: The Way of the Celibate," deal with this stage of the journey toward a holier, simpler life. "Awareness" is about specific exercises or disciplines of the spiritual path—ascetical practices developed in ancient times to train the body and the mind in new ways of acting and thinking. Each was developed as a method of teaching people about the effects of desire and passion. Disciplines such as fasting were not about earning spiritual points or about self-punishment but were instead "experiments on the self." For the early ascetics, the laboratory for these experiments was the desert, where they could focus without distraction on what it was they were trying to learn.

In addition to providing self-knowledge, the disciplines acted as strengthening exercises. "Purity" shows that the goal of these disciplines was a human being no longer troubled at every turn by his constant need for food, warmth, or entertainment. Certainly, the ascetics also hoped to be freed at some point from the distraction of sexual desire—or at least from the pain it caused them. The practice of chastity, one of the most important of these early disciplines, was thus meant not to block or deny sexual energy but to channel it in more useful ways.

The cleansing stage—gradually abandoning self-destructive, wasteful, or selfish habits—can go on for a long time. In fact, it can become a new kind of obsessive passion, a problem of which the early ascetics were quite aware. For this reason, they insisted that the goal of ascetical practices was never spiritual athleticism, but love. These practices were not a competition, they were not the "extreme sport" of the spiritual elite, but training in gentleness and humility.

St. John Cassian (A.D. 360–435), who spent fifteen years wandering the deserts of Egypt and Palestine where most of the early ascetics were living, wrote extensively on this phenomenon. St. Augustine of Hippo (A.D. 354–430) is of course famous for his *Confessions,* a long autobiographical work in which he examines, with unflinching honesty, his own sexual nature.

CHAPTER 3

Awareness:
The Way of the Ascetic

Suppose you were to be given an axe
for some necessary use, and preferred
to abuse it by killing the innocent, you
could not blame the smith who made
it, if you were to use for murder what
he provided for uses both necessary
and beneficial to life.[1]

St. John Cassian (A.D. 360–435)

Isometimes reflect fondly on the fact that I was a *normal*
teenage girl, regardless of what an odd adult I finally
became. Such girls are notoriously enthralled with male
prowess, and I'm proud to say that I was no exception. For
me, the football stadium was holy ground where noble
warriors fought for the honor of our school. My own hero
was a 245-pound tackle named Greg who went on to play
for the Oilers. What intrigued me so about this unsuspecting target of my attention was the fact that he also
played piano. I thought this a mark of admirable complexity—also a hopeful sign in terms of my own desire to

finally attract his attention. I was already aware that the single-mindedness of serious athletes does not bode well for the girls who worship them. Maybe he was different.

The football players may have been our heroes, but in terms of sheer focus nobody could match the wrestlers. One of them, John, was a member of my Lutheran youth group. It was John who introduced me to the prolonged fast, the weeklong voluntary starvation of the wrestler trying to "make weight." Until I watched him go through it—seven days of sweats and pallor and strange metallic breath—I did not believe people could fast for a week. That he suffered was clear. I remember him gripping my forearm once as we were getting to our feet after a meeting, a hard, sudden grip as though he were keeping himself from passing out. I remember how miraculous I thought it was that he could so easily forego the social-hour brownies after not eating for *five whole days.*

What struck me most was his lightheartedness during what had to be an unspeakably painful and difficult ordeal. He actually seemed to be enjoying himself, despite his increasing lassitude as the day of his wrestling match approached. His great effort, though debilitating, was just as clearly energizing. I didn't understand how this could be. More than anything, however, I was baffled by this level of self-denial in service of a goal.

St. Cassian and the Monks of Egypt

I did not think of John's long fast again until years later when I stumbled onto a section of the fourth-century

Institutes by St. John Cassian entitled "On the Training of a Monk." Cassian compares the disciplining of the novice brother to the training of a secular athlete, who must first prove himself in the "colt's division" before he is allowed to compete with grown men. Eventually, "if he can consistently hold his own against them in competition, as well as often winning trophies of victory among them, then at last he may deserve to compete in the great games, in which those alone may take part who have won prizes and have been rewarded with many wreaths." [2]

For the young monk, this meant ascesis, or the practice of deliberate self-denial in order to master the desires and passions. The body with its incessant demands for food, sex, warmth, and sleep was trained to do with less and less until it finally learned (quietly and obediently) to accept its proper place. Experienced ascetics could, for example, spend the night on their feet praying, or sleep on cold stone floors without a mattress, or regularly go two, three, or even five days at a time without eating.

More subtle ascetical practices were aimed at controlling psychological dependence on money, social status, intellectual achievement, or a sense of moral superiority. A monk could own no private property, and once he had divested himself of anything he'd brought with him to the monastery, he was taught to continue the relinquishing process through laboring for the communal good instead of his own benefit.

The goal was a monk entirely liberated from the normal distractions of human life, a monk free from both physical and psychological constraints. This process, however, was not to be seen as an end in itself, for down that road lay the demon of pride. The purpose, instead, was to clear the vision, to enable a person to both see and focus on the one true thing, the treasure in the field, the pearl of great price. In addition, ascetical experimenters who had undergone this kind of profound personal transformation found that when they attained this level of focus, they were graced with tremendous powers, powers that allowed them to accomplish feats far beyond the usual human limitations. Psychic gifts such as clairvoyance and telepathy were commonplace, as was the gift of healing. Some of the more famous ascetics could command obedience from wild animals, multiply loaves for the hungry during time of famine, and appear in more than one place at the same time.

John Cassian was a firsthand witness to both the experiments and the spiritual accomplishments to which they eventually led. Though his early life is shrouded in mystery—we do not even know exactly where or when he was born—in about A.D. 380 he arrived in Palestine with an older friend, Germanus. The two of them joined a monastic community in Bethlehem, near the Cave of the Nativity. At some point, an elderly visitor who was put up in their cell told them stories about the great spiritual flowering in the Egyptian desert. Cassian was intrigued, particularly when the identity of his mysterious guest was revealed by a band of monks who arrived in search of him. The man was Abba Pinufius, a famous cenobitic abbot. Cassian learned that Pinufius had tried several times before to escape his high-level position in Egypt, a position that he feared tempted him to pride.

The old abbot was once again carried off by his "sons" to the desert, but the hook had been set; Cassian could not stop thinking about what he'd been told. He and Germanus applied for permission to make a short tour of the monasteries of Lower Egypt and the Nile Delta, a tour that ultimately lasted (with several breaks) some fifteen years. During this time, the two men not only visited anchorites but also went to the renowned monastic center of Scetis in Wadi al-Natrun, Nitria, and its outpost Kellia ("the Cells"). All three were famous for their asceticism, but it was Scetis that became Cassian's Egyptian base, and he used the holy men of Scetis as literary characters in his great treatise on monastic theology, the *Conferences*.

Sometime around 410 he arrived in Marseilles, Gaul. Though there were monasteries in the West at this time, Cassian did not see anything that compared to what he'd experienced at Scetis. The only hope for reform of these undisciplined communities in the West, he thought, was *ex oriente lux,* or "light from the East." Monks needed the kind of training he'd had in Egypt, but not many people with Egyptian ascetical experience were bilingual in both Greek and Latin and therefore able, as he was, to communicate freely with Western monastics.

Like Anthony and Pachomius before him, he now had a clear vision of what his work would be. Eventually, he founded two new monasteries in Gaul—one for women and the other, St. Victor, for men. The instructions for these communities ultimately became the foundation for his other major written work, the *Institutes*.

Cassian saw the spiritual life as an ongoing struggle to free human beings of the passions and desires that distract them from their real purpose in this world. Ascetic disciplines were a means, not an end: For Cassian, the final goal was always perfected love. The term "purity of heart" appears often in his writings; for him, as for Plato and other ancient writers, Christian and pre-Christian alike, this meant a "simplicity hard-won through experience." [3] This, as Cassian scholar Columba Stewart points out, was "not a trait of the untested." [4] The person who stepped on this path could count on some measure of suffering. [5]

Asceticism was a kind of ongoing experiment on the self that quickly revealed the obstacles that lay in the path that led to genuine simplicity. It was a set of exercises—sometimes quite harsh by modern standards—that were designed to vastly sharpen one's awareness of the complexity and imperfection of human nature, especially one's own. Thus armed with the truth, no matter how unwelcome, a person could move forward. The opposite condition—naiveté or fantasy about one's own "goodness"—killed even the possibility of growth.

Cassian's predecessor, Pachomius, provides a good example of what asceticism was meant to accomplish. At the beginning of his spiritual life, long before he could envision the great *Koinonia* he would someday found, he sought out the best-known ascetic in the area, Apa Palamon, and knocked on his cell door. He was given some blunt instructions that included the following: "Try yourself in every point to find out whether you can be steadfast. . . . When you come back we will be ready, in so far as our weakness allows, to labor with you *until you get to know yourself*" [my italics].[6]

Apa Palamon here sums up both the experimental nature of ascesis and the fact that it is tailor-made to reveal our individual preferences and aversions, vanities and inferiority complexes, weaknesses and strengths. The ascetics that Cassian studied could thus be called scientists: they were finding out what happened to the "behavior and reactions of the body and the mind when they were subjected to precise material influences," as Jacques Lacarrière puts it in his *Men Possessed by God.*[7] Their laboratory was the vast solitude of the desert; their equipment was their own minds and bodies.

Self-Study at the Refrigerator Door

Though contemporary psychology has pretty much become *the* modern path to self-knowledge, I was utterly intrigued by this alternative method of self-discovery. My growing love for silence and my new sense that words were precious and meant to be hoarded made me wonder if modern, talk-dependent therapy was really the path to self-knowledge. The great ascetics trained others to become self-aware, but they did not rely on speech to do so. Instead, the novice watched and imitated, silently comparing his own results with that of the experienced practitioner, until he, too, understood what Apa Palamon meant by getting to "know yourself."

I was more than intrigued; I felt compelled to try this in my own life. What could other people see in me that I could not? If Cassian were right, the answer to this question was embarrassingly blunt: way too much. I went back to the *Institutes,* specifically to his discussion of the "eight deadly sins" that are so handily revealed through asceticism.

On Cassian's list of sins, the first is gluttony and the third is avarice; both, he points out, are types of greed, and greed is integral to the human condition. Anyone who has tried to divvy up a birthday cake in a crowd of kids can attest to this. The pained yowl of "She got a bigger piece than me! Not fair, not fair!" really means "I want the most for myself and I don't care what happens to anyone else." According to the ascetical tradition, this primitive self-interest contaminates almost everything we do. If life *were* a birthday party, I thought, blushing, then guess who never thought she got a big enough chunk of the cake?

What could I do? Could I figure out some self-shaping exercises of my own without moving into the cave of an experienced ascetic? Soloing did not seem wise. I did have the *Institutes* and my friends at the hermitage who lived by the Camaldolese Rule and were only a telephone call away. Surely, there could be no harm in a very small experiment. I asked myself what my first venture should be. Then I had my great revelation: My self-study would begin at the door of our well-stocked refrigerator.

Like most folks with Midwestern Scandinavian farm roots, I grew up with the attitude that good food, and plenty of it, is *the key* to a good life; not art, not adventure, not even romance: food. My earliest memories are of a garden: rich dark loam; baby lettuce thin as green silk; ruby tomatoes bowing the vine, fat with sugar and sun.

My grandmother, wearing the apron she never took off except for church, would move briskly down the rows, snapping off pea pods from beneath the leaves and tossing them behind her into the big crockery bowl I balanced against my stomach with both arms. Later, we'd sit shelling at her kitchen table while the aroma of baking bread slowly filled the room, bringing me to the edge of a delighted swoon.

I always managed to get the first piece of bread: white, hot, yeasty, and smelling faintly of mashed potatoes. My grandfather, who'd never been off the farm, did not believe in margarine. Thus, I slathered that hot bread with pure creamery butter, letting it melt completely before I dipped the spoon into my grandmother's strawberry jam—the jam she'd made with berries I helped her pick.

This, I thought, was *real* food, not like what we had in the city. You had to have a garden; you had to stick your hand beneath a warm and irritable hen to get your eggs; you had to buy your milk from the dairy farm down the road, where black-and-white Holsteins rolled their eyes at you in a dim, lofty barn that smelled of alfalfa. You did not buy ice cream in a grocery store; you cranked it in an old wooden freezer under huge cottonwoods on a hot July evening as the fireflies were starting to glow. You picked your peaches from the tree, slicing them straight into the bowl of cold, melting vanilla.

By age five, I was a connoisseur already, a hopeless food snob who would grow up willing to go to unbelievable lengths to re-create for family and friends that everlasting banquet on the farm. From my early twenties on, for example, I've baked all our bread—not the steamy white potato bread of my grandmother's day, but brown loaves heavy with oats, flaxseed meal, sunflower seeds, and wheat germ. Loaves far too weighty for bread machines, which is the excuse I give to people who suggest I finally buy one. A bread machine indeed: my grandfather (in case these well-meaning folks have forgotten) *didn't even believe in margarine.*

I have a garden far too big for a person with my schedule and far too complicated, with oddball heirloom seeds that, year after year, I cannot resist trying. Maybe *this* tomato will be my grandmother's—or *these* early peas. Maybe *these* red potatoes are the very ones. What about these New England pie pumpkins? Were these what *she* used? Naturally, everything in this gigantic garden of mine is grown organically (which means it all takes six times longer than normal). The result is that *nothing but the best* goes into the mouths of the people I love. No doubt my grandmother, still in her apron, is looking down upon all this effort and smiling approvingly.

My ascetical experiments have not worked any miracles in regard to the way I view what my family and I eat. One thing is quite different, however. Nowadays I can laugh at myself for being so fierce and unbending about the quality of broccoli. Food has finally taken its rightful place in my life.

This did not happen overnight. First, I had to read and reread the famous account of Christ's prolonged fast, a fast much longer than anything John the high-school wrestler ever dreamed of: Jesus was in the wilderness for forty days, not eating for the duration. I tried to imagine it, then gave up and instead tried to imagine relinquishing just one thing: my precious cup of coffee in the morning. No, no—I couldn't fathom it. All my reading in Cassian's works about those admirable spiritual athletes, those ascetics who survived on a nightly meal of bread and salt and water, had not prepared me in the least to give up a simple cup of coffee.

This constituted my first lesson about ascesis: It can't be read about or thought about—it must be practiced to have any effect whatsoever. Like those endless diets in the women's magazines, ascesis works only when we do it.

Chagrined, I went back to Christ in the desert and the sudden appearance of Satan, who seemed to know exactly when his intended victim would be at his hungriest and, therefore, at his weakest. He suggests that Jesus simply change the stones that lay scattered about him into nice hot loaves of bread. Of course, I knew Jesus' response to this by heart—who doesn't?—but not until the day I, myself, was about to begin fasting did it strike me with such power: "One does not live by bread alone, / but by every word that comes forth / from the mouth of God" (Matt. 4:4).

Gloomily, I stared across my kitchen at the countertops covered with just-picked fruit, at the steaming pie I'd pulled from the oven moments before, at the soup merrily simmering on the stove. My kitchen was the closest place to heaven I could devise. How could I give it all up and replace it with a growling stomach? I hadn't even started the fast yet, but I was already getting seriously irritated, even cranky. This might have some detrimental effects on my character, I thought—*permanent* effects. Who was I to inflict such nastiness on my beloved family?

I went back to Matthew. This time Jesus was talking to his disciples, who were apparently having some of the same thoughts I was: "When you fast, do not look gloomy like the hypocrites. They neglect their appearance, so that they may appear to others to be fasting. Amen, I say to you, they have received their reward. But when you fast, anoint your head and wash your face, so that you may not appear to be fasting, except to your Father who is hidden" (Matt. 6:16–18).

This made me cringe. Suddenly, I'd caught a glimpse of an unsavory trait in myself, something I'd suspected but never seen quite so clearly before: my tendency to exaggerate whatever I did, be it good or bad, delightful or trying. It was all larger than life—even legendary: the goodness of food, the beauty of my grandmother's preserves, the necessity of my morning coffee, and the dank horrors that awaited should I try to give all this up, even for half a day.

The awful part was that even as I wallowed in this exaggerated self-pity over the deprivations I had not yet experienced, I knew full well that there were people in this world—I'd traveled among them—who lived whole lives on a monotonous diet of rice and lentils. Worse, there were people in this world who didn't even have that—stick people who staggered across the North African savannas in search of water and a handful of grain. This tendency of mine to hype the importance of my own response to things was more than humorous—it was both selfish and blind: in a word, *greedy*.

This was not a self-imposed guilt trip; it was reality. My exquisitely fine-tuned taste in food was simply that— a taste I could afford to develop, a taste to which I could pander. I had a choice, and I'd chosen to put my faith in food. What if, someday, the system collapsed? What if famine struck, or if we simply lost our jobs and could no longer afford this taste of mine?

I thought about the people I knew who fasted regularly and smiled while they did it. My friend Janet, who, Catholic from birth, takes only bread and water on Wednesdays and Fridays. The monks at New Camaldoli, who observe the calendar fasts and various forms of abstinence. My friend Jah'Shams, a Muslim who always keeps the Ramadan fast—no food or drink from sunrise to sunset for an entire month.

I'd asked him about this: How did it feel? Did it take a long time to adjust? Did he get cranky or weak? Did he slip up along the way? I could not recall his answers, only his striking last comment, which was that he never thought with such clarity as he did during that long hungry month of Ramadan. It was time, I thought, to call Jah'Shams.

He, along with a well-known Benedictine monk who has written much about fasting, Adalbert de Vogüé, convinced me that the long-term results would more than make up for the initial discomfort. De Vogüé, who has practiced the one-meal-a-day "regular fast" since the late 1970s, says in his book *To Love Fasting* that the very last portion of the twenty-four-hour cycle is the best: "A feeling of freedom and lightness invades my whole being, body and mind. Work, either intellectual or manual, becomes easier, as does prayer. When I walk in the forest just before the meal, while reciting the scriptural phrase that I 'meditate' on for that day, spiritual joy comes over me as by appointment."[8]

De Vogüé also mentions that his practice of fasting has curbed his "anxiety and irritation, sadness and nervousness, . . . vanity, touchiness [and] envy."[9] Jah'Shams reported a similar effect—after, of course, the first three days of grouchiness while his body adjusts to the change. In this, both fasters are in agreement with Cassian, who says, "We have discovered that the reason for practicing bodily restraint is that by this fasting we may attain purity of heart."[10] For de Vogüé "The habit of fasting effects a profound appeasement" of our instinctive, self-protective responses to the world.[11] He believes that "a certain mastery of the primordial appetite, eating, permits a greater mastery of the other manifestations of the libido and aggressiveness."[12]

I decided to try this kind of fast first—skipping breakfast and lunch and eating my one meal after 6:00 P.M.—rather than Janet's more traditional Catholic fast of bread and water. My theory was that no food at all would be easier for my system to handle than not enough of it. Both Jah'Shams and de Vogüé had emphasized the sense of lightness that came when the body was entirely freed up from all digestive duties. I was afraid that bread—especially *my* weighty version—would interfere with that.

I chose Sunday for my first attempt, mainly because I did not have to be in the classroom. De Vogüé stresses that a quiet, nonsocial environment is far more conducive to successful fasting than one in which we must meet the demands of the public. Plus, Sunday *is* the Sabbath, after all, our designated day of rest. Why not also make it a day of rest for my overworked system?

I settled a few basic issues ahead of time. I would not try to forgo water, as Jah'Shams and de Vogüé did, and I *would* have my morning cup of coffee. Other than that, I would simply attempt to experience the fast as an observing scientist might: objectively and indifferently. I would also try to squelch any uprushes of the impulse to exaggerate what was happening to me.

Morning dawned clear and lovely with a few low clouds floating in the eastern sky. I saw this because I was already up and sitting on the bench under the jack pine with both hands in a death grip around my half-full coffee cup. Never, I thought, has coffee tasted *this good*—then sternly cut off this self-pitying drivel before it could carry me away. No storytelling, I told myself. Just go on about your normal business.

Normal business on Sunday morning, however, includes Mass. I had forgotten to decide how I would deal with this specific event. If you were fasting, could you take communion? Did the wafer and wine invalidate the fast? This question put me in minor turmoil for a while, but it seemed silly (and counterproductive) to skip communion when I'd had that cup of coffee. I'd also read that as far back as the year A.D. 200, Tertullian criticized Christians who abstained from communion just to preserve their fasts. He offered them a solution not open to a modern-day parishioner dealing with hypervigilant eucharistic ministers: preserve the consecrated host to consume right before the one meal of the day.[13] I decided to take communion and not worry about it.

Church was not until 10:30 A.M., which was well past my usual breakfast hour. I was still feeling fine except that my body was starting to get . . . nervous. This was the only way I could describe it. My body was like a Labrador retriever that had not been fed on time and whose owners were nowhere in sight in a still-dark house. Loyally, my body was still assuming I'd show up soon and feed it, but there was a touch of hysteria lying right beneath that thought.

Perhaps it was partly for this reason that Eucharist that morning was imbued with a rare splendor. The wafer, always holy, had taken on a new dimension. I moved reverently to the chalice and sipped the wine—and suddenly the internal dog (still, strictly speaking, unfed) plopped to the floor with a contented sigh and fell asleep. What a strange thing, I thought when I was back on my kneeler, that a morsel of bread and a few drops of wine could so completely satisfy me.

Then I realized how it was that those old monks of the desert—Anthony, Pachomius, Cassian—could talk about being sustained by the Eucharist. I couldn't see this until I isolated the bread and wine out from the mountains of food that make up a normal diet. So one reason for fasting, I was already starting to see, was to put things into their proper perspective—to achieve, as Jah'Shams told me I would, a kind of clarity not available to the contented eater.

The day went on—3:00 P.M. was the biggest hurdle, for some reason—and dinner, taken at 6:30 that evening, had never been so purely lovely. After years of praying either perfunctorily or not at all before my meals, suddenly I was filled with a deep and honest gratitude for what I was about to eat. It seemed a minor miracle, this food on my plate, for the possibility that it could be taken away had been opened to me for the first time. I was now not nearly so fussy about freshness and presentation. Variety was also irrelevant; I didn't care if we'd had the same meal the night before or for weeks straight, for that matter. It was food, tasty and nourishing, and I was a hungry animal.

But never again would I be *just* that. After a single day of voluntary deprivation, a strange new connection had been forged between flesh and spirit. The body itself had seemingly done what it always did: demanded to be fed as soon as it felt the pangs of hunger. My deliberate choice not to respond to it, and the fact that my body had survived just fine—in fact, had been surprisingly acquiescent about the whole thing—was a big clue that the hunger I so dreaded was probably not even centered there, but somewhere else entirely.

Where? I went back to Cassian, who had this to say: "The needs of the flesh are no hindrance to purity of the heart, if we consume only what our bodily weakness requires, not what the appetite demands."[14] What the *appetite* demands: Of course—the desire for food was a completely different thing from the actual physical need for it.

I knew that every diet counselor in the country was aware of this interesting fact: Our psychological responses to food must be changed if we are ever to lose weight. However, I was pretty sure Cassian meant something more—that food was just one of the many things we desire, and that desire and the will are tightly intertwined. We want something (for example, my grandmother's perfect tomatoes), and we then act to obtain what we want (going through hell to grow those heirloom seeds).

This is not such a big deal, perhaps, if the outcome of desire is merely more hours spent grubbing in the garden; but what other unthinking actions, far more self-destructive, had followed hard upon the heels of my desires? For the first time, I felt that I was getting what Plato must have meant in the *Republic* when he said: "When the desires lose their intensity and ease up, then what happens is . . . freedom from a great many demented masters." [15]

In one short day of fasting, I'd become aware of the hold desire had on me. Clearly, fasting and the other ascetical disciplines had something important to teach me about myself, something that I could not afford to ignore. I decided to continue fasting and thereafter tried to do it on a regular basis. I never became much better at it, in the sense that it was any easier to actually begin each time, but I persisted.

Eventually, I tried my friend Janet's fast—bread and water for a full twenty-four hours. A year or two later, during an unusual time in which Ramadan and the six weeks of Lent overlapped, I joined Jah'Shams and a Catholic friend in a monthlong, one-meal-a-day fast like the one de Vogüé practices. At no time did I ever feel weak, ill, or deprived of necessary nutrients. If anything,

I felt as Jah'Shams told me he did: extra clear, extra alert, very aware.

The Desires that Define Us

For Cassian, food is the obvious place to start, the aspect of our lives over which we must establish some control before we are strong enough to move on to the more complicated desires that manipulate us. There are a myriad of these, some of them completely innocent, some of them fairly innocuous, and others leading straight to the devil. The ultimate goal of ascesis is to strengthen ourselves through regular self-denial so that we are no longer enslaved by any of these, good or bad. If we are to live simply, our choices must be deliberate ones.

Cassian advises that if we can do only one thing, "it would be better to moderate the forbidden foods of the soul than to fast from the permitted and less dangerous foods of the body." [16] To figure out what he might mean here, I went back to Christ's forty days in the desert.

Just as I suspected, Satan starts with the dangerous foods of the body ("command that these stones become loaves of bread" [Matt. 4:3]) and moves on to the forbidden foods of the soul. After Jesus refuses to break his fast, Satan first strikes at his faith. He takes him to the parapet at the top of the temple and says, "If you are the Son of God, throw yourself down" (Matt. 4:6). Then Satan attacks Jesus' humility. He takes Jesus up to a very high mountain, shows him "all the kingdoms of the world in their magnificence," and says to him, "All these I shall

83

give to you, if you will prostrate yourself and worship me" (Matt. 4:8–9).

Christ's response is, of course, clear and unequivocal ("The Lord, your God, shall you worship / and him alone shall you serve" [Matt. 4:10].)—and far more straightforward than one I could ever make. This gave me the sinking realization that I was still at that birthday party. It was a more sophisticated version, perhaps, in which promotions with nice raises instead of slices of chocolate cake were being offered, but it was still a place in which there was seemingly never enough to go around: not enough money, not enough interesting jobs, not enough book contracts. This meant that I was in a state of perpetual competition for those limited resources—in short, ripe for temptation.

This is what Cassian is talking about when he categorizes avarice, or the desire to *have* (no matter what sort of negative effects this might have on our neighbor), as a form of greed. He allows for the fact that the belly has its natural functions and that the desire for food is strongly connected to our being physical creatures. Avarice, however, he calls a "created vice," one for which we develop a taste that turns into an addiction.

He describes, for example, a young monk who has taken the usual vows of poverty, chastity, and obedience but who can't stop feeling anxious about no longer having a denarius to his name. What if he gets sick and needs outside medical help that the monastery cannot provide? What if his clothes wear out and the community cannot afford to replace them?

The young monk figures out how to get just one coin to store away against future need. To do this, he has to work at something he has not obtained permission to do, and then sell his handiwork in secret. He gets the denarius, but immediately begins to worry about how to double it, where to hide it, or with whom he might entrust it. This leads him to invest it (still secretly, of course, which means through lying), and soon "the unhappy man is constricted in the serpent's coils." Ultimately, the overwhelming desire for that single coin, a desire he supposedly set aside when he made his public vows, leads him by stages to break those vows and leave the community entirely.[17]

Some might call Cassian's reasoning here fallacious, a typical "slippery slope," but what struck me in his description of this wayward monk was how believable the story was. It seemed as though it was not a parable after all, but a real event to which Cassian had been a sad witness. Was there something in this story for me?

There was. I recognized that poor monk's anxiety and the impatience it led to. I understood why he couldn't just relax and trust that God and his brothers would meet his needs. I'd been in the anxiety trap for most of my life, and anxiety had led to many of my more selfish actions over the years. I could not seem to wait for things to unfold naturally; I had to make sure they unfolded the way they were *supposed* to.

Our house is a good example. When Mike and I married, we had between us four children ranging in age from three to eight years old. Though they did not all live with us on a full-time basis—his visited, mine went back and forth—there were definitely times when they were all present and needed to be housed in what was still a run-down, two-bedroom house. Clearly, we had to add on in spite of having no money to do so. Mike, however, was not at all put off by our lack of funds and (whistling, with a pencil behind one ear) assured me that, given enough time, he could handle the job pretty much by himself. "We'll pay as we go," he said. "No debt that way."

This was a fine idea and a heroic one besides—most husbands I knew would not have made such a cheerful offer—but all I could do was scowl at him anxiously.

"What?" he asked.

"It'll take forever," I said. "We can't wait that long."

"We can't?"

"No," I said. "If we're going to do this, we're going to hire people."

This precipitated the first real argument of our marriage. We did not hire people, and Mike's insistence that the job would get done and that I should not worry only led to more anxious tooth gnashing on my part. Where I could have been a real partner in the enterprise, instead I stood around nagging and criticizing and suggesting that we "get some professionals on the job." Finally, with an enormous expanse of one-and-a-half-pound Mexican tiles staring him in the face, he gave in. "Okay, okay, go ahead—hire somebody."

I did, borrowing money to do so. Not only were the results disastrous (all the tiles had to be torn up and redone by guess who), we were now in debt, a debt that would continue to grow every time I gave in to my anxious impatience that we immediately have what I thought we needed. I was not a spendthrift—my purchases were almost always practical, and usually edifying besides—but I could *not wait* to have something once I'd decided we needed it. The desire, at first rather innocent, soon became a burning itch, dominating all my thoughts until it was assuaged.

I could not see anything wrong with this behavior of mine. After all, my going into debt had to do with the betterment of my family, not just myself. One day, however, I awoke to the realization that we were in serious financial trouble, caused by me. Not only were we now carrying thousands of dollars in credit-card debt, but I had opened an equity line of credit on the house, and we'd reached the limit on that as well. We also had four young teenagers hoping to go to college, plus our own retirements looming somewhere in the future.

How in the world had I gotten us to this terrible moment? E. F. Schumacher, in his famous book *Small Is Beautiful,* sheds some light on my situation. He says that our modern economy "is propelled by a frenzy of greed and indulges in an orgy of envy, and these are not accidental features but the very cause of its expansionist success." [18] The plain fact was, I'd fallen for the notion that my desires—for a roomy, artistic house in the country near the ocean, for "cultural" trips to Europe with our kids, for famous writers' conferences, for an advanced degree in middle age—were trump; and my society validated this attitude.

According to Schumacher, our culture believes that economic progress is possible only if "we employ those powerful human drives of selfishness, which religion and traditional wisdom call universally upon us to resist."[19] In such a society, we will never hear a message of restraint. In fact, we are constantly told by advertisers that we "owe it to ourselves" to satisfy our every desire. Our economists validate the "wisdom" of the advertisers: If we don't spend, spend, spend, the system will collapse.

No wonder it seems unnatural, even unhealthy, to deny ourselves anything. In spite of having directly experienced the painful results of living by such a philosophy (it took us several years and much overtime to extricate ourselves from the debt I'd created), I found that this rarely questioned societal belief was still a major obstacle for me. At some level, I was afraid that if I lost my desires, or at least trained them into submission, I would not be myself anymore—that, in a nutshell, my desires were who I was.

Seen in a certain light, this is probably true. Benedictine contemplative Laurence Freeman says, "It is generally agreed among the religious traditions that the human being is an animal of desire, a wanting being. At times it even seems we define ourselves by what we are wanting and explain meaning in terms of our desires."[20] An old battle still wages over this issue: how best do we handle this powerful aspect of our nature? At least some contemporary Christian thinkers believe we do better when we seek to transform rather than to deny our wantings. To deny desire completely, they say, is to deny some crucial aspect of our humanity.

Both camps, the ancient and the modern alike, agree that unmodified, unrestrained desire can never take us where we wish to go if our goal is a simple, focused life. In this regard, ascetical disciplines can make us aware, perhaps for the first time, of just what it is that we want and of how much time and effort we are spending to get it.

My first small experiments with asceticism brought this home to me with a bang. As soon as I began looking, I became aware that the stamp of my desires was firmly impressed on everything that surrounded me, including other people. I saw that others—Mike, for example, or the kids, or my friends—were aware of how I liked things to be, and they changed their behavior in a hundred small ways to please me or to avoid conflict. This realization led me to count up the times in a given day that I felt myself wanting something: the number was astonishingly high.

My "wantings," I discovered, even the most innocent of them, were a constant interruption to my concentration. They pulled me away from my writing desk for a handful of almonds. They sent me upstairs in the middle of a serious conversation to change into a warmer pair of socks. They sent waves of self-righteous anger churning through me when a colleague failed to correctly "read," and then capitulate to, my unexpressed desire to teach the class he'd been assigned. Each time a desire arose, I had to mentally deal with it—and this was taking literally hours out of my days.

Just becoming aware of all this helped me start dealing with my habits. Duane Elgin discusses the importance of self-understanding in his book *Voluntary Simplicity:* "As we develop the skills of living more consciously, we are able not only to examine the underpinnings of our personally constructed reality (as habitual patterns of thought and behavior) but additionally to examine our socially constructed reality (as equally habitual patterns of thoughts and behavior that characterize an entire culture)."[21] Once we begin to look more closely at our patterns, we are more able to penetrate through "the glib advertisements and cultural myths that sustain the status quo" and thus be strengthened in our resolve not to be misled by them.[22]

I found that I was now aware of something else: I was suddenly far more likely to notice the people who did not seem to know what their culture expected of them. Instead of shopping, they made do. Not just made do, they lived in a different way than I did, a lighter, less encumbered way. Not surprisingly, many of these folks could be found at the hermitage: Fr. Bernard with his "holey" jacket and mismatched sandals; Br. Joshua and the old pickup he's driven for years; Br. Emmanuel, who prays over broken generators. Just as Cassian claimed it would, this lightness in their lives has led to possibilities most people cannot envision. "With no concern for the present, no thought about personal likings, no anxiety about the future," says Columba Stewart, "[the freed-up monk] remains undisturbed by avarice, pride, contentiousness, envy, or the remembrance of wrongs."[23]

In his "Time in the Desert Fathers," David Fagerberg suggests that the freed-up monk is able to love in a way the rest of us cannot. For

> charity is always the supreme law. As serious as these ascetics were about maintaining their discipline, there is no hint of rigidity which would begrudge a charitable act. To the contrary, one has the sense that if one applauded them for having interrupted their regimen, they would have replied, perplexed, "What interruption?"[24]

My teenage awe at the single-minded self-denial of the high-school wrestler now makes more sense to me. My friend John's strange lightheartedness and the inexplicable good cheer that only seemed to increase the longer he fasted, now fall into place. He had a goal—making weight—and the goal was so important to him that it counterbalanced the "suffering" of self-denial. In addition, he hoped that by achieving his immediate goal, his struggles might someday end in his becoming a great wrestler. His joy, perhaps, grew out of the knowledge that he was moving directly toward that deliberately chosen point.

On a much larger scale, the goal of the ascetic is control of desires. The hoped-for end, however, is always love. Stewart could have been describing my grandmother when he said of Cassian, "A farmer works day in and day out, through all weathers and seasons, pursuing the 'goal' of a field kept clear and tilled so as to attain the 'end' of a good harvest. The prospect of a good harvest makes even heavy labor endurable, for every turn of the spade brings the farmer closer to both goal and end." [25]

As the author of Hebrews writes, "At the time, all discipline seems a cause not for joy but for pain, yet later it brings the peaceful fruit of righteousness to those who are trained by it" (Heb. 12:11). St. Gregory of Sinai, who must have been God's poet, says it most beautifully of all: "The waters of passions, having troubled and muddied the sea of silence, flood the soul, and can be crossed only in the light and empty boat of complete self-mastery and unpossessiveness." [26]

CHAPTER 4

Purity:
The Way of the Celibate

> But whatever is done either through
> fear of punishment or from some
> other carnal motive, and has not for
> its principle that love which the Spirit
> of God sheds abroad in the heart, is
> not done as it ought to be, however it
> may appear to men.[1]
>
> St. Augustine (A.D. 354–430)

Until I was forty-five, I never thought much about what I wore (I was from California, after all). Then, I was suddenly presented with the opportunity to take a round-the-world trip, and clothing became a significant issue—maybe even *the* significant issue. I was a lone Western woman making my way through conservative countries in the Middle East and Asia; I was going to attract enough attention as it was without adding to the problem by accidentally violating local dress standards. I knew that India insisted on women covering their shoulders and legs. Other societies would be offended if I wore pants. At times (when entering an Orthodox church, for example), I'd need a scarf to drape over my head.

I went shopping for what frankly seemed to be the dowdiest clothes on which I'd ever spent good money: ankle-length skirts, voluminous tunic-like blouses meant to conceal my money pouch, and chunky walking shoes. Everything, of course, in plain, dull colors—the duller the better. I also seriously considered dyeing my blonde hair dark so as to blend in more easily, but finally decided instead on a toad-brown hat. It not only concealed my hair, but most of my head.

On the day of my departure, a male friend remarked that I'd never looked less attractive—which was precisely the reaction I'd hoped for. I could not afford to be "attractive," even in the most casual and innocent way, for along with the possibility that I might unintentionally give offense loomed a larger and more sobering one: I could become a target.

Benedicta Ward, in her book *Harlots in the Desert*, talks about the female counterparts of St. Anthony and Pachomius—women who fled the cities for the solitude of cave and sand and sky. Very often, no one knew that they were women until after their deaths because, for safety's sake, they disguised themselves as men. I, too, felt as though I were in disguise, not my usual self, as I embarked upon my solo journey. This was a surprisingly disconcerting feeling, knowing that I didn't look like me. It raised an interesting question: Just how much of my self-identity was based on appearance?

In American culture, the answer for most of us would have to be "a lot." A competitive consumerist society such as ours requires that we constantly "sell" ourselves to get ahead, and thus the good-looking take the prizes. Though I'd never in my life consciously set out to be seductive (well, maybe not *never*), I was just as aware as anyone else of the edge that came with dressing attractively.

I had the strong feeling, as I boarded the plane swathed from head to foot in my dull robes, that such attire went far beyond unattractive—all the way, in fact, to "unnatural." Here I was, about to set out on the most challenging adventure I'd ever undertaken, and I was voluntarily giving up one of my "powers," a power that, however meager it happened to be in my case, had always helped me get the job done.

St. Augustine and Sexual Obsessions

One of the most famous works of Western literature, *The Confessions of St. Augustine,* deals directly with this interesting connection between sex (for the term "attractive" always implies an element of sex) and power. In fact, Augustine is notorious for dwelling so long and so intently on the issue of sexuality in what is ultimately a spiritual autobiography. In his particular case, the greatest obstacle on the spiritual path happened to be a sexual one. His deep attraction to "beautiful bodies" led to what moderns might term an addiction. This addiction to *cupiditas,* or erotic passion, began at a relatively young age—sixteen—and took him many years to overcome.

Augustine's proclivities are at least partially explained by his era. Born in A.D. 354 in the North African town of Tagaste near the eastern border of Algeria, he grew up in bloody and decadent times. Though the most violent forms of persecution against Christians had by then subsided, the emperors relied upon the spectacles of the circus in Carthage, where Augustine went to school, and the savage gladiatorial games in Rome, where he eventually lived and worked, to keep the populace of the empire entertained.

His mother, Monica, was a devoted Catholic; his pagan father, Patricius, was a minor government official. Even in the smaller and more provincial Tagaste, the family had links to the Roman ruling class and thereby to the cultural standards of the day. Augustine's early years were famously wild. In *The Confessions,* he attributes his delinquency not only to the general moral decay of his time but also to a misguided love on the part of his parents.

On his father's side, he says, there was too great a respect for book learning for its own sake. On his mother's side, there was an overly intense focus on education in hopes that it might lead him to Christianity someday. His parents made great sacrifices so that he could go to the best schools. Meanwhile, nobody noticed the trouble into which he was drifting, the "brambles of unclean desires" spreading thick over his head; there was "no hand to root them out." He began running the streets with a crowd of bad youngsters, and his status in this group became the most important aspect of his life.[2]

One night, for example, they stole great loads of fruit from a nearby pear tree for the sheer joy of stealing. They did not consume the pears themselves but instead threw them to the pigs. "Even if we did eat a little of it," he says, "we did this to do what pleased us for the reason that it was forbidden."[3]

Far more enticing than stolen pears was the forbidden fruit of sex. Augustine says that in this same year, the year of "youth's seething spring," he became increasingly driven by desire. "I could not distinguish the calm light of chaste love," he says, "from the fog of lust. Both kinds of affection burned confusedly within me and swept my feeble youth over the crags of desire and plunged me into a whirlpool of shameful deeds."[4]

At school in Carthage, the situation only worsened. Here, he discovered firsthand the price extracted by a devotion to *cupiditas.* "For I was loved, and I had gained love's bond of joy. But in my joy I was bound about with painful chains of iron, so that I might be scourged by burning rods of jealousy, and suspicion, and fear, and anger, and quarreling."[5]

In time, he took on a mistress, a woman he lived with for many years, who bore him a son, Adeodatus. Apparently, Augustine never even considered marrying this woman—primarily, it seems, because of his friendship with Alypius, a young man who convinced him that unmarried, he was free to live the life of a philosopher, a life of "unbroken leisure in love of wisdom." Still, Augustine writes, "I thought I would be too wretched if I were kept from a woman's arms."[6]

This admission led to great anguish. He very much admired Alypius's life of "strictest chastity" but was sure that he himself was incapable of giving up sex. "I believed," he says, "that continence lay within a man's own powers, and such powers I was not conscious of within myself. I was so foolish that I did not know that . . . no man can be continent unless [God] grant it to him."[7]

Struggling to find some relief from the conflict, he gave up his mistress and betrothed himself to a girl too young to marry—and while waiting the requisite two years for her to be of age, took on yet another lover. However, "not yet healed within me," he says, "was that wound which had been made by the cutting away of my former companion. After intense fever and pain, it festered, and it still caused me pain, although in a more chilling and desperate way."[8]

Our Confusion over Romantic Passion

I must confess that this passage made me cringe. Somehow, in a single sentence, Augustine manages to catch all the confused anguish of a broken love affair—a love affair that has nothing to do with another human being but instead with a certain celebrated *notion* of love. I knew exactly what Augustine meant, for I'd been in that place myself for many, many years.

Since almost nothing in our culture is placed on a higher pedestal than this notion of love, my situation was not uncommon. Passionate, romantic love is, for many of us, our be all and end all, our highest good. At age fifteen I went out with a boy for the very first time and decided, in the space of less than an hour, that I would someday marry him. When I finally did so, he was twenty-one and I was nineteen. The marriage was doomed from the start—not because he was a bad person or because we were deeply incompatible, but simply because I had not married *him* at all.

When I left that marriage thirteen years later for another man—somebody, I thought, who would *complete* me in a way my increasingly baffled first husband could not—it was because of this allegiance to romantic ideals. Nobody could have lived up to my romantic expectations, however. One human being cannot possibly provide all inspiration, all meaning, all sustenance for another. Yet because of what we are taught to believe about love, we think we can demand this, especially, sad to say, if we are women.

As a result, I felt justified, even self-righteous, about being brave enough to leave what I termed an "unsatisfying marriage." That phrase had the ring of somber inevitability—what else could I do, after all? I was not "fulfilled"; I had to be with someone who could fulfill me. Off I went, banners flying, to learn exactly the same lesson all over again.

In my own way, I was just as enslaved to *cupiditas* as Augustine had been. My notion of love may have been more romanticized than his frankly sexual one, but my self-built prison was made of the same stuff. It was also windowless, and this is actually what I remember most about those years of being obsessed by eros: Romantic passion can lead to strange, cruel, lonely blindness.

Precisely because romantic passion is a form of idolatry, the worship of a false god, it can sometimes lead us, via profound disappointment, to the real thing. This is what happened to both Augustine and me. This is also what ultimately led to my return to religion after a twenty-year hiatus—and to some of Augustine's most profound theological insights.

First, however, someone had to help us break the chains.

In the case of Augustine, this turned out to be a fellow North African who came to visit, a devout Christian who noticed that Augustine was reading a book by St. Paul. During the ensuing discussion, Ponticianius told his unhappy young friend about St. Athanasius's *Vita St. Antonii,* published only twenty years before. Augustine was not only riveted by Anthony's life story, he felt convicted by it. He describes his reaction thus: "As he spoke, you, O Lord, turned me back upon myself. You took me from behind my own back, where I had placed myself because I did not want to look at myself." [9]

Augustine's famous spiritual crisis had begun. He realized that for years he had prayed, "Lord, give me chastity and continence, but not yet!" [10] Much as he longed for healing, wholeness, and peace, he was unwilling to give up sexual pleasure to get them. Now, torn nearly in two, he found himself weeping uncontrollably in the garden while his friend Alypius sat by in silent support. Suddenly, Augustine heard what sounded like the voice of a child chanting the words, "Take up and read. Take up and read." [11]

Remembering Anthony's pivotal moment—the words of Christ to the rich young man—Augustine ran for the book by St. Paul. He opened it to this passage: "Not in orgies and drunkenness, not in promiscuity and licentiousness, not in rivalry and jealousy. But put on the Lord Jesus Christ, and make no provision for the desires of the flesh." [12] "Instantly," Augustine says, ". . . all the dark shadows of doubt fled away." [13]

My version of Augustine's North African friend was a patient philosophy professor who, over time, managed to convince me that every aspect of my life was being affected or directed by romantic fantasies—that, in fact, I was not thinking about life at all, but instead creating a world in which I'd always feel charmed and pleased. It was he who one day handed me an essay by philosopher and novelist Iris Murdoch entitled "The Sovereignty of Good over Other Concepts."

In this essay, Murdoch spends some time talking about art and artists, and about two different ways that art presents reality to us. The first kind of art is "consoling fantasy," which simply reassures the needy ego. No doubt many of my notions about romantic passion came from this kind of art—for our culture has produced hundreds of books and movies on the subject, some of them quite famous and respected. From *Gone with the Wind* to *Titanic,* we can't resist a dramatic love story.

The second kind of art, however, presents life as clearly and truthfully as possible. These books and poems and movies may also present stories of great erotic love, but in an honest, realistic way that also follows through to the consequences. This art does not set out to supply us with the fantasies to which we so easily become addicted.

These are the stories, says Murdoch, that can open our eyes to the dangers and the glories of love, "the general name of the quality of attachment."[14] Our human tendency to attach ourselves to things and people and ideas is "capable of infinite degradation" (for we are always ready to distort for our own egoistic purposes what is essentially good). In spite of all the temptations that surround love, however, "its existence is the unmistakable sign that we are spiritual creatures, attracted by excellence and made for the Good. It is a reflection of the warmth and light of the sun."[15]

One of the most important turning points in my own life came when I realized this very thing: My obsessive romantic passion was actually spiritual passion in disguise.

Augustine was struck hard by the same insight, but he went on to share it with the world. In fact, he became a major—perhaps *the* major—influence on the development of Western Christianity for the next sixteen hundred years. At least partly out of his own long struggle with sexual enslavement and the abuse of sexual power was born a simple conviction about God and his relationship to humans, one that serves as the groundwork for Augustine's own theology: "You have made us for yourself, and our heart is restless till it rests in you."[16]

What Augustine calls *cupiditas* can never bring peace, for ephemeral pleasures can never satisfy when what we are really seeking is God. Peace comes instead with *agape,* the love displayed by Christ, the kind of love that does not lead to possessiveness, dependency, jealousy, wrath, or other self-centered emotions. This *agape* love is what

Murdoch seems to be talking about. Augustine's celebration of chastity and continence can only be understood in this light: These two acts of self-control help simplify and purify the heart, making it possible to love other people in a genuine, nonmanipulative way.

For Augustine, a chaste life is a life that acknowledges and honors the original goodness of all flesh: "Both soul and body, man was made good by a good God." [17] The physical passions are a divine gift. It is only the perverse will (we would probably call this "egoism") that leads to abuse of this gift. "Do not accuse the nature of flesh when you hear: 'If you live according to the flesh, you shall die,' for it could have been said thus, and most truly so: 'If you live according to yourselves, you shall die.' " [18]

In addition, chastity is very difficult to maintain, and the struggle to do so is humbling. Augustine admits to being plagued for years with "images as [his] former habits implanted" in him, and "so great a power [had] these deep images over my soul and my flesh that these false visions persuad[ed] me when asleep to do what true sights [could not] persuade me to do when awake." [19] He was a powerful and intelligent man but helpless in regard to his sexual appetite. He finally concluded that "continence is a gift of God," that he had to give up the illusion of his own strength before he could be healed of his weakness. [20]

In spite of some of the disturbing problems in our society today that are directly linked to sex and its abuse, Augustine's hard-won commitment to chastity can seem antiquated, even misguided, to modern readers. We believe we have "moved on" from the days when people denied themselves sex for the sake of their religion. We secretly pity those celibates left among us (priests, monks, nuns). How can they experience *life,* we think, if they never make love?

Laurence Freeman attributes at least some of our cultural attitudes toward sex to the "cult of desire" that emerged during the late medieval period by way of the troubadours and their romantic ballads. "A culture that so exclusively identified love with the passion of erotic desire finds it particularly difficult to hear about the goal of elimination of desire or its transformation into a desire for God." [21]

Another tradition that contributes to our attitude comes out of nineteenth-century Romanticism with its near worship of nature and its elevation of the natural over the artificial. This combined with the flowering of the new science of psychology in that same century has made us hyperaware of the "power of biology." Sexuality is natural, we are taught, and we only hurt ourselves when we deny what is natural in us. Repressing healthy desire can cause psychological problems, even emotional crippling. While I did not hear this from the cradle (my mother and father were typical parents of the fifties, reluctant to talk about sex at all), by the time I was a young adult, the sexual revolution of the 1960s and 1970s had done its work in me. Like many other people my age, I believed that "free love" (whether or not I personally indulged in it) was the symbol of a new utopia, open only to the courageous.

Nowadays, Augustine's renunciation of sex is often interpreted negatively, and he himself is portrayed as a dour, self-hating moralist. One popular spiritual writer blames him for the notorious mind/body split bequeathed to us by Western philosophy, and another refers dismissively to his "prejudice against the body." Women (including me, when I first began to read him) seem particularly offended by his dramatic repudiation of sex.

The Unacknowledged Desire for Approval

Given my commitment to simplicity, I realized that I could not afford to overlook the complex layers of sexuality in my life. Though I was no longer enslaved by obsessive romantic fantasy, I was still inundated on a daily basis with the subtle and not-so-subtle erotic images that were meant to create in me the yearning for beauty, wealth, status, and sophistication. The disheveled ingenues staring moodily from the magazine racks at the grocery store, the movie-star couples-of-the-week, the smart, sexy models on the cover of *Cosmopolitan*—all bore the same message: You are somehow inadequate unless you wear makeup like ours, dress like we do, live in the kinds of houses in which we live, take the vacations we take, spend the money we spend, and attract the people we attract.

I realized that if I took the message of the advertisers seriously, my own course was set. The beautiful, unconscious simplicity of the Amish farmers on their way to church, the white-robed Camaldolese monks filing in for Mass, or the black **V** of ducks flying over the jack pine in early morning would never, ever be mine. I began to think hard about how a person like me, a married woman living a nonmonastic life in a sex-centered culture, might embrace the spirit of loving chastity.

The Gospels did not provide a lot of help, at least not in the sense of directives or injunctions. Christ is anything but a finger-wagging moralist when it comes to sex—in fact, he offends the local moral experts when he shows compassion toward the woman caught in adultery, Mary Magdalene with her seven famous devils, and the Samaritan woman who lived with five different men. Instead of focusing on the act, he focuses on what's in the heart: "You have heard that it was said, 'You shall not commit adultery.' But I say to you, everyone who looks at a woman with lust has already committed adultery with her in his heart" (Matt. 5:27–28).

Scrupulosity in outward behavior means nothing if it does not spring from a genuinely pure heart/mind. As Augustine discovered to his great chagrin, even when he gave up his mistresses, he went right on fantasizing about and longing for the sexual passion that had once enslaved him.

Though my outward behavior had changed a lot from the days when I centered my life around romantic love, I realized that I was not so very different from Augustine when it came to these old patterns of thought and emotional response. Much of my self-identity was still tied to my ability to attract and hold male attention (hence the weird sense of *losing* my identity as soon as I clapped that toad-brown hat on my head), though I'd consistently denied this. I told myself instead that I liked men for *themselves,* not for the ego boost their friendships gave me. I insisted that men were more straightforward, more honest, and less self-absorbed than women.

One side effect of this unacknowledged desire for male approval was that I'd become scornful toward most women. They were silly, frivolous things, I told myself—always worrying about how they looked. I'd been extra cold to young women for this reason. Their insecurities were so obvious, the overcompensation (push-up bras, heavy makeup, tight pants) so blatant. I'm different, I thought. Men like me for myself because I don't play those games.

I was also contemptuous of another kind of person: the occasional poor soul who fell for my unspoken but powerful need for sexual approval—people who became smitten with me. This didn't happen much, but when it did, I heaped coals upon the head of the offender. It was terribly important for me, a woman who'd been to hell and back on the tail of an illusion called romantic passion, to crush out with prompt cruelty any sign of starstruck fantasy in someone else.

Once at a large writers' conference, for example, a kindly professor in his fifties tearfully confided to me on an evening walk back to the dorms that he'd had an affair with a student—an affair that was apparently going to cost him not only his job but his wife and children besides. I listened to his sad story—the sort of tale that is endemic in a culture that worships romance—and when asked, I offered my bit of advice.

My apparent sympathy, however, was too much for a man so addicted to female consolation. He became a hopeless pest, tagging along behind me everywhere I went for the entire two weeks of the conference. I found myself increasingly plagued by insomnia. When, in frustration, I pulled back the curtains late one night so I could look at the moon instead of the drab dorm-room wall, whom should I spy but my pest, keeping faithful vigil beneath my second-floor window.

His growing obsession was not only obvious to me, but to others. I noticed people giving me sympathetic looks—in fact, rolling their eyes—when they saw him trudging mournfully along in my wake. I could not have been more disgusted. What was with this guy, anyway? Couldn't he get a life?

As I tried my best to examine my own attitudes toward sexual passion and romance, I thought of this poor beleaguered soul—how quickly he'd become re-enslaved to the same kind of fantasy that had already blown up his life. Had I dealt with him compassionately? Not quite. I put up with him for the duration of the conference, then sent him a scathing and condemnatory letter the moment he tried to contact me after my return home.

Why? I had done so because he'd had the audacity to reveal to me and to others something I did not want to know about myself—that my preference for male friendship was in some part a power trip. Male attention did something important for my needy ego. At some level, sex still drove me. By falling so hard and so publicly, this man had called attention to this unsavory aspect of my character. He'd become a living, breathing bit of evidence for something I mightily resisted having to acknowledge. No wonder I'd sent him straight to the outer darkness, "where there will be wailing and grinding of teeth" (Matt. 13:42).

In addition, he was a painful reminder of my own humiliating years of romantic enslavement. He was like a mirror, reflecting back a self I never wanted to see again. This was a shocking realization—that he was I. How had I responded to him in his weakness? I gave him the bitter fruit of self-hatred.

Who else had I hurt without knowing it?

The answer became obvious to me: the rare man who could attract *my* attention. Rare, because I was so nervous about slipping back into fantasy that I might as well have been wearing spiked armor. It was one thing to know that others found *me* attractive—that left me entirely in charge of the situation. It was quite another to feel that old tug myself. Woe to the poor unsuspecting soul who triggered it.

I remembered a dimly lit restaurant and a table full of writers, especially a tall, handsome, and quite famous one with whom I'd had to briefly share a chair. As we chatted quietly, sipping wine and exchanging personal histories, it became clear to me that, contrary to all my internal swaggering, I was still very much a human being, as subject as anyone else to inconvenient desire.

My response? In its own way, it was just as unloving as the one I'd made to that poor pest at the conference. I deliberately wrecked the budding friendship by pouring salt in an open wound that had been trustfully revealed to me. Perhaps I did well to flee. Perhaps he was the kind of person who abused his power over others; but how on earth would I know that? *He* was not part of the equation. I never allowed him to show his character. I was far too absorbed in my *own* anxieties to focus on the person beside me.

What could heal this hidden sexual turmoil that caused me to hurt and condemn others? How might I stop viewing sexuality as a power game? How might I become simple and loving toward every single human being, regardless of gender or erotic subcurrents?

Augustine discovered through years of frustrating failure that we cannot run the show when it comes to our sexual natures. Doing battle with ourselves, putting our trust in personal strength or willpower, is ultimately a lost cause. Worse, we can fall into unconscious self-hatred, as I did, when we attempt to rule or dominate some God-given aspect of our natures. "Peace, then," Augustine says, "will be perfect in us when, our nature clinging inseparably to its Creator, nothing of ourselves fights against us."²²

I thought about my friends at the hermitage, all of whom have taken a lifelong vow of celibacy, and I wondered how they had calmed and redirected the tremendous force of eros, for (with varying degrees of success) they have. This is one of the most striking differences between life on the mountain and life "in the world."

Fr. Bernard of the mismatched sandals has watched retreatants come and go for nearly forty years. One night while we were walking the road together, he told me what he had noticed about the women visitors. "I think they feel safe here," he said, "especially the ones who have been hurt by men. They realize they can trust the monks, and you can just see them relaxing and starting to smile."

I realized that this was one of the reasons I kept going back—because it was safe, and not just in the usual sense (freedom from attack; freedom from all the other real and imagined threats I had worried about on that long, solo trip around the world). It was safe to love, warmly and wholeheartedly, with no holding back. This was one thing that united the far-flung group of regular visitors to the hermitage: our deep and abiding affection for the monks.

After nearly a decade of retreats, there were people whose names I still wasn't sure of—was the tall guy with the round face and black glasses Br. Mark or Br. Anthony? how about the little one with the longish hair?—but even those I loved. I loved them in the sense that I expected them to be in their places in the choir and missed them when they weren't. I loved them because, whether I passed them on the road at dusk or stood beside them in the dish line after Sunday dinner, I could feel love coming back at me—a sort of beaming benevolence that lay self-consciousness to rest.

Here there were no speculative looks, no sidelong, implicative glances—none of the automatic assessments that we are so tediously, boringly subjected to, men and women alike, as we move through the world. There were none of the silent judgments that tempt us to give up on love entirely and simply go cold. There was no suggestion that there are limits on who may take delight in the world, that only the young and beautiful are permitted to offer their hearts to other people.

The Liberating New Rules of *Agape* Love

These, however, are the rules of *cupiditas,* not *agape.* Augustine, when he finally saw the difference, lamented, "Too late have I loved you, O Beauty so ancient and so new, too late have I loved you! Behold, you were there within me while I was outside: it was there that I sought you, and, a deformed creature, rushed headlong upon these things of beauty which you have made. You were with me, but I was not with you. They kept me far from you, those fair things which, if they were not in you, would not exist at all." [23]

This grief is genuine; chasing the ephemeral butterfly of erotic beauty, Augustine had missed the real thing. It should not therefore surprise us that he became an influential proponent of the vow of celibacy for clergy, which was finally adopted at the fifth Council of Carthage in 401. Augustine thought that celibacy would free men to love God and others without the distraction of eros. Such a difficult rule is only rightly obeyed, he said, "when the motive principle of action is the love of God, and the love of our neighbor in God." [24]

This was the freedom I felt at the hermitage—the freedom to love my neighbor without fear of sexual entanglement. This was the gift of celibacy, the difficult sacrifice made for the sake of *agape.* I was deeply grateful to be a recipient of that generous gift.

At home in the world, however, I still had to deal with the fact that *cupiditas* ran the show and that it still lived in me. I realized that I must find a way to transform its unruly energy into something more useful—and that this was no longer an option, but an obligation.

As Laurence Freeman says, "Desire can lead us to create. But disordered desire starts the chain of events that leads to evil when in its pain and ignorance it imagines the unreal and attaches itself to these images." [25] Precisely. Other people had also suffered because of the consoling fantasies to which I'd so stubbornly clung. "In this understanding of evil," adds Freeman, "illusion cannot be lightly explained or dismissed. Responsibility for it sits squarely with human beings." [26]

Bede Healey, a New Camaldoli monk and a psychoanalyst, has also written about desire. That which Augustine calls concupiscence, lust, or *cupiditas,* and I have termed sexual enslavement, Healey, like Freeman, refers to as "deformed or distorted desire." [27] Desire is built in, he says; as humans, we are naturally desiring creatures. It is when fear attaches itself to desire that it becomes dangerous.

What is the nature of this fear? "It is a pervasive, overt and yet subtle questioning of our own worth, goodness, abilities, motivation, and desirability. Over time it undermines our basic sense of selfhood and self-worth." [28] It makes us entirely vulnerable to both real and imagined negative judgment. The smallest things can stir it up—for example, having to wear that toad-brown hat and those dull, dull travel clothes.

Under fearful conditions, we crave what we think will calm our self-doubts. Our natural desire to be loved, for example, becomes an obsessive craving that can only be assuaged by fantasy—a fantasy that allows us to become more beautiful, intelligent, and accomplished than we really are. This, in turn, allows us to attract astonishing people like ourselves into love affairs—affairs that, even if we never acted them out physically, are legendary for their passion and depth. Absorbed in fantasy, we cannot see who is really in front of us; and certainly we cannot love.

The unwelcome truth was beginning to dawn that a serious effort in the realm of chastity would be just as disorienting as my efforts to obtain solitude, silence, and awareness had been. My attitudes toward sexuality were indeed a tangled mess, and the process of finding and unraveling all those knots was no doubt going to occupy me for the rest of my life. It was also becoming clear that genuine simplicity was impossible without such an effort.

The problem has not gone away, but recently I came across a heartening story, one that gave me hope. It was the story of Pelagia, a well-known actress in Antioch who lived during the days of the desert hermits, perhaps even as a contemporary of Anthony and Pachomius. Young, beautiful, and heedless, she rode one day with a group of laughing companions past a meeting of bishops and monks. Most of the men turned away or hid their eyes so as to avoid being seduced by the lovely sight. One of them, however, a monk-bishop called Nonnus, "did long and most intently regard her and after she had passed by, still he gazed and his eyes went after her. Turning to his fellows, he asked, 'Did not her great beauty delight you? Indeed, it delighted me.'" [29]

In time, Pelagia, who had noticed his frank joy in her natural loveliness, came secretly to see him and was so overwhelmed by the gentle *agape* he extended to her that she was converted. Voluntarily setting aside her considerable sexual power, she disguised herself as a man and went to the desert to live out the rest of her days as a hermit.

What I found inspiring in the story was not so much Pelagia's part in it, the giving up part, remarkable as that was, but instead the beautiful way that Nonnus loved her. For him, she was yet another proof of God's astonishing goodness, just as, one would guess, the desert flowers of spring or the starry night sky might be. Her beauty was not in his case an occasion for sin, as it was for the others, but instead a hymn to the glory of God. This could mean only one thing: Nonnus had achieved genuine chastity—that is, a pure heart no longer troubled by disordered desire.

With such purity, he was able to reach out to others with the love that St. Paul so famously celebrates:

> Love is patient, love is kind. It is not jealous,
> [love] is not pompous, it is not inflated, it is not
> rude, it does not seek its own interests, it is not
> quick-tempered, it does not brood over injury,
> it does not rejoice over wrongdoing but rejoices
> with the truth. It bears all things, believes all
> things, hopes all things, endures all things.
> (1 Cor. 13:4–7)

Augustine, commenting on this passage, adds, "Now the end of the commandment is charity, out of a pure heart, and of a good conscience, and of faith unfeigned." [30] St. Paul, who is accused nearly as often as his disciple of a cold and unloving severity, answers with joy, "So faith, hope, love remain, these three; but the greatest of these is love" (1 Cor. 13:13).

PART III

DISCOVERING A NEW COMMUNITY

Though the early ascetics did not adopt the disciplines as a moral enterprise to make themselves in some way "better" than others, this sort of cleansing and strengthening process can separate us from our fellow human beings if we are not careful. When in our solitude and silence we become more self-aware, we cannot help but become more aware at the same time of others and how they handle life. Since we ourselves are so engrossed in the transformation process, we cannot seem to avoid the fact that most people aren't. How do we deal with this? What sort of judgments do we pass?

If we are not careful at this stage, we can become angrily obsessed with the *im*purities of the world. We ourselves have worked so hard and been disappointed so often in our struggles to overcome the habits that distract us from our quest. We have suffered in a certain way. We've learned to deal quietly with misunderstanding, even scorn. We've lost friends and our easy relationships with relatives. We've come to terms with our essential aloneness. Why can't others take this journey as seriously as we do?

Waste disgusts us. Selfishness horrifies us. Greed in all its ugliness has become nearly unbearable. The sexual obsessions of our culture are beyond belief. No longer do we feel sad about withdrawing from the world. Now the problem is how to continue living in it. To protect ourselves from a chronic sense of outrage, we pull back even further; we emotionally disconnect. We separate the world into "us" and "them"—the few who understand what life is about and the many who amble like sheep through their unthinking days—or, worse, manipulate the sheep for their own ends. We are, at this stage on the path, seriously at risk of becoming pious cynics, toxic people who do more harm than good.

If we are to avoid cynicism, we have to keep caring, even when it makes us angry. Yet an angry moralist can become an ugly creature indeed—a puritan who tries to force others to "straighten up," either through legislation or military strength. History is full of such zealots.

What is the answer? How can we continue to shed the kind of clutter that keeps us from simplifying and purifying our lives without condemning others for not following suit?

Christ knew from the very beginning that this would happen to us if we tried to walk this path alone. We cannot separate ourselves forever; we cannot become lofty critics, refusing to see the deep connection we have with our fellow human beings. If we do, we become guilty of the greatest sin of all: we fail to love. This is why Jesus directed his followers to become "one body" in the church. This is what communal worship is all about. Here we find others at various stages of the path, people who understand our deep longing for a better life. Here, we find fellow travelers. The chapter called "Devotion: The Way of the Psalm Singer" focuses on this aspect of the journey.

Even today, monastics know that it is their times of common prayer that maintain the health of the community. Like them, when we worship and pray with others on a regular basis, we continually reorient ourselves on the basics. We protect ourselves from the very real temptation to go it alone, to be proud and disdainful of others. We learn that the community can accomplish more good on this earth than we ever can on our own. We are humbled by the struggles of others and by their faith and hope in the face of adversity. We are inoculated against cynicism.

From this base, we are strengthened for our return to the world as changed creatures. We begin to understand that this, in fact, might be the whole point of the journey—that we are meant to be "salt and light" to those who have no community at all and to those who flounder in darkness. St. Benedict (A.D. 480–547) was convinced that love is learned best in community and that anyone who wishes to become a solitary must first learn love in the tough and humbling school of communal worship. His insistence that the *Opus Dei,* or Work of God—the daily hours of liturgical prayer—take precedence in monastic life was in part prompted by this conviction.

CHAPTER 5

Devotion:
The Way of the Psalm Singer

Let us consider, then, how we ought to
behave in the presence of God and his
angels and let us stand to sing the
psalms in such a way that our minds
are in harmony with our voices.[1]

from the Rule of St. Benedict (A.D. 480–547)

Surprisingly enough, it was my mother who first told
me about them. She actually got the newspaper out of
the trash just so she could show me their picture—the
four members of a new rock group with oafish haircuts
who were causing a major sensation. It was 1964, I was
twelve, and they were the Beatles. That week they sang "I
Want to Hold Your Hand" on *The Ed Sullivan Show,* and
on the playground the day after their performance, I realized that I now understood the term *devotee.* This was a
word I'd recently guessed right on a vocabulary test:
"someone set apart for a special use or service; someone
who has given up himself to some purpose, activity, or
person."[2] Now I had a visceral, heart-pounding sense of

what it meant: a devotee was a person like myself, twelve years old, who was ready to lie across the railroad tracks for her particular Beatle (mine was George; I chose him because John, Paul, and Ringo were already taken).

As I found out later, this was only Level One; genuine devotees engage in rituals, make solemn promises, collect and display relics, write loyally impassioned entries in their diaries, dream nightly of their gods, and most importantly, go together to massive concerts where they scream themselves hoarse, become hysterical, and sometimes even swoon. By that standard, I ultimately did not make the devotee cut. It was one thing to gather with the faithful each day at lunch and endlessly talk Beatles or to go see *A Hard Day's Night* en masse. It was quite another to actually make the pilgrimage to the Hollywood Bowl and put myself in their *live presence.*

I don't remember even bothering to ask my parents if I could go. The urge must not have been strong enough to fight that fight. I suppose I knew at some level that my devotion was really a pretty thin thing compared to, say, Stephie's—Stephie who had scrapbooks filled with Beatle memorabilia, Stephie who was willing to save her money for months to pay for the ticket. I sensed that, unlike hers, my devotion was primarily peer-generated, something you professed just so people knew you were normal. I admitted to myself, guiltily, that I really didn't spend that much time thinking about George anymore, certainly far less than I'd led my friends to believe.

The night that Stephie went to see them, I had a talk with my mom about this disturbing realization of mine.

She described a Frank Sinatra concert she'd been to as a teenager, the shrieking and the fainting, the helpless pubescent passion of the female crowd. "I didn't scream," she confided. "I didn't feel like it. I thought it was fake anyway." This was one thing I respected about my hardheaded mom; she didn't fool easily when it came to what she called "mob hysteria." She gave me a couple of helpful analogies. "It's the same thing that happened during the Russian Revolution," she said. "People just lost their heads. Or you could also think of it like one of those big religious revival meetings. You know—the kind they have in tents?"

Though this explanation left me mildly confused—Communism, Pentecostalism, and Beatlemania, all in the same package—I was left with the conviction that crowds of devotees were not to be trusted. You could apparently lose your normal personality in one of them. You could be swayed into doing things you wouldn't normally do. My short stint as a worshipper in the cult of George Harrison pretty much fizzled to an end that night.

As the 1960s unfolded, I continued to be haunted by the issue of devotion and drawn to the lives of people who inspired it: Tolstoy, Gandhi, and Martin Luther King Jr. I read their biographies and wondered what fueled their ability to change the course of other people's lives. For a long time, I wanted to *be* one of those people—not a devotee, never again a devotee, but instead the focus of other people's devotion, a force to be reckoned with. Most of this, of course, was nothing but ego inflation; the remainder seems to have been an early manifestation of a call that would grow stronger throughout the decades—

the call to be better than the oftentimes miserable creature that I was.

I was reminded of this call years later in a philosophy class when I read a book called *After Virtue* by Alasdair MacIntyre. In it, he describes a "crucial turning point in history," a moment when at least some people in the Western world gave up on the hopeless task of holding the crumbling Roman Empire together and began seeking another way to live instead. MacIntyre writes that they sought a way in which "both morality and civility might survive the coming ages of barbarism and darkness." He suggests that we moderns are in the same boat as the Romans were, except that the barbarians "have already been governing us for quite some time." He says, "We are waiting not for a Godot, but for another—doubtless very different—St. Benedict." [3]

St. Benedict—I'd heard of him, but that was about it. Here he was, being offered up as a possible savior for my own chaotic age. I was intrigued then, and thought that I should read about Benedict, but it wasn't until one of my retreats at the hermitage that I finally picked up a biography of his life. In it, I discovered that nearly 1,500 years before the Beatles, St. Benedict got a startling taste of what it must have been like for John, Paul, George, and Ringo in the Hollywood Bowl that night. As a young man seeking to live a holy life, he inadvertently became an object of veneration—and this not once, but several times. Unlike my former idols, however, his initial response was to get as far away as he could from his would-be devotees.

St. Benedict and the Price of Fame

Benedict was born about A.D. 480 in a small town called Nursia, nestled among the Sabine Hills. This area of Italy was famous for its old-fashioned virtues—Cicero called its inhabitants *severissimi homines,* or "most severe men"—and among these, the people of Nursia were seen as particularly austere.

At the time of Benedict's birth, the political situation in Italy was bordering on chaos. Rome had been sacked and burned by the Visigoth Alaric seventy years before, and in 476, the barbarian Odoacer replaced the last emperor of the Western empire. Though the imperial structure had still not completely collapsed, disintegration seemed imminent—not only of the secular system but perhaps even of Christianity itself. Despite its official recognition by the emperors, Christianity did not have much moral or spiritual clout in Rome, which had become a famously wicked city.

Sometime between the ages of fourteen and eighteen, Benedict arrived in the imperial capital to study either rhetoric or law—scholars are unsure. He was accompanied by Cyrilla, a woman whom his first biographer, St. Gregory the Great, refers to as his "nurse." She came along to cook for him, to keep his lodgings clean, and to watch over her young charge as he faced the temptations of the big city for the first time.[4]

Whatever it was he was studying, the strictly raised young Benedict soon found himself in a life crisis. He could not commit himself with a clear conscience to the path laid out before him. Soon, and in somewhat the same manner as his famous predecessor Anthony, he abandoned both his studies and his father's money in order to seek "some place where he might achieve his holy purpose."[5] This turned out to be the small village of Enfide, less than fifty miles from Rome, where others of like mind were already living in lodgings near the Church of St. Peter. There, he spent his days in silence, prayer, and the study of Scripture and the works of the Fathers, particularly Cassian's.

He might have stayed in the small community of Enfide for years, for the peace and quiet suited him and he was slowly finding his way to God in the manner outlined by theologians Tertullian and Origen: through a "solitary life within the social framework."[6] Under this model, lay Christians understood themselves as contemplatives within a wider secular community, a separate people who were to practice their way of life regardless of circumstance.

Overnight, however, everything changed. His faithful housekeeper, Cyrilla, accidentally broke a borrowed earthenware sieve. He found her weeping disconsolately, and in an attempt to comfort her, picked up the two pieces and went down on his knees to pray over them. When he stood up, the sieve was again whole. News of the miracle spread rapidly, and soon the healed utensil was on display in the porch of the local church. Realizing how much attention he was attracting, he made his escape, this time all alone.

Benedict hiked to the northwest out of Enfide, following the river Anio. Eventually, he met a monk named Romanus, who pried out of him his plan to become a hermit. Romanus apparently took the young man seriously, for it was he who gave Benedict the traditional garment of the Eastern monk, a sheepskin "melota," and showed him the way to an almost inaccessible cave in the side of a precipice near Subiaco. Every day for the next three years, this same Romanus, who lived in a clifftop monastery above the cave, lowered whatever bread he could spare from his own small allowance down to his young hermit friend below.

As had happened in Enfide, however, Benedict once again began to attract attention, this time for his austerity and holiness. Eventually, a band of monks who were living in a series of hand-carved caves called Vicovaro begged him to become their abbot. He resisted for a time, telling them that his discipline would be too harsh for them, but eventually gave in. Here I found an interesting devotee twist: after a while, they began to agree that his rules were indeed too austere and decided to poison him. The assassination attempt failed, however, when he made the sign of the cross over their offering of wine and the jug obligingly shattered.[7]

He made his way back to the cave at Subiaco but never again to the solitude of the previous three years, for by now his reputation had begun drawing large numbers of prospective novices. Eventually, he established twelve monasteries in the valley beneath the mountain. Each housed twelve monks overseen by superiors who came to him for direction—a small-scale Pachomian experiment in the north of Italy. These communities, in addition to observing their hours of prayer, did the hard work of the local peasants, and the valley prospered.

Eventually, however, his holiness put him at risk once again. A local priest named Florentius, who for a long time had been jealous of Benedict's spiritual authority, turned murderous. Choosing not to imperil his other monks, Benedict and a small band left Subiaco in search of a new building site. Eventually, they constructed a monastery on the site of an ancient mountaintop acropolis, ringed by sacred woods and shrines dedicated to Apollo and Jupiter. This was Monte Cassino, where (most scholars believe) he composed his famous Rule.

What interested me about Benedict's story was the way that other people had become such obstacles in his search for a simpler life, not just the evil priest Florentius or the irritable monks of Vicovaro but his eager young disciples, too. In fact, there were many more loyal followers than there were enemies, and at certain points Benedict must have felt weary under the weight of their dependence on him.

I had a small inkling—very small—of what he may have gone through. By the time I picked up his biography, I had been questing after holy simplicity for quite some time. I was long past my ambivalence about silence and solitude and the necessity for retreating at regular intervals. I knew what I needed to do and how often I needed to do it. Yet the more I tried to quietly withdraw from the world, the more the world seemed to come looking for me.

This could be frustrating at times—especially when those arriving on the doorstep wanted to watch, but not do; to question, but not try a way of life that had to be personally experienced to be "gotten." Meanwhile, my own solitude was once again stymied, as my friends the monks could sadly confirm. I admired Benedict for his patience with that vast flock of seekers.

I was also drawn to his steady, almost plodding persistence when it came to working out his discipline. He didn't move fast or change his mind quickly, yet he made a serious try at almost all forms of early Christian living before he invented a hybrid version that allowed his disciples to flourish. This was again familiar territory; I seemed to be perennially wrapped up in the problem of how to be simple in the midst of our extremely *un*simple society. Just as often as I found this simplicity, I felt myself missing the point entirely.

I sympathized with Benedict's goals, I respected his patience, and I understood how it was he kept attracting devotees. I found his Rule, which ultimately provided the rock on which Western monasticism was built, to be extremely helpful even for someone like me, a layperson living in the world. What I didn't understand was why he should have insisted that the *Opus Dei,* or the Liturgy of the Hours (communal prayer and psalmody), take priority over all other monastic activities.

"Let nothing be preferred to the Work of God," he said. What he meant by this was that monks should rise in the middle of the night to gather for vigils, then gather again, during the daylight hours, for lauds, prime, terce, sext, none, vespers, and compline, for in this "we fulfil the duties of our service."[8]

On the one hand, part of me loved this crazy notion— loved it the way romantics love: theoretically, ideally.

What a wonderful way to live! How inspired! To deliberately interrupt the workday for group prayer, to let go of the anxious striving long enough to chant some psalms: how rejuvenating this must be! How sad that I could not do it myself.

On the other hand, as far as I could see this forced communal worship effectively destroyed whatever remnants of solitude monks could still find in a crowded monastery. How could somebody who'd lived alone in a cave for three years insist on such a schedule? How could the contemplative Camaldolese, who'd given me my first taste of the hermit life, continue a tradition that seemed so antithetical to their basic orientation toward solitude? Though they observe only four of Benedict's original eight offices, that is still a *lot* of time in church.

I wondered how the guys who actually had to live under such a rigorous schedule managed to handle it. It was a battle that even I, a sporadic visitor, often lost, this business of getting out of bed when the hermitage bell rang for vigils. It wasn't the hour (5:15 A.M.); it was the principle of the thing. I wondered how they stood it, that relentless, clanging dawn bell. That four-times-a-day call to worship, regardless of head colds, insomnia, bad dreams, depression, or simple human resistance to being told what to do.

I was far from the first person to wrestle with these issues. Benedict's famous statement about the Work of God taking precedence in his monasteries has inspired controversy for years, both within and without the Benedictine community. Adalbert de Vogüé, for example, finds the roots of the *Opus Dei* in Paul's injunction to "Pray without ceasing" (1 Thess. 5:17), roots that he thinks may have been forgotten over the centuries. In Anthony and Pachomius's era, he reminds us, Christ's words were followed, as much as possible, literally; monks kept to their cells, chanting the psalms and praying, for most of their waking hours. The first practice of the hours was simply a way for monks to "help each other, by dint of a common rule, to bear a personal obligation which each one [felt] too weak to discharge by himself." [9]

In addition, de Vogüé insists that Benedict never meant his statement to be taken rigidly, that he wrote his Rule for rural communities where there were crops to grow and animals to tend, not for urban monasteries where choir monks chanted before the congregations of great sanctuaries. In a rural situation, "the monks perform[ed][the office] not only all together in the oratory, but also, if need be, in little groups and even individually, in the kitchen, cellar, garden, the fields, or on a journey." [10] It was primarily a way to assist one another in the lifetime effort to pray without ceasing rather than as a special "strong moment" in the midst of the monastic day. [11]

Nowadays, de Vogüé says that the hours of the office at their best are meant to "mark the beats at which the monk can recollect himself. If need be, they relaunch the impetus of incessant prayer." [12] This, in fact, is exactly what the celebration of the hours did for me when I could let go of my struggle and simply comply with the schedule—it relaunched me, refocused me, and sent me back to my writing or my sitting with renewed enthusiasm.

The Snob in Church

Rarely did I make it to daily Mass at home, however, despite the fact that I only had to drive a few minutes in either direction to get to a church. Without the bell outside my window, without a community who might notice my absence, I found it easier, more convenient, more *me*, to simply take my cup of tea and the daily missal down to the turtle pond at home or the herb garden on campus. What's the difference? I asked myself. Can't I think spiritual thoughts just as well out in nature?

The fact was I had a capricious relationship to organized worship. I wondered if this persistent ambivalence might be connected somehow to that ancient conversation with my mom the night of the Beatles concert in the Hollywood Bowl—our discussion about groupthink. Perhaps the conversation had simply confused me that night, and I had never sorted it all out. Perhaps (and here I breathed a sigh of sudden relief) it was *all Mom's fault.*

Certainly, she'd struck a deep chord in me with her talk of "mob hysteria." Even at twelve, I recognized what she was saying and could see what was at stake. It was a matter of the individual versus the crowd. A few years later, I stumbled onto the novels of Ayn Rand. Rand's fierce defense of the isolated human person swept me away. I was too young to grasp the political implications of her position; I only knew, caught as I was in the stormy seas of my own teenaged rebellion, that she was speaking directly to me. According to Ayn (what a *fascinating* name, I thought, not having the slightest clue about how to pronounce it), one had to fight hard for autonomy. It was one's most noble lifetime endeavor.

It wasn't difficult to figure out, then, why my childhood religion was the first thing to go. Who needed that Lutheran curmudgeon in the sky, that long, bony, wagging finger of judgment? If I were to be genuinely free, Ayn-ishly free, I could no longer be saddled with any Transcendent Beings; nor could I be saddled with church, where people were so homogeneously Scandinavian you could hardly tell them apart. Week after week, it was the same old hymns, same old liturgy, same old prayers. It was a travesty against the individual, I thought with enormous disgust. Ayn would be appalled.

I stopped going to church and didn't return for nearly twenty years. Spiritual yearning returned first—vague restlessness, followed by desperate seeking. Eventually I found myself perched on rocks by flowing streams, trying to remember how to pray. I read, I pondered, I asked discreet questions of people who seemed to know something I didn't—but at no time did I even think about returning to the pews. I told myself that church was for people who didn't think—followers who needed to be led: weak and domesticated devotees. I was not one of those; God had not made me that way. He and I had our *own* relationship, and church would only interfere with this.

Then one day, a friend invited me to a service—a Catholic service, though he wasn't Catholic. His wife was singing in the choir that day. We would sit with the kids in the front row and listen to the "Hallelujah Chorus."

At this point, I can only bring back impressions of that morning: the unforgiving feel of the wooden pew against my spine, the swirl of dust motes caught in a high slanting beam, the thud of kneelers hitting the floor. I do remember being in a state of hyperalertness, like a concealed deer with hunters ranging close by. What was going to happen to me here? Despite the years of fumbling my lonely way toward God, I was not yet ready for this, whatever "this" was going to turn out to be.

Then the singers stood before us, a small and motley crew in robes that had not, it was clear, been individually tailored. They were going to sing the "Hallelujah Chorus," the fabulous chorus from Handel's *Messiah,* with only an upright piano to back them up? I shrank in embarrassed pity for them, getting in return a sharp rap in the vertebrae from the pew. Then they began to sing, and what came out of them was joy, waves of it, and it knocked me flat. Suddenly, the candles, which had been lit all along, were blazing gold. Suddenly, the flowers at the foot of the altar burst into living color. I was a goner. This was an experience of God I'd never had before—not as a supercilious Lutheran delinquent, not as a middle-aged seeker by the side of trickling streams. This was (the term came out of nowhere) an experience of the Mystical Body, although at that point I had but the vaguest notion of what this term might mean.

The service that day, and the equally ecstatic experiences of Mass that followed it during those first few years after my return to organized religion, set a fairly high standard. For a while, I couldn't get enough. Dailiness, however, was bound to take its toll. Finally the tug, the old Ayn-ish tug to do it my way, began to reassert itself in a life that had been in many ways transformed by the experience of church.

Ironically, the problem grew in proportion to the amount of time I spent practicing the disciplines. If I happened to be fasting, for example, I couldn't help but take smug note of how many buttermilk crullers were disappearing down the hatches of my fellow parishioners during hospitality hour after services. If I'd been trying hard to live frugally, I couldn't seem to keep from looking askance at the brand-spanking-new, paid-for-by-credit, gas-guzzling SUVs littering the church parking lot.

I noticed a certain peevishness setting in, an impatience with freeform homilies or a tremulous cantor. I was working *so hard* to be more focused; why couldn't they? Where was the sense of excellence, the pride in doing a job well? I found myself analyzing a visiting priest's drone: What, exactly, was he was trying to project with that? Ennui? Cynicism? The state of living death?

To put it simply, I had become a critic, hyper-conscious of slip-ups on the part of the celebrant or choir. Worse, I became increasingly irritated by signs of slovenliness in the congregation, especially in those who slouched up for Eucharist in T-shirts with Harley Davidson symbols or Slayer death's-heads on the back. What was up with these people? Did they have no respect? More often than not, Mass in a parish church ended with me tense with frustration. The temptation, of course, was simply not to go, to wait until my next visit to the hermitage, where I could refuel in a place with some of the—let's face it—*class* that seemed so woefully lacking in the average, garden-variety parish.

As my personal piques began to control my decision about whether or not I would worship communally that day, I felt a corresponding slippage in other parts of my life. My students, for example, seemed ruder, less prepared, far sleepier than in the past. My colleagues on campus *had* to be more dazed and disconnected; I could swear it. People were wilder drivers than they used to be. I couldn't even make a simple phone call anymore without running into six days' worth of instructions from a disembodied voice.

I was becoming a hopeless crank, old overnight and far before my time. My capacity for love was shrinking by the minute. Could this have anything to do, perhaps, with my reluctance to mingle with the hoi polloi in church each day?

In John 4, Christ has his long discussion with the Samaritan woman at the well. In the course of their conversation, he tells her facts about her life that nobody else knows—for example, that she's lived with five different men. She is appropriately impressed and also possibly annoyed at his insight—whichever it is, she begins a little argument about the proper place of worship, which has long been a controversial subject between Samaritans and Jews. Jesus replies that "the hour is coming, and is now here, when true worshipers will worship the Father in Spirit and truth; and indeed the Father seeks such people to worship him" (John 4:23).

He was saying, in effect, "Don't get stuck in the physical details. Don't get trapped in a pharisaic ritualism." For "even if every least rubric is scrupulously observed," the Benedictine directory *The Monastic Hours* warns, "a celebration can be cold, formal, pseudo-sacred, and dehumanized."[13] It *will* be, one would expect, if it becomes an end in itself. Christ also seems to be saying that a person shouldn't become caught up in the criticizing of ritual. For the "quality of prayer assuredly does not depend on the number of psalms recited, nor on the number of hours celebrated, but on the inner disposition of mind and heart."[14] Neither of these—mindless ritualizing or critical intellectualizing—are the point of going to church.

What *is* the point? I wondered. My shilly-shallying about organized worship did me no good—I could see that now. It was time for me to develop an adult perspective on this issue; time to let my poor mother off the hook. I needed to answer these questions once and for all. Why communal worship? Why can't we meet God just as well in the privacy of our own space? Why on earth must we saddle ourselves with the crowd?

The Price of Privacy

Maybe that was the problem: the privacy part, the "own space" part. "I am the vine," Christ says, "you are the branches. Whoever remains in me and I in him will bear much fruit, because without me you can do nothing" (John 15:5). Where was the "privacy" in that image? Shortly before he is betrayed by Judas, and knowing full well that in the first horrified hours after his execution his group of loyal compatriots will be tempted to disband

and flee for their lives, he tells them, "This is my command: love one another as I love you" (John 15:12).

Jesus' final requests to God are for their protection: "I gave them your word, and the world hated them, because they do not belong to the world any more than I belong to the world" (John 17:14). He also speaks of future believers: "I pray not only for them, but also for those who will believe in me through their word, so that they may all be one, as you, Father, are in me and I in you. . . . I have given them the glory you gave me, so that they may be one, as we are one" (John 17:20–22). Finally, he envisions the relationship that must hold between his followers if they are to survive in a world in which they're now aliens and strangers: "that they may be brought to perfection as one" (John 17:23).

The Benedictine directory *The Monastic Hours* says, "We shall truly see God in the Work of God, that is, we shall receive the revelation of his agape-love, only if we are joined with our brothers or sisters in genuine communion."[15] In other words, we will only receive this revelation from God if we are *part of* what's going on in the worship service—not an "objective" critic or an individual praying in public but *in* one another as though we are one thing. We must be a single human body, singing our meager praises to what is "utterly inexpressible and indescribable," as Basil the Great puts it. "Divine beauty blazing like lightning; neither word can express nor ear receive it."[16] We must help each other try to express the unexpressible, however, or at least that seems to be Christ's point. Communal worship seems to be nothing more or less than the ongoing effort to do so.

Dostoyevsky, speaking of the spiritual price we have paid for our precious modern autonomy, says of Christian ages past, "There must have been something stronger than stake and fire. . . . There must have been an idea stronger than any misery, famine, torture, plague, leprosy and all that hell, which mankind could not have endured without that idea, which bound men together, guided their hearts, and fructified the 'springs of life.'"[17] Sometimes, in a crowd of Sunday-morning devotees, I did see what he must have meant. People you'd normally find handling cash registers or fixing jammed drains or coaching soccer were all on their knees, waiting with great hope to be healed and forgiven.

According to Josef A. Jungmann, "In the Christian religion it is the assembled community, the gathering of the congregation, that is the main thing. . . . Not the holy place, not the lifeless walls, not the gold and silver of its decoration are the primary things. No, it is rather the holy community, the *plebs sancta,* the gathering of the new people of God, who worship the father in spirit and in truth."[18] In communal worship, says Paul, we become the "temple of the living God" (2 Cor. 6:16). More than that, we experience the great split between ourselves and others, ourselves and nature, as momentarily healed, for as Paul Delatte explains, "creation as a whole possesses in a true and special way a liturgical character" that only we humans can put into words.[19] We worship on behalf of the cosmos itself.

Perhaps it was this image that inspired Benedict's deep commitment to the Work of God or Liturgy of the Hours.

Perhaps he believed that this formal coming together, day in and day out, would lead, finally, to a transcending of individual quirks, likes and dislikes, private peeves and objections—to a genuine humility. Benedict says in his Rule that the monk who has achieved this "will presently arrive at that love of God which, being perfect, casts out fear." [20]

Christ Within and the True Self

Seen in this light, my ambivalent relationship with formal worship started to seem insignificant, in the same category, perhaps, as a hormonally caused mood swing—nothing you'd rely on if you needed to make a serious decision. It was maybe even something to be grown past, the way I'd finally grown past (at about age thirty-four) my stormy teenaged rebellion—or, for that matter, the seductive philosophy of Ayn Rand.

My youthful investment in hyperindividualism may have been, all along, the single biggest impediment to a simple life. The belief that my personality—that peculiar combination of habitual responses to things—was my most precious possession made it extremely difficult to do things differently. For example, if I stopped reacting with vociferous moral indignation whenever I heard about some flagrant corporate misdeed, I wouldn't be Paula anymore. If I stopped anxiously imagining the worst before I climbed on board an airplane, I wouldn't be me. This held true for my tendency to flatter others, my secret passion for macadamia nuts, and my self-consciousness in front of a camera. I'd always assumed that, quirks though they were, they were my own, and thus inherently valuable.

The notion that I could simply ignore my occasional restlessness during worship services, that I could stop listening to the effete proclamations of my internal critic, was brand-new. At the same time, it was entirely consistent with what I'd learned during my experiments with silence, solitude, fasting, chastity, and the other disciplines. I had already learned that habits could be changed, attitudes could be relinquished, and life could become fuller, richer, and simpler, but not without giving up the proclivities of the personality for something perhaps less obviously "personal" though quite a lot deeper.

I'd seen references to this deeper self in a number of different places: the Hindu Atman, Merton's true self, the Quaker Divine Spark, the Ground of Being, presence, essence, spirit, soul—the image of God within. According to most religious traditions and some schools of psychology, this deep self is universal—we all have it— though it is usually hidden from us under the complex layers of our personalities.

It is through this deep self, so mysterious and seemingly inaccessible, that we meet the Divine. Seen in this light, the spiritual journey becomes a long process of giving up the layers of the personal so as to uncover the hidden Self. In the process, of course, we become far less predictable to ourselves—and to others, who have come to think they "know" us and often prefer that we remain our old idiosyncratic but familiar selves.

Fr. Bruno Barnhart, a monk of New Camaldoli, says, "Awakening to the Self introduces a duality and tension between this deep center of a person and the practical center of the personality which is the ego."[21] In the New Testament, the "tension between 'spirit' and 'flesh' represents . . . the contrast of two orientations of the whole person: toward the 'old world' which is centered in the unredeemed self . . . or toward the 'new world' which is participated [in] through self-giving in faith and love."[22]

This, I thought, might explain that first overwhelming experience in Mass the day of the "Hallelujah Chorus"— the sense of being momentarily caught up in the Mystical Body or corporate Christian being. This could only happen, of course, because I was so swept up in what was happening around me that for once I forgot to check in with headquarters. I had no time to draw back, assess, weigh, judge, or dismiss; no time to dig trenches, fortify the barricades, boil the oil. By the time I realized I was exposed and vulnerable, it was over: my naked and shivering little self had surrendered, and, for a moment, I was seeing through brand-new eyes.

I remembered the sudden flare of the candles, the swell of the music, the light falling from that high window, and I wondered if this had been what we were all looking for so very long ago when, twelve years old and filled with nameless yearning, we'd become Beatles devotees. Perhaps the urge to worship is so powerful that, denied, it comes bursting out anyway and carries us, tumbling and exhilarated, toward almost anything that seems larger and more magnificent than our own wee selves.

This could explain the peculiar joy that sometimes hits without warning during the most mundane morning Mass, bringing tears in its wake. I had felt it many times, but only when I was not feeling "me" at the same moment, when I had briefly let go of my precious individuality and oriented myself instead toward the "new world" that Fr. Bruno talks about, the world of "self-giving and love."

From his prison cell, Paul writes a wonderful letter to the young church at Ephesus, a church that has experienced in a visceral way what Jesus warns his disciples that they too will feel: the weight of the world's hatred. Paul reassures them that despite their set-apart condition, they are not, after all, alone: "So then you are no longer strangers and sojourners, but . . . fellow citizens with the holy ones and members of the household of God" (Eph. 2:19). The apostles, prophets, and Jesus Christ himself provide the foundation for this communal habitation into which they have been welcomed. Paul informs both the Ephesians and us that, "Through [Christ Jesus] the whole structure is held together and grows into a temple sacred in the Lord; in him you also are being built together into a dwelling place of God in the Spirit" (Eph. 2:21–22).

The notorious existential loneliness of the contemporary individual cannot withstand such an experience. When "our minds are in harmony with our voices" as Benedict puts it,[23] we are no longer thinking and behaving as isolated selves, but have found our place in the Whole. When we do, we see what is normally hidden: we see that we are not alone at all, but, in joining worshipfully together with our fellow human beings, we have become the very dwelling place of God.

Benedict's own life seems to bear this out. St. Gregory the Great reports that Benedict, shortly before he died, had what has come to be known as his "cosmic vision." Praying in a tower, "he saw the whole cosmos gathered before him as if in a ray of sun,"[24] a stunning image that Gregory explains this way: "It was not that the world grew small, but that his heart was enlarged."[25] His heart was enlarged, rendered capacious, opened to universal love—and all after a rigorous lifetime practice of psalmody, liturgical prayer, and the holiness of genuine communion with his fellow devotees.

PART IV

FACING THE DEMONS

Once we are made self-aware by solitude and silence, cleansed and strengthened by the disciplines, and steadied by community, we are ready for a greater challenge—the confrontation with our own most primitive fears. It is one thing to clear away the clutter of bad habits, another to deliberately place ourselves in what feels like terrible danger. Fear keeps us trembling at the very edges of security, wanting to move into the next stage of the journey, but unable to let go of self-protectiveness. Even though we can sense that fear is the opposite of faith and that a life of holy simplicity requires far more "letting go" than we've done up to this point, we still cannot make that step.

This step is exactly the one that all the great saints have taken; this is in fact the hallmark of saintliness: complete self-abandonment, nothing held back. What we'd like is to be "good" enough to avoid the rigors of sainthood. The saints gave too much, we think; it wasn't healthy. Where was their natural self-regard, their common sense? Besides, we have enough saints out there already; the calendar is jammed with their feast days.

We admonish ourselves: Who am *I*, to think about saintliness anyway? Isn't that awfully conceited? I am a lot better than I used to be—why don't I just quit while I'm ahead? One can get too big for one's britches, after all. Life is a lot smoother than it used to be. I'm much calmer and more content. People like me better, or at least those who didn't reject me at the beginning. Surely, I can just rest easy now? Be thankful for the progress? Daily Mass is good, my prayer life is deep and sincere; I can't believe I used to be so scattered. Isn't *this* holy simplicity?

No, Christ tells us, just as he told his disciples. This is spiritual comfort: nice, but meant to be fleeting. There's work out there that needs doing—the harvest is ready, but the laborers are few—and you didn't go through all this so that you could rest on your laurels. It's time to confront your enslavement to fear. It's time to develop the courage to return to the world . . . not as critic, but as healer.

The next three chapters, "Right Livelihood: The Way of the Laborer," "Confidence: The Way of the Mendicant," and "Integrity: The Way of the Reformer," are devoted to the *big* demons: fear of not measuring up, fear of physical harm, fear of our basic needs not being met, fear of speaking the truth in a public arena. St. Aelred of Rievaulx (1110–1167) wrote extensively about vocation, St. Francis of Assisi (1181–1226) about "Lady Poverty" and what she can teach us, and St. Catherine of

Siena (1347–1380) about telling the truth at whatever cost, including the threat of death. Together, these three speak of a kind of spiritual courage we cannot approach unless we have already given up our self-pleasing behavior, along with most of our habitual responses to being crossed by others.

CHAPTER 6

Right Livelihood: The Way of the Laborer

In this wretched and laborious life, brethren, Martha must of necessity be in our house; that is to say, our soul has to be concerned with bodily actions. As long as we need to eat and drink, we shall need to tame our flesh with watching, fasting, and work. This is Martha's role. But in our souls there should also be Mary, that is, spiritual activity. For we should not always give ourselves to bodily efforts, but sometimes be still and see how lovely, how sweet the Lord is. . . . You should in no wise neglect Mary for Martha; or again, Martha for Mary. For, if you neglect Martha, who will feed Jesus? If we neglect Mary, what use is it for Jesus to come to your house, when you taste nothing of his sweetness?[1]

St. Aelred of Rievaulx (1110–1167)

A few years before my round-the-world trip, I saw Europe for the first time. The experience was overwhelming—not only because the Old World is, under its accumulated millennial grime, so very lovely but also because we were traveling in an eight-passenger van with all four of our teenaged children, our Dutch exchange student, and my mother—and we were camping.

At some point amid the happy and not-so-happy chaos of that ill-conceived adventure, we found ourselves on the windswept Brittany Coast. Up ahead of us, just visible through our bug-smeared windshield, was one of the genuine wonders of the world: the miraculous Mont St. Michel. The grumbling teenagers behind us fell silent. My eyes grew hot with fervid tears. Out of the gray gloom of the sea, a holy mountain rose, an abbey cathedral so married to the rock on which it was built that you literally could not tell where one left off and the other began.

We parked and walked over the long causeway to the sea mountain, which for centuries was cut off (by intention) from the mainland at every high tide. A small town clung to the lower face, two- and three-story medieval buildings looking no more significant than barnacles in comparison to the massive church above them. Before anything else, one had to bow before that original vision: what sort of holy fool had first conceived of such a thing?

Up close, it was even more astonishing. In fact, the collection of buildings on the north side of the rock is called *la merveille,* or "the wonder." Three stories tall and built to face the oncoming waves, it is made of intricately fitted blocks that were carved by master stonemasons from granite quarried on the mainland. The abbey church with its Norman nave is laid out in the shape of a great cross. In the choir hang narrow windows of clear glass many stories tall, carefully positioned to catch the sunlight diffused through ocean mist. A building more suited to its environment I'd never seen; we in our time have nothing that compares with it. Henry Adams, that nineteenth-century connoisseur of high medievalism, had this to say about it:

> Mont St. Michel, throughout, even up to the delicate and intricate stonework of its cloisters, is built of granite. The crypts and the substructures are as well constructed as the surfaces most exposed to view. . . . The thirteenth century did not build so. The great cathedrals after 1200 show economy, and sometimes worse. The world grew cheap, as worlds must.[2]

I spent some time in those crypts, deep beneath the soaring church, and Adams was right. No effort, apparently, was too great for those long-dead craftsmen, even those who knew they'd spend a lifetime on this immensity and never live to see it completed. Who had they been? What had kept them at it, year after endless year?

Several years after our visit to Europe, my first novel was published. It was the exciting culmination of many years' work. For some months, I lived in a state of irrepressible exuberance. I loved the readings, I loved the signings, I loved the reviews. Well—the ones I was getting; the *big* one hadn't actually appeared yet. It would, my agent assured me. You're getting too much attention for the *New York Times* to ignore you. They'll come through.

They did, finally. Six months later, and after what I'm sure was considerable pressure on the part of my agent, they published a dismissive little review in their (of all days) Christmas issue.

I was irate—more than that, distraught. How many readers had seen this scandalously unfair—nay, *unprofessional*—attack on what everybody else in the *whole country* had so loved? (Here I patted my thin stack of reviews from places like the *Rocky Mountain News Press*.) This would not stand. Surely somebody would write to them, an elegant but vehement protest against the damage done to a genuine work of art.

Nobody did. In fact, the few people who mentioned they'd seen the review simply patted my hand the same way I'd patted that stack of clippings and silently shook their heads. Pity there was, but no offers to take vengeance on my behalf. Finally, still boiling, I approached a good friend, somebody I'd chosen primarily because he actually subscribed to the *Times* and because he had a different last name than me. Okay, okay, he said, shaking his head, though not quite so pityingly as the others. You write it, I'll sign it.

So I found myself faking an indignant letter to the editor of the most prestigious book review in the country. Not only faking it, but sending it. Naturally, they never ran it. Not only are they astute reviewers, but apparently they are equally good at recognizing a fraud when it bites them in the toe. On my end, however, the ramifications of this nasty little exercise in self-promotion were more profound, though I did not realize this for some time, not until I took a serious look at my attitude toward work.

The impetus to do so came, once again, from the hermitage, where, one Sunday after lunch while waiting in the dish line at the sink, I noticed that the prior was in suds up to his elbows. I'd seen this before—at the hermitage, no one is exempt from kitchen duty—but we'd just come from Mass, where this very same man had delivered a truly outstanding homily, one rich in scholarship and intellectual interest while vibrant with experiential wisdom.

It had moved me deeply, and I was still thinking about it when I happened to glance up and see him there, all covered in bubbles. The two images—scholar and dishwasher—were suddenly and somewhat crazily juxtaposed in my mind, like an icon I was supposed to read but could not because of some heretofore-unsuspected blindness. It was not the sight of a man doing menial scullery work that bothered me (this was the twentieth century, after all) but the sight of such a gifted man wasting his time over the sink.

I went back to the guesthouse and reread the Brief Rule of St. Romuald, which did not say anything about K.P. duty. So I went to the bookstore, where I browsed through a history of the Camaldolese, who in eleventh-century Italy had attempted to recapture the original eremitical vigor of the Desert Fathers. According to this book, St. Romuald's monks "lived a solitary life of perpetual silence and severe fasting in small huts."[3] There were probably not many dishes involved.

Pages later, however, I found a description of similar reform movements in eleventh-century France, where the Cistercians, similar in many ways to the Camaldolese, began in the forests of Citeaux. Known as the White Monks because of their rough, gray-white habits, they sought a return to the original simplicity of monastic life, which included hard manual labor. They believed that, under the prevailing Cluniac influence (the Abbot of Cluny eventually oversaw 1,300 monasteries),[4] Benedictines of the day had become overly concerned with liturgical magnificence and the accumulation of wealth and had thereby lost the humble communal spirit of St. Benedict's Rule.

The early Cistercians rejected Cluny's feudal system of administering its monastic property (for example, its manorial bakeries, courts, serfs, and fairs), repudiated all moneymaking ventures, and pledged themselves to self-sufficiency. Like the Desert Fathers who were their model, they took seriously the biblical injunction in Thessalonians: "Nevertheless we urge you, brothers, to progress even more, and to aspire to live a tranquil life, to mind your own affairs, and to work with your [own] hands" (1 Thess. 4:10–11). This meant that monks and lay brothers had to till the fields themselves rather than use serfs to do their heavy agricultural labor. Nearly a thousand years later, the Order of Cistercians of the Strict Observance, known as the Trappists, still strive to meet this ideal.

This was interesting. I knew that Thomas Merton, one of our most famous modern monks, was a Trappist. I pulled a copy of his *Seven Storey Mountain* off the shelf and turned to this description of life in the Abbey of Gethsemani, where he lived for many years:

> Now, at the beginning of July, we were in the midst of the harvest, getting in the wheat. The big threshing machine was drawn up at the east end of the cow barn, and wagons loaded with sheaves were constantly coming in . . . from the various fields. You could see the cellarer standing on top of the threshing machine, outlined against the sky, giving directions, and a group of lay brother novices were busily filling the sacks and tying them up and loading trucks as fast as the clean new grain poured out.[5]

Despite the grinding labor and the terrible Kentucky heat, Merton—who'd spent most of his secular life studying, reading, writing, and discussing—found himself loving the physical toil:

> How sweet it is, out in the fields, at the end of the long summer afternoons! The sun is no longer raging at you, and the woods are beginning to throw long blue shadows over the stubble fields where the golden shocks are standing. . . . And when the undermaster claps his hands for the end of work, and you drop

your arms and take off your hat to wipe the
sweat out of your eyes, in the stillness you realize how the whole valley is alive with the
singing of crickets, a constant universal treble
going up to God out of the fields, rising like the
incense of an evening prayer to the pure sky:
laus perennis! [unceasing praise!][6]

St. Aelred and the Land of Unlikeness

In 1134, a brilliant youth with a promising future ahead
of him had almost exactly the same revelation. Sent on a
diplomatic errand to the Yorkshire District of northern
England by his lord and guardian, King David of
Scotland, young Aelred was told about monks in white
robes living a primitive but amazingly harmonious life in
the woods on the banks of the River Rye. Immediately, he
rode out to see them. He was fascinated by this still-new
Cistercian mission of Rievaulx, and the next day he
returned and asked to join the community.

In order to adopt their simple life, Aelred had to give
up his place in the royal court, his bright ecclesiastical
prospects, his high social standing, and the wealth he
would someday inherit. In return, he was given the back-
breaking job of moving stone; the group was ready to put
up permanent buildings. Throughout his early years at
Rievaulx, he participated fully in the required manual
work, served as novice master, and helped establish the
daughter house of Revesby. At thirty-seven, he became

the now-much-larger Rievaulx's abbot, a role he filled until his death in 1167.[7]

Aelred also wrote more than twenty books. His most famous, *The Mirror of Charity,* was directed at young novices struggling to re-form their individual personalities in order to be able to live in communal brotherhood. For Aelred, it all came back to love—God's great love, expressed first of all through his initial act of creation, and then through his "rest," or cessation of activity on day seven: "Great day this, great this rest, the Great Sabbath! Let not its meaning escape you."[8] Aelred thought that somehow God's love is most purely apparent to us when he is not actually doing anything, but instead is simply being himself, for his very nature is love: "God's rest . . . is his love."[9] We are to imitate God in this as best we can: "Bind, then, the whole world in one embrace of love. There remember and rejoice with all the good. There behold the evil and weep for them."[10]

Two notions about human beings sit at the heart of Aelred's anthropology: First, because we are made in the *image* of God, as it says so clearly in Genesis, we are at our cores divine love. It matters not whether we recognize this fact: we cannot change our essential nature, no matter how we resist acknowledging it and no matter how unapparent it may be in us. Second, we are also meant to manifest the *likeness* of God, which is akin to living in imitation of Christ, and this is where, for Aelred, monastic asceticism and Benedict's Rule begin to make sense. Likeness is achieved when we freely choose it, and it is developed in us only through hard and unremitting work on ourselves, aided always by God's loving grace.

He spoke much about the "land of unlikeness," the shadowy realm of Augustine's disordered loves. Here, most people, including himself before he found the monks beside the Rye, abide: "I, no other, am that prodigal. Selfishly I clung to my inheritance. Serve thee I would not. I went instead to that far-off country, the land of unlikeness."[11] In this realm, we strive for recognition, wealth, and success; we surround ourselves with beautiful things and indulge our desires. We *desire* to desire, he said, because in this way we feel fully alive. Ultimately, however, none of this satisfies.

Aelred thought that only if we became disillusioned enough to leave that land behind could we then choose, like the prodigal son, the unimaginable joyous homecoming that awaits us. If we, like that wayward son, will only open our eyes to our true condition, then "peace, quiet, happiness . . . await[ ] us in the homeland of our hope."[12] Go on with your seeking, he tells us, "but not as hitherto. Seek rather for what alone will quiet your longing and bring you rest. Yes, seek that."[13]

Longing. Yearning. Seeking. These were words that resonated for me—as they have, perhaps, for the whole 1960s generation. If there is any combination of emotions that has characterized my life, it is this unhappy state of perpetual dissatisfaction coupled with the conviction that there's something better elsewhere, just out of reach.

One of my very earliest memories—I was three—is of standing mournfully inside our living room behind a closed screen door, watching the neighbor kids troop off to school and being told I could not go with them. Where were they all headed? Somewhere mysterious and grown-up and not for babies, that was clear. It looked like a children's crusade, though I couldn't have known about that then. They seemed so purposeful, marching along in their black-and-white saddle shoes and swinging their metal lunch boxes. Some of them (this hurt) were even pushing *bicycles* across the street. Little spokes twinkled in the morning sunshine, and from one back wheel pink streamers fluttered.

By the time I was old enough to go to school, my longing had become continuous and no longer just for bicycles and lunch boxes. I longed for something I couldn't even name because it was so high, so lofty, so *not* like mundane family life. Out there in the world, I thought, it would *have* to be different. There, people would recognize my specialness, would see that I was made for some better place and time.

What this place or state might be, I had no idea—only that it was very hard to get there and it involved a lot of serious work. Beginning in kindergarten, no less, I plunged into my lifetime quest for straight As, my unceasing effort to be the most studious, the most reliable, the most intelligent. This goal generated prodigious energy in me, and soon detached itself from that original gauzy, but noble, vision and became an end in itself.

In adulthood, my once clear-cut path became frustratingly complicated. Suddenly, duty was part of the standard, and I couldn't get the A without fulfilling its demands. For example, if I hired a babysitter so that I could spend a day writing a short story, no matter how "good" it turned out to be, no matter if I eventually sold it to a fine literary magazine, I was stuck with a guilty conscience because exemplary wives and mothers put the needs of their families first. If, on the other hand, I spent all day cooking a great dinner and never made it to my writing desk, I felt remorseful for caving in to outmoded standards for womanhood, thereby abandoning my "real" work.

Not surprisingly, the pressure of duty made me cranky and resentful—it had been so much easier in the days when I could lock on to the Girl Scout merit-badge program and power my way through, oblivious to everything but my own goal. It was so much less confusing when teachers automatically loved me for my perfect penmanship and excellent spelling, my little hand ever waving in the air. As an adult, however, my *character* was open to judgment, which meant I couldn't ignore my obligations to the people around me. Somehow, I had to figure out how to be the "best" and the "goodest" at the very same time.

On certain memorable occasions, I was shown, beyond the shadow of a doubt, the impossibility of what I was trying to accomplish. This happened on my daughter Andrea's third birthday. It was a very big event at her particular preschool, a day on which the birthday lamb wore a huge silver crown and the lamb's mother brought homemade cake and ice cream to serve at snack time. This particular mother, however, was so deeply engrossed in writing that she forgot not only the time but the cake, the candles, and the ice cream as well.

It was only after a shocked phone call from the teacher that I flew into action, roaring to the scene by way of the local market, which (thank God) had a bakery, and arriving, soaked with mortified sweat, to a scene still—*still,* after all these years—singed into my memory: my beautiful little girl at the head of a long table filled with other children, sighing at the sight of her mother with a relief so profound it was as though she'd been spared death.

Less dramatic reminders that I was not Superwoman came regularly. They caused me to feel guiltier and to redouble my already mighty efforts. Not surprisingly, I was often exhausted, anxious, and frustrated. I was also convinced that I was underappreciated. How could anyone, no matter how generous, heap enough praise on my head?

Most of the time, people didn't even know what I did to myself—the long hours of writing or studying in the middle of the night to avoid conflict with my daytime chores, the stomach cramps when I took on yet another challenge. Increasingly, I felt driven by something I could no longer control—something that had become more habit than vision. That original nameless longing for a better place had become so weakened by the long years of focusing on the means and ignoring the ends that the chances I'd ever find it had almost disappeared. The truth was, I didn't think much about that better place anymore—only occasionally, when I was in a wistful mood with a little wine in me. The hopeful yearning had been crushed under an endless round of work.

Aelred, too, felt the pressures of duty. As abbot of Rievaulx, which under his leadership grew to a population of 140 choir monks and 500 lay brothers and lay servants, his administrative tasks were monumental.

Rievaulx itself gave birth to five daughter houses, one of them as far north as Scotland. Every year, he made official visits to all of them, plus to the annual General Chapter of the Order at Citeaux, in Burgundy, France. His diplomatic skills put him in constant demand; he arbitrated disputes between reform movements and within orders other than his own, he preached at major events, and he corresponded regularly with King Henry II, King Louis VI of France, and Pope Alexander III.

The work took its toll on him:

> "Your messenger was telling me of your
> request," he wrote to a friend, "and I was feeling
> in my heart what strong and loving affection
> had prompted it, when I suddenly recalled
> where I once was, what I once felt, what effect
> those words of the gospel [the story of Jesus at
> twelve] often produced in me when they were
> being said or sung. Unhappy man, I looked
> back. I looked back and saw how far behind I
> had left those pleasant feelings of joy, how far
> from those delights the bondage of business and
> of cares had drawn me, so that what my soul
> would then have disdained to touch is now in
> my anguish my daily bread." [14]

Even without the pressures of his administrative role, he sometimes felt the sheer grind of Cistercian monastic life, especially in his last ten years, which were plagued by terrible arthritis. In *The Mirror of Charity*, he has one of his novices describe the situation: "The food is rather scanty, the clothes are quite rough; spring-water is the beverage; a book often cradles a sleepy head. Weary limbs don't make the couch any softer; the bell for rising is sure to ruin a good sleep. . . . We are no better than beasts of burden." [15]

Ultimately, and despite the years of endless labor, Aelred's life, unlike mine, was characterized by serenity and a profound joy—a radiance, according to his biographer Walter Daniel, that drew "to Rievaulx from foreign nations and distant lands, a stream of monks who needed brotherly mercy and true compassion, and there they found the peace and sanctity without which no man can see God." [16]

Clearly, at some point along the way Aelred had managed to leave behind him the land of unlikeness, had somehow found that "spiritual Sabbath [which is] rest to the soul, peace to the heart, quiet to the mind." [17] He had found a way to harness his galloping energy, a vision to replace the enslaving habit of work for work's sake. In so doing, he had learned certain things about labor: how to plunge his hands into the soil and carry stones on his back, how to stop when stopping was needed, and how to discern what it was God had created him to do. In other words, he had discovered his vocation.

Lessons in Doing Nothing

I had been making retreats at the hermitage for many years before I finally asked to meet with the oblate master, Fr. Michael Fish. Even then, the meeting was, in my mind at least, for information only and certainly not an expression of any kind of commitment on my part. I didn't even know what oblates did, though I suspected that whatever it was would be too much for me. After all, my schedule was already packed, my life overburdened. No doubt, oblates were supposed to rise at dawn—not just when they felt the need for some solitude and silence, but every day, just like the monks. No doubt, they were supposed to go to Mass seven times a week and follow the Liturgy of the Hours all by themselves. Right—I would just fit that in around my teaching, my writing, and my household chores. What was I even thinking, really? I almost turned back at the door.

Fr. Michael, after I finally made myself sit down and talk, seemed to have an inkling about the sort of mental churning I was going through. He sized me up, beaming, then said, "The hardest thing for you will be learning how to stop."

"Stop what?"

"That," he said, with an airy wave in my direction. "Look how you're sitting in that rocking chair. Look at the grip you've got on the armrest—good Lord."

I looked down at my hands, and, yes, my knuckles were distinctly pale, if not completely white, with the effort of . . . what? "Are you by any chance," he asked me, leaning in with an appealing twinkle, "the oldest child in your family?"

"How did you know?" I was beginning to feel flabbergasted.

"Because I am, too," he announced triumphantly, "and I sit just the way you do! Look!"

I looked. He was being kind—he wasn't nearly as tense looking as I was—but I could see the shadow of what he was talking about even in his relaxed lounge. For some reason, I thought of a PowerBar, one of those vitamin-and-amino-acid-stuffed snacks that lean-legged runners chow down. Fr. Michael looked like pure potential in a state of alert repose.

"It's been the hardest thing on earth for me," he said, "to learn how to watch a frog."

"A frog?"

"You know," he said. "A frog." He made a little hopping motion with two fingers. "Just to sit by the edge of the pond, watching a frog instead of getting some useful task out of the way. It's been hell, let me tell you."

This was what oblates did? I was getting more and more confused. In the course of our conversation, however, he revealed enough about his own life to convince me that I'd just met someone far more than my match in the arena of the "best" and the "goodest." Here was a man who'd spent twenty-six years as a Redemptorist priest in South Africa, ten of them in a Zulu village where he was the only white person in residence. Here was a man who'd been face to face with death by lightning strikes, death via disease, death through political upheaval. In the midst of all this, he'd also taught, given spiritual direction, harvested honey from hives of killer bees, and fulfilled his role within his busy order. Now he was trying, as a Camaldolese monk, to learn how to watch a frog.

"Did you know," he said, "that this is a Jubilee Year?"

I did not know. He explained to me that the ancient Jews had instituted the practice of celebrating Jubilees every fifty years, during which time no crops were planted, debts were cancelled, prisoners were released, and, generally speaking, all was deliberately allowed to go fallow. "A yearlong Sabbath!" he said. "Isn't it marvelous? What a perfect time for you to start."

I gulped. Apparently, I was starting. I was not doing so because he was pressuring me, either, but because what he was saying was somehow so utterly compelling—so absolutely appropriate to my situation—that I couldn't *not* respond. Just like that, he'd touched, very gently, that old longing of mine and brought it back to life, full force. There is a better land, he seemed to be telling me—a better place and a better time—and you, personally, are invited to go there. This, my dear, is how you begin.

The first task he gave me was simply to sit outside with a glass of wine in the evening. "You can do it when we're having vespers, if you'd like, but the point is, you are not trying to keep to a rigid prayer schedule or force yourself into a tougher regimen than you're already keeping."

"Then what *am* I doing, exactly?" This sounded vaguely like my longtime practice of silence on the bench under the jack pine, but not really. *That* was a discipline, a commitment I kept each day if I possibly could, and over the years it seemed to be having a salutary effect on my tendency toward nonstop talk. There was a useful purpose, in other words. This glass of wine business, on the other hand, sounded suspiciously like . . . resting. A childhood nursery rhyme, oft repeated by my mother, floated to the surface: "Lazybones, lazybones, lying in the sun, when are you going to get your day's work done?" It was a perfectly legitimate question, I thought. I could feel the homesteader genes deep inside me stirring in self-righteous indignation.

"It'll feel very strange at first," Fr. Michael assured me. "Disruptive and vaguely sinful. Ignore that."

"O-*kaaay*," I said. "And then what?"

"Then nothing. That's it for a while. Just the wine. Half a glass, preferably during sundown so you can watch the show."

He was right. It *was* disrupting—and very interesting to realize how rooted in my soul was the value of unending work. That term he'd used—"vaguely sinful"—perfectly described the guilty pleasure I felt during my first intentionally taken rest in years. Vacations, of course, weren't for resting. They were for hitting the road—figuring out exchange rates or trudging through the woods with a pack on one's back. Weekends were dedicated to laundry, yard work, grocery shopping, and paying bills. Nowhere was there room—or justification—for an actual *rest* in all of that. With any luck, you rested when you were asleep. If not, you just drank more coffee.

Three days into the experiment, I began to feel a kind of loosening inside, as though I were being slowly and gently unraveled at the seams. It was both enjoyable and disconcerting. What was happening here? I felt as though I were being lulled into something I hadn't actually agreed to, that parts of me were starting to ignore, ever so subtly, their usual orders from headquarters—that my arms and legs, for example, were becoming quietly rebellious. I found myself stretching a lot, though these stretches were not like my usual vigorous Marine Corps-style morning warm-ups but instead were spontaneous, catlike affairs that sent ripples of pleasure down my weary limbs.

I went, all on my own, for my first massage ever and was both startled and humbled by the number of little knots nesting unsuspected in my ligaments and tendons. The masseuse, kind-hearted woman that she was, did not even attempt to wrestle them out but instead worked gently all around them, promising me that when the territory felt safe enough, they'd dissolve on their own, which, after a couple more sessions, they began to do.

This was a new world for me, this world of resting. Very soon, I began to realize just how bone-deep tired I was—and that this resting business, which Fr. Michael referred to as "Sabbath time," was going to precipitate some big changes, though I knew not what. This part made me nervous, when I let myself think too hard about it. Mostly, however, I was too busy adapting to the dawning of a new delight.

When the wine experiment had gone on for four months, Fr. Michael gave me a new task. "I want you to write down every single responsibility and duty in your life," he told me on the phone. "Obligations that are so important that you simply can't get out of them. Then give me a call, and we'll talk."

I wrote. I wrote and wrote and wrote. When I finally finished, I had sixty-two extremely important items on my list, tasks that I absolutely could not abandon, no matter how much I wanted to. Just looking at the list made me weary all over again. The progress of months seemed to be wiped out in a single depressing moment of truth. I called Fr. Michael and glumly reported in. "Wonderful," he said briskly. "Sixty-two items, you say?"

"That's right. Sixty-two it is."

"Splendid," he said. "The next thing I want you to do is to cut that list in half."

I laughed, though it was more maniacal than happy.

"No kidding," he said. "It's the next step."

Cutting that list in half, despite my strong conviction at the beginning that it couldn't be done, turned out to provide the same kind of stern fun that, say, cleaning out closets or discarding tax files older than three years can provide. It was downright bracing, like a boiling-hot bath with eucalyptus oil in the water. At first I trembled—how could I possibly abandon *this?* Or this? No way, no way! Then, I grew increasingly ruthless. Item fifteen, I'd say, tapping my teeth with a pencil. Hmmm—that wickedly humorous, two-page, single-spaced Christmas letter I send out to three hundred of our closest friends each year. Can I really give it up? Won't people be puzzled? Or even hurt? Well—too bad for them if they are! I'm done with it! Off to the Dumpster with you, item fifteen.

When the list had been cut in half—it took me three weeks—I left a giddy message on Fr. Michael's machine, reporting my progress. I could hardly wait to see what he had up his sleeve next. I should have known. Now he expected me to actually *live* by the cut-in-half list. I had to follow through.

Suddenly, this Sabbath business was getting serious. Suddenly, I was reducing next year's teaching schedule by a third—regardless of the fact that my paycheck would be suffering the same fate. Suddenly, I was withdrawing from committees, skipping the readings of visiting writers, turning down speaking opportunities, and telling my agent that I needed more time—quite a bit more—for the new book. This was extremely uncomfortable business for a person like me, old Ms. Reliable. What would my colleagues think? What would happen to my careers? Wasn't I going to look like a person who no longer took her professions seriously? Didn't professions require that one give all one had?

Yes, I found, they do. At least in the eyes of the world, they do. I was becoming somewhat weird (or perhaps weird*er* is more accurate). I was slowly, deliberately, giving up my place in the center of things, my spot in the busy hub. I, a healthy middle-aged person, was disengaging for no apparent reason, walking away from new challenges at the very time that I should have been pursuing them with even greater vigor. On certain occasions, I caught a look of actual moral disapproval in someone's eyes: This would not stand, this shambling off from responsibility. Their disapproval inevitably triggered my own self-doubt, which was lurking just beneath the surface.

Work had pretty much defined me. There wasn't a whole lot there, really, when you took the straight As out of the equation. What was I going to become if I continued on this path of so-called simplicity? Would I simply . . . disappear? Would I become identityless?

The true test came during my first summer off in years (I usually taught summer school). I was out in the garden weeding, reveling in the warm sun on my back, the smell of the earth, the songbirds. I thought of how many years I'd dutifully rather than joyfully weeded this very garden. I wondered why things were so different now that I'd given up so many other chores—and then it hit me: There was something I hadn't yet even considered giving up, a form of work so ingrained in me that I couldn't imagine myself as myself should I stop doing it. It was the discipline I began to develop as a wee seven-year-old: my writing.

Had I ever, in all my adult life, been free of *that* particular task? Hadn't there always been some project in the works—stories, a book, or research for a new book? Had there been any weekends, any vacations, when I didn't feel obligated to put in some desk time or haul along research material? In fact, it was a joke in the family, Mom's stacks of books, sandwiched in among the sleeping bags and camping equipment.

Suddenly, I realized that this Sabbath time I was taking had to include writing, too. Maybe (the thought made me downright shaky) this might even mean a moratorium without limits. As long as writing was sitting out there in the distance, I would be likely, as I daydreamed my way down the corn rows, to cheat. I'd be unconsciously working out a plot for a novel or thinking about a new essay I wanted to tackle. While I was writing in my journal, somehow story notes would appear. Maybe I would have to give up writing entirely before I could truly experience the Sabbath.

This was becoming serious. In fact, this was starting to feel not like rest, but a renunciation of that which gave life meaning. Now I can see that this was the point. Somehow, before I could move on, the idol that I'd made of work had to be overturned.

What sustained me during that long creative drought—which lasted nearly seven months before I woke up one morning knowing that it was time to get back to my desk—was, curiously enough, those weeds. A task that had often seemed onerous in the past now took , on new dimensions, primarily, I think, because it was no longer "competing" for my precious time. With less grading because of my reduced teaching schedule and the last of the four kids out on her own, my list of duties was shrinking all by itself.

Life was becoming so different, in fact, that one day I actually found myself praying in thanksgiving for weeds and their eternal presence in my garden. Whatever other kinds of work were taken away from me, there would always be weeds: I could count on them. This made me straighten up, rub my back, and laugh. Could there be a more anonymous task? One less calculated to win me straight As, glory, honor, and immortal fame? I looked around me; aside from three crows intently watching everything I did, my audience had long since disappeared. I was a nameless middle-aged woman in an old straw hat, sore of back and dirty of hands, stooped in the dirt—not exactly the world-beater I'd imagined I might someday be when I was that three-year-old yearning behind a closed screen door.

Still, I was doing good work; this was indubitably "right livelihood," as the Buddhists would call it. What more honorable work could there be, really, than growing food? What more necessary, useful chore than weeding?

I glanced over at the crows, who were watching me hungrily. This was it, I thought. Work at its most basic level. Turning the soil, planting the seeds, pulling the weeds, holding the crows at bay. How many generations of human beings have devoted whole lives to these tasks? Then I thought of all the other anonymous chores out there: cooking, cleaning, building, transporting, record keeping, documenting, filing, nursing, drilling, digging, navigating, piloting, bulldozing. The world is not sustained by the achievers. This revelation had a solid feel to it, the heft and weight of truth.

"Be eager to present yourself as acceptable to God," said St. Paul to his disciple Timothy, "a workman who causes no disgrace" (2 Tim. 2:15).

Then I thought of art, my long love affair with the beauty of art, the reason I'd spent so many years developing the twin crafts of writing and teaching literature. Could it be that art was, in the final analysis, worth less than these humble, but life-sustaining, tasks that made the world go round? Could I be a better human being— really and truly—if I never wrote again and instead spent my life in this garden, growing food? It was a somber moment, more wistful than frightening. I realized I *could* do it, if I had to. Something had changed, and I suspected that the change was permanent.

In almost the same moment, however, came another thought—actually more of a picture. I had to ponder it a bit before I realized what it was: Mont St. Michel, that incredible unsigned work of art and craftsmanship. I saw the soaring, clear glass windows of the choir, the hand-carved granite blocks, the graceful arches and slender pillars, so beautifully offset, the cloister walk overlooking the sea. That had been honorable work, too—right livelihood—in the same way that all the beautiful and anonymous workmanship of the ages has been honorable. It was work done for its own sake, not for the glory it brought to the workmen. I wondered if I would ever be able to approach my own work that way.

Aelred, who shortly before he died called himself "the handmaid of the lord," spoke at length on this subject.[18] Referring to his reputation as a great scriptural teacher, he insisted that "whatever progress I make . . . is not so much given to me as sent to you through me." He refused to take credit for anything he did, saying:

> I neither ascribe this [his teaching] to my merits, since I am a sinner, nor to my scholastic training, since, as you know, I am almost unschooled, nor even to my study or hard work, since I am rarely at leisure and often engaged in business. So it all comes from God, committed to me, transmitted to you, that "he who glories may glory in the Lord."[19]

He also taught that no useful work is better or more worthy of honor than any other kind of work, for "each has his own special gift from God; one in this way and another in that." For Aelred, particular gifts and talents are nothing more than offerings ("One offers more work, another is better at watching, another at fasting, another at prayer, another at reading or meditation."), which are meant to be used "for the common good of all." He warned especially that no one should "take exceptional pride in any gift God has given him, as though it were his own." [20]

Contemporary Cistercian Francis Kline, abbot of the Trappist Mepkin Abbey, points out in his book, *Lovers of the Place,* that the Rule of St. Benedict is very specific about how we are to use our gifts and talents. He quotes the Rule of St. Benedict 57.1–3: "If there are artisans in the monastery, they are to practice their craft with all humility. . . . If the artisan becomes puffed up by his skill-fulness in his craft, and feels he is conferring something on the monastery, he is to be removed from practicing his craft." Says Kline, "This now gets transformed into last-ing virtue, since what I do, while it is still all for the com-munity, is no longer part of my persona which I must defend against all comers, and constantly declare its value. And when I choose not to protect myself by pride, then humility is my gift." [21]

Outside the monastery walls, however, he acknowl-edges that the situation is somewhat different. Turning over the idol of work and the rewards of honor it brings means loss of social esteem. I found this out myself when I began to withdraw from my professional life: "Since I am not playing the game the others are, they ignore me, think me dry, or gone out of step. . . . Instead, I must be content with the polite dismissal of the me who used to be, when my fur was shiny, when I was the center of attention. For a sophisticated person, at least, this is the most menial treatment imaginable." [22]

This humiliating experience is counterbalanced, however, by a slowly growing sense of freedom, freedom from the heavy weight of public approval or disapproval, freedom from one's own demon of ambition. Merton describes the Cistercians of Aelred's day, who "worked with their hands, silently plowing and harrowing the earth, and sowing seed in obscurity," as genuinely liberated people, primarily because they had discovered this fact about work: "They were poor, they had nothing, and therefore they were free and possessed everything, and everything they touched struck off something of the fire of divinity." [23]

When our identities are no longer tied to what we do for a living, we are also freed up to love in a way we cannot when others represent, on the most primitive level, competition, or even just frustrating interruptions. During all those years of jealously guarding every spare moment for writing, I learned to shudder at the arrival of an unexpected guest, to cringe when the phone rang. How could I bear giving up that hour when I could be at my desk? How could people be so inconsiderate? Didn't they know I was *working*?

Aelred reminds us that our real work is to love:

> [L]et the plight of the poor, the complaints of
> the orphans, the desolation of the widows, the

> sorrows of the sad, the needs of the pilgrim, the
> vows of the virgins, the perils of those at sea,
> the trials of the monks, the worries of superi-
> ors, the fatigue of warriors all come to your
> mind. Open the breast of your love to all these,
> for these shed your tears, for these pour forth
> your prayers.[24]

Finally, to be freed from bondage to the idol of work is (ironically) to be released into the possibility of vocation. If each of us really has "his own special gift from God," then one aspect of the simple life is to discover what that gift is and how we are to use it. Aelred speaks of the land of unlikeness, where we stumble about looking for ways to satisfy our deepest desires; Merton speaks of the "false self," that performing persona in us so tuned to public approval that we never have the time or energy to discover why we were really set down here on earth. Both metaphors speak of realization, then renunciation—our realization that the public arena cannot assuage our long- ing for Aelred's "homeland of our hope," and our renun- ciation of whatever impedes our progress toward that "blessed quiet and quiet blessedness."[25]

If we, like the prodigal, finally return to that long-lost home, one thing we will know, both men assure us, is who we really are and what we were made to do. No longer will we have to compare the size of our paychecks, scan our curricula vitae for reassurance, and glance at the framed citations on the wall to know exactly what our value is and why. *That,* I realized among the weeds and crows that day in the garden, is pure freedom we can never give up.

I could only hope for enough courage to claim it, to let myself believe, along with St. Paul, that, "For freedom Christ set us free; so stand firm and do not submit again to the yoke of slavery" (Gal. 5:1).

CHAPTER 7

Confidence:
The Way of the Mendicant

Let all the brothers strive to follow
the humility and poverty of our Lord
Jesus Christ, and let them remember
that we ought to have nothing else in
the whole world, except, as the
Apostle says: "Having food and
wherewith to be covered, we are
content."[1]

St. Francis of Assisi (1181–1226)

M y "entry into womanhood," as my mom put it, was
far more traumatic than it was triumphant. I was
nearly fourteen, downright elderly compared to my
friends who'd had to start wearing bras two or three years
earlier. I'd seen the Disney movie, I'd stocked up on
"supplies," I was ready. Then I woke up one morning,
sicker than I'd ever been in my life, sicker than an
extremely sick dog. This is what I'd been longing for all
these years? I couldn't believe it. No wonder they called it
"the curse."

The older I got, the worse it became. By the time I was eighteen, my monthly infirmity put me in bed for a day and a half—extremely inconvenient for a person with a job and classes to attend. Nothing seemed to help. My doctor, clearly frustrated, finally suggested that I might as well cheer up and forget about it because "having a baby someday's going to be a piece of cake—you've been going through labor for years!"

My problem was not a funny one. Traveling, for example, could become a nightmare if the cramps caught me during a long bus trip or on an airplane. Even keeping up with my daily schedule could be tough; sometimes I miscalculated and found myself stuck miles from home, too sick to drive. During my last couple of years in high school, the school nurse automatically rolled out the wheelchair when she saw me coming. College was even more challenging in this regard—the campus was large and anonymous, and it was usually easier to try to make it home than to the crowded lobby of the health center.

One day I found myself in the campus parking lot, knowing I shouldn't try to negotiate traffic, but unable to walk any farther. I got into my 1965 Dodge Dart and pointed the nose toward home. The next thing I knew, I was blacking out, right in the middle of a crowded intersection. My hands were doing their usual thing when I got sick: my fingers, icy cold, were fanning rigidly, preventing me from gripping anything. I took my foot from the accelerator and leaned against the wheel, and somehow we, the Dart and I, drifted up against a curb and came to a gentle stop. There, I promptly passed out.

The next thing I knew, a male voice was speaking insistently in my ear. "Are you all right, miss? Are you ill?" I nodded dopily. "Can you walk?" I shook my head. "All right," he said, and then the car door was open and this stranger's hands were gripping me by the shoulders, half-dragging me from the car, and I was trying to flop along, my knees buckling crazily at every step. We stopped, breathing like twin steam engines, while he held me upright through sheer willpower. "I'm going to have to carry you," he puffed. "Is that okay?" Again, I gave him a dumb nod, too out of it even to feel embarrassed. With a great "oomph," he scooped me up and lugged me another few feet up some stairs and into a dark, cool office where he laid me out on the floor and hollered for help.

As it turned out, my trusty Dart had drifted to a stop in front of a Methodist church. The man who helped me was a Methodist minister, a slight man—far too slight, I thought when I returned to the church two days later to thank him—to have had to muscle my inert carcass up those steps. Plus, he looked old—early forties at the very *least*—and had a full beard that made him look even older. There were pictures of his pretty wife and their many small children all over his desk. We could not seem to meet one another's eyes, especially when I shyly explained what had been going on with me. He said, "Oh!" in what sounded like surprised relief, then admitted that both he and the office secretaries had been sure I was overdosing on drugs. "After all," he said, "that sort of thing seems to be happening a lot these days."

I was utterly chagrined—I'd never even tried pot, for heaven's sake—and even a bit offended (Ms. Straight As, wrongly accused). It wasn't until years later that I realized what a good Samaritan he'd been, if that's what he'd been thinking. He could have called the police instead, or simply turned his head and left me hunched over in the front seat of my car. He'd helped me, though, an all-out effort that had probably thrown his back out for weeks. He'd taken a chance. I, on the other hand, had endured the somewhat rare experience of complete helplessness. For a short time, I'd been utterly dependent on the goodwill of a stranger.

St. Francis of Assisi and the Risk of Vulnerability

St. Francis of Assisi, possibly the most beloved saint who ever lived—a man chosen, as Gerard Straub points out in his *The Sun and Moon over Assisi,* by *Time* magazine as one of the top ten most influential figures of the last millennium—believed that this experience of complete vulnerability was the central message of the Gospels.[2] Around it he built a spiritual movement that rocked the medieval church and electrified the common man. Like the Buddha, the current Dalai Lama, and Jesus himself, Francis went straight to the heart of our most recalcitrant spiritual problem—our natural tendency to shield and protect ourselves at any cost—and quietly dismantled it.

He did not do this through argument, though he was by all accounts a riveting preacher, but instead by example. For Francis, experience was what taught us. If self-protectiveness was such an obstacle between humans and God, he thought, then we must deliberately place ourselves in vulnerable positions, learning thereby to rely solely on divine providence. The more we were forced to lean on God, the more quickly we gave up our illusion of control. Only then could God do something with our lives.

Francis's legend is familiar; even as a Lutheran child, I heard it—St. Francis kissing the leper; St. Francis preaching to the birds; St. Francis and the stigmata. Gerald Straub says that between 1920 and 1926 alone, "254 books and essays on the life of Francis were published in Europe and the United States."[3] When he himself tried to count the books in the Francis section of the Collegio Sant'Isidoro, he stopped after a thousand, probably less than half of what was there. Despite its familiarity, Francis's is a story that continues to thrill people because it is so radical.

His radicalism can be partly explained by his era, which was an extreme one. Paul Sabatier says in his biography of Francis that by the end of the twelfth century, public worship, still conducted in Latin, had been reduced in the minds of the unlettered masses to a kind of magic ritual; "it was more and more becoming a kind of self-acting . . . formula." In addition, "among the populace there was superstition unimaginable. . . . Those who deemed themselves pious told of miracles performed by relics with no need of aid from the moral act of faith."[4]

Much of the clergy had become decadent, swollen with the power it held over an uneducated public. The great monasteries of Italy had grown wealthy on the patronage of the aristocrats, losing the original simplicity of the Benedictine Rule. Some of them were shamelessly commercialized; Sabatier says that "members of the chapters of most of the cathedrals kept wine-shops literally under their shadows, and certain monasteries did not hesitate to attract custom by jugglers of all kinds and even by courtesans."[5] The backdrop for all of this was constant warfare between neighboring cities, between countries, and between Europe and the Middle East, as crusaders marched off to Jerusalem to do battle with the "infidels."

Francis himself was born in Assisi in 1182, at the height of the monastery-founding phase in Europe. His father, Pietro Bernadone, was a wealthy merchant who sold fine cloth. This meant that Bernadone spent much of his time on the road, buying materials to sell at the great fairs of Europe, which went on for weeks and drew salesmen and customers from as far away as Africa and the Middle East. Textile merchants were the bankers of the day, in some places considered to be a second class of nobles because of their great riches. Francis grew up knowing that he would inherit his father's lucrative business and would someday be wealthy in his own right.

As a young man, however, he spent his future inheritance with reckless abandon, carousing through town with the other youthful aristocrats of Assisi, throwing party after party. Pietro Bernadone seems to have been remarkably relaxed about his son's profligacy; this was what young heirs apparently did before they took over the reins.

Francis was equally reckless when it came to his health, eagerly marching off when barely twenty-one to war against the neighboring city of Perugia, where he was taken captive and imprisoned for a year. Upon his return to Assisi, he immediately resumed his party life and soon fell very ill, nearly dying. After weeks in bed, he went out into the countryside, which was just then bursting into spring, hoping, says Thomas Celano, one of his earliest biographers, to recapture his usual joyful insouciance. Instead, "he felt in his heart a discouragement a thousandfold more painful than any physical ill. . . . He was seized with a disgust of himself, his former ambitions seemed to him ridiculous or despicable."[6] He had figured out that seeking pleasure leads to a profound emptiness, but thanks to the decadence of the church at that time, he had little inkling of where a better way might lie.

A movement was afoot, however. Prophets, holy men, and heretics were beginning to make their presence felt. Gioacchino da Fiore, a former Cistercian abbot who received permission from Pope Lucius III to give up his position in the monastery and become a wandering preacher, may have been the catalyst for Francis's own thinking about voluntary poverty and about the efficacy of lived experience over study. A spirit of "apocalyptic mysticism" was in the air. For example, earlier in the twelfth century, St. Elizabeth of Schönau had a vision of her guardian angel, who warned that the church could not much longer continue down the wrong road it had taken:

> Cry with a loud voice, cry to all nations: Woe!
> for the whole world has become darkness. The
> Lord's vine has withered, there is no one to tend
> it. The Lord has sent laborers, but they have all
> been found idle. The head of the Church is ill

and her members are dead. . . . Shepherds of
my Church, you are sleeping, but I shall awaken
you! Kings of the earth, the cry of your iniquity
has risen even to me.[7]

Francis's internal struggle came to a head one day as he
prayed by himself in the small chapel of St. Damian:
"Great and glorious God, and thou, Lord Jesus, I pray ye,
shed abroad your light in the darkness of my mind. Be
found by me, Lord, so that in all things I may act only in
accordance with thy holy will."[8] Afterward, he had a profound vision during which he understood what his life
was to become. Then, like Anthony and Benedict before
him, he proceeded to give away most of what he owned.

In Francis's case, however, his violent father refused to
accept his decision, hunting him down with the help of
neighbors. Francis hid for many days, then decided that
the inevitable showdown must be gotten through and
made his way back to Assisi, pale, thin, and wearing rags.
There, his father attacked and beat him, then tied him
up, near death, in a dark closet. His mother, Pica, secretly
released him several days later, and he made his way back
to St. Damian to await his father's next move. It came
quickly: Bernadone applied to the magistrates to have his
son expelled from the territory of Assisi, an application
that was denied. The most that he could do was formally
disinherit a son who was already in the process of repudi-
ating his wealth.

In a dramatic scene made famous by Franco Zeffirelli's
film *Brother Sun, Sister Moon,* Francis appeared before his

father, the local bishop, and a great crowd in the Piazza of Santa Maria Maggiore to hear his sentence. Guido II advised him to give up all his property; his response was to vanish inside the bishop's palace, reappearing a few minutes later completely naked and holding in his hands the packet of his folded-up clothes and a few remaining coins.

"Listen, all of you, and understand it well," he then said, according to his early biographers. "Until this time I have called Pietro Bernardone my father, but now I desire to serve God. This is why I return to him this money, for which he has given himself so much trouble, as well as my clothing, and all that I have had from him, for from henceforth I desire to say nothing else than *'Our Father, who art in heaven.'*"[9]

From that moment on, goes the legend, Francis's life, despite its severe hardships, was characterized by a profound and irrepressible joy.

Shaped by Our Fears

My rescue in front of the Methodist church was atypical; I'd been taught from a very young age that one should not ask for help from others. Both of my parents were Depression-era children, and both of their families suffered, though my mother's experience seems to have been more traumatic than my father's. I no longer remember the details of her stories (food baskets brought by the neighbors; an awful Christmas in which the only present she received came from a community tree at the church). What she planted in me instead was the sense of bitter shame she felt, like the puckering aftertaste of something rotten. She had been the object of pity, and this, I learned young, was degrading.

Unfortunately, my own childhood experiences lent some credence to this belief. I was the oldest of five, and my hardworking father's salary was just adequate. We had what we needed—food, shelter, books, even a piano—but there was not much left over for, say, school clothes in the fall. As a result, these often came from my cousins, who were a few years older than me. Despite the fact that their clothes were nicer than anything we could afford, I learned to hate the term *hand-me-downs* for the same reason my mom had hated those Depression-era food baskets. They made me feel like an object of pity. They weren't really *mine*.

In my early twenties, I took a job with the welfare department in which I had to interview families applying for aid, then drive to the nether regions of the county to make home visits with these prospective clients. Often the visits took place in buildings that should have been condemned years before. More than once, I found myself walking into shacks with no floors or windowpanes, or stumbling over babies sleeping on piles of dirty laundry. Nothing was sadder, I thought, than people who had somehow been cut out of the economic system—the unwed teenaged mothers, the mentally deficient, the homeless alcoholics I saw on the street corners downtown mutely displaying their cardboard "Will Work For Food" signs.

Money was clearly the divider between people who did what they wanted in life and people who took whatever came. When I married Mike and we found ourselves supporting our unwieldy stepfamily, money became an even bigger issue for me, especially when we made the tough decision that I would return to college to finish my B.A., then go on for a master's degree. Right in the middle of renovating the house so that we could all fit inside it, we were suddenly down to one income. Sometimes in my zeal to get these building projects wrapped up, I became impatient and spent what we didn't have.

Our rapidly growing debt made me shudder. My secret yearning was for a hefty savings account. Savings meant that you were safe, that you had something left over after all the bills were paid. When we managed to put a few dollars away, I gloated like a miser. That habit took root in me and continued to influence my attitude toward money long after we were through the worst of it. It lingered long after we'd finished the building projects, paid off that monster debt, and gotten the kids through college. Somehow, I'd been seared by money worry, just as my mom had been during her Depression-era childhood.

This happened in spite of my knowing at some deep-down level that money cannot buy security. Certainly, I'd been taught this in Lutheran Sunday school—Jesus even had something specific to say about my youthful attitude toward hand-me-downs: "Why are you anxious about clothes? Learn from the way the wild flowers grow. They do not work or spin. But I tell you that not even Solomon in all his splendor was clothed like one of them. If God so clothes the grass of the field, which grows today and is thrown into the oven tomorrow, will he not much more provide for you, O you of little faith?" (Matt. 6:28–30).

Jesus also spoke to my nagging need to have all the financial bases covered, my unacknowledged bedrock conviction that having enough money took care of most problems: "Are not two sparrows sold for a small coin? Yet not one of them falls to the ground without your Father's knowledge. Even all the hairs of your head are counted. So do not be afraid; you are worth more than many sparrows" (Matt. 10:29–31). He addressed my secret reveling over the savings account that slowly began to grow as our responsibilities diminished: "Do not store up for yourselves treasures on earth, where moth and decay destroy, and thieves break in and steal. But store up treasures in heaven, . . . For where your treasure is, there also will your heart be" (Matt. 6:19–21).

I may have *heard* Jesus' admonitions about money, but Francis actually *understood* them, and he wasted no time in acting on them. For Francis, it was so simple as to be obvious: "No one can serve two masters. He will either hate one and love the other, or be devoted to one and despise the other. You cannot serve God and mammon" (Matt. 6:24). Very well, Francis apparently said to himself, then I will not deal with money at all. For the rest of his life, he lived entirely outside the economic system of his day.

This was a rather harsh interpretation of the Gospels, I told myself when I first read about Francis. How could you be a biblical literalist about something as crucial as money? You had to provide for your own, didn't you? It was not hard to find easier explanations of this passage, readings which left the door to a money-centered life wide open: these passages did not mean that we should not concern ourselves *at all* with money and security, but instead that we should not make money a higher priority than serving God.

There was something in these more "reasonable" interpretations that left me feeling uneasy, however, as though both they and I were purposely avoiding the point. It was all very fine to talk about making God the priority, but what did we do when money had so clearly become the only credible hedge in our society against chaos, darkness, and fear? When tax-sheltered annuities had eliminated the need for faith, both in the goodness of others and in the providence of God? When credit cards worked faster than prayer? What did we do when we lived in a system that *depended* on a vast flow of money for its continued existence? Could we so glibly declare that we were putting God first in spite of all that?

When I began reading about Francis, this most radical of saints, I had already had my first sessions with oblate chaplain Fr. Michael. I was still on the same path I'd so tentatively entered years before, but this time there was a difference: somebody was helping direct my feet. When I wasn't reeling in disbelief at my next assignment, I could even sit back and smile a bit at what an adventure it all was. My life seemed to be on a more solid footing than it had ever been before. I knew I could give things up if I had to: food, sexual power, a "social life," certain kinds of status. I was feeling freer all the time. Still, Francis somehow put my cautious efforts into instant perspective; he showed me, without many words, where I was still holding back and to what extent my fearful insecurity was still in charge.

In Francis's Rule for the brothers, and for the sisters who chose to follow him under the direction of Clare, he went straight to the heart of *what must be done* if we truly wish to overcome our fearfulness, rather than focus on how we should explain things to ourselves. Not surprisingly, he instructed his little band of friars to simply forego money and possessions: "The Rule and life of these brothers is this: namely, to live in obedience and chastity, and without property, and to follow the doctrine and footsteps of our Lord Jesus Christ, who says: 'If thou wilt be perfect, go sell what thou hast, and give to the poor, and thou shalt have treasure in heaven, and come, follow Me.'" [10]

In practice, this meant that the community did not traffic in any way, no matter how piddling, with mammon. If a man wished to become a friar, Francis said, and

> if he be willing and able, with safety of conscience and without impediment, let him sell all his goods and endeavor to distribute them to the poor. But let the brothers and the ministers of the brothers be careful not to interfere in any way in his affairs, and let them not receive any money, either themselves or through any person acting as an intermediary; if however they should be in want, the brothers may accept other necessities for the body, money excepted, by reason of their necessity, like other poor. [11]

Certainly they would need to work, so he declared, "[L]et every man abide in the art or employment wherein he was called. And for their labor they may receive all necessary things, except money."[12] At times it might be necessary to ask for others' charity, but if so, "let the brothers in nowise receive money for alms or cause it to be received, seek it or cause it to be sought, or money for other houses or places; nor let them go with any person seeking money or coin for such places."[13] The bottom-line for Francis? "[W]e ought not to have more use and esteem of money and coin than of stones."[14]

This was startling, invigorating stuff. It was so uncompromising, so sure of itself. It vanquished, in one blow, all the hemming and hawing over how much, how little, what was justified, and what wasn't. Surely, such a radical stance toward money meant that at times the little band of friars went hungry. Surely, it meant that at times they had to *ask others for help.* I shuddered. How on earth could I even begin? Every value I held with respect to self-sufficiency, providing for one's own, not being a burden to others, planning for the future, seemed to be under fire. How did Francis ever overcome the *shame?*

Francis actually talked at some length about this subject:

> And when men may treat them with contempt,
> and refuse to give them any alms, let them give
> thanks for this to God, because for these shames
> they shall receive great honor before the tribu-
> nal of our Lord Jesus Christ. . . . Alms is an
> inheritance and a right which is due to the

poor, which our Lord Jesus Christ purchased for
us. And the brothers who labor in seeking it
shall have great recompense, and they will pro-
cure and acquire a reward for those who give.[15]

It might be true that it was better to give than to
receive—except in those cases when becoming a recipient
allowed somebody *else* to give, somebody who might
need, as I did, to give up fearful insecurity about letting
go of stored-up treasure. Underlying Francis's words was
a calm disregard for the need to hold one's head up in
public. He completely refused to negotiate with pride. If
accepting help from others makes us squirm, Francis
seemed to be saying, then *good*—these moments of shame
show us exactly how proud we are.

This was interesting. Francis's extremism was starting
to make more sense to me now. I'd noticed that what I
was most proud of—my grown-up kids, Mike, our lovely
renovated home, my writing—I most feared losing. What
I was most proud of in myself—my diligence and loyalty,
for example—I most feared I would not live up to consistently. Pride and fear were linked, and the prouder I
became of something, the more I secretly feared having it
taken away. To keep myself from actually having to *experience* that terrible unease (it's far too painful), I'd come
up with a million self-protective devices. Money, magic
money, was just one of these.

The real issue, the deep issue, was fear itself.

Francis, of course, figured this out very early. The legends collected in the fourteenth-century *Fioretti* often

focus on the way he deliberately placed himself in danger. One of the most famous of these stories, the conversion of the giant wolf of Gubbio, has him calling the marauding creature to come forth while the townspeople trembled in hiding behind him. When the wolf appeared, ready to devour him, Francis gave it a stern but gentle sermon about its bad behavior. The wolf, apparently convinced, renounced its wicked ways and became an honorary town guardian instead.

In other stories, Francis went walking alone in crime-infested places, was beaten, robbed, left for dead—and ultimately managed to convert his attackers. When three well-known robbers showed up at his monastery requesting hospitality and were turned away by the monk in charge, Francis insisted they be overtaken on the road and brought back for a good meal and a bed that night. Not surprisingly, all three later asked to become friars.

Whatever grain of truth exists in these medieval legends (a very debatable issue), the point is clear: Francis had even less regard for fear than he did for pride or money. I thought about my own life and how many of my decisions were driven by unacknowledged fear. I thought of how many times I took complicated evasive action instead of facing up to what scared me. I thought of how much energy that required, energy that could be focused on more useful or creative endeavors. Clearly, a simple life required courage—quite a bit more, unfortunately, than I'd ever displayed in the past.

However, soon thereafter, I experienced my own small version of the giant wolf of Gubbio episode. Though I was anything but fearless, somebody else was—and suddenly I thought I saw what Francis had been up to when he seemed to flirt so casually with danger.

Walking with Mountain Lions

An ongoing controversy at the hermitage has to do with mountain lions. Certainly, they are in the area; people have seen them to the north and to the south, and everybody knows they are widespread in California. They are nothing to fool with, either. Cougars are attracted to fast, repetitive movement, like jogging or cycling, and when they do attack humans (which happens every few years), they usually go after children.

The controversy is over whether or not there are any *resident* lions, lions who consider the eight hundred plus acres of hermitage property their own. Occasionally, a flustered guest will report seeing one; an out-of-breath out-of-towner claims to have just witnessed what most monks never have. Eyebrows go up. Are you sure it wasn't a bobcat? They can look plenty big in certain lights. Did it have a puffy tail? Could it have been a lynx, maybe?

One morning, I was walking the mountain road at 6:00 A.M. As I neared the last switchback before the descent to Highway 1, I looked up and saw a medium-sized cougar, perhaps 150 feet ahead of me, eating what must have been his breakfast. I froze, then ran through the mental checklist: Small ears, close to the head? Affirmative. Long curved tail? Another yes. Extremely scary-looking? Absolutely. I raised my arms high to make myself look bigger while the lion, not interrupting his meal for one moment, watched me carefully, tail twitching. We eyed each other for some time, then ever so slowly I began backing up until I'd made it past the higher switchback. There, giving in to panic, I turned and ran the mile back to the bookstore, where I duly made my breathless report, receiving in return some courteously raised eyebrows.

Embarrassed, but not recanting—I *had* seen a lion, I knew a lion when I saw one, thank you very much!—I was already worrying about my upcoming evening hike with Fr. Bernard, the head of the no-lions-on-the-property faction. Would he believe me? More important, would he prudently cancel our hike? If he did not offer to do so, would I have the courage to admit my cowardice and insist that we not go?

He met me at sundown in our usual spot, wearing his blue beret. Seventy-four years old, five foot two inches tall (child sized, I thought—a cougar McNugget), he's walked this road twice a day for most of his adult life, often in pitch darkness, often in rain or billowing fog. He knows every crack in the asphalt, every bunny, every bird, and in his French-Canadian way, takes the time to read up on all these phenomena. I was pretty sure, for example, that he had a book on large felines. I gulped and asked him whether he'd heard about my sighting. "What kind of tail?" he asked mildly. I told him. "How about the ears?" I told him. "Ah, yes," he said, just as mildly. "It appears that you have seen a lion."

I let go of the breath I had been holding. He believed me! I waited; surely he would now cancel our walk.

Instead, he pointed himself downhill, then threw me a twinkling glance. "I heard a very funny thing on the radio today," he said. "Someone reading a story called 'A Pig Is a Pig'—have you read it?"

I had not. By the time he'd filled me in on the details, we were already past the second switchback, heading for lion territory. I could not believe I was going back down there, especially with darkness falling so rapidly. Just as I began to raise a feeble protest, he said, "Are you ready to do the rosary?" This was another of our traditions, the ostensive purpose of our nightly hike, in fact, and there was nothing I could do except cross myself and dutifully recite, "In the name of the Father, the Son, and the Holy Spirit . . ."

The dark indigo sky deepened to black, and the edges of the waves far below turned phosphorescent. Handfuls of stars came pricking on as we walked through a pool of warm air—leftover noonday heat lingering in sage and sandstone. I looked for the ever-present fog bank, but it had vanished. Circumstances aside, it was a truly exquisite evening in Big Sur.

"Hail Mary, full of grace," intoned Fr. Bernard, "the Lord is with thee. Blessed art thou amongst women and blessed is the fruit of thy womb, Jesus."

"Holy Mary, mother of God, pray for us sinners now and in the hour of our death." My voice sounded fairly normal, considering that we were now walking past the place where my lion had been eating—here we were, two not-very-big people with soft voices and dark clothes. Someone was playing the xylophone on the back of my neck with small icy hammers. Fr. Bernard, of course, seemed completely unruffled. He stopped right at the *very worst place* to tie his shoe, a position which cut him down to four-year-old size. "Oh, my Jesus," I said breathlessly, casting wild glances about, "forgive us our sins, save us from the fires of hell, lead all souls to heaven, especially those in most need of your mercy!"

He straightened up, then moseyed over to the drop-off edge of the road to stare out at the dark horizon. "That was a good one," he said, pointing toward a vanishing arc of glitter. "Did you see it?"

Fr. Bernard, I wanted to moan, for God's sake! Then, suddenly, I got it—the difference between a true monk and myself. In this circumstance, at least, he literally had no fear; it did not matter if the lion came or didn't come. His job was to pray the rosary and admire the beauty of the cosmos, to laugh with a friend and take in draughts of sun-warmed sage. He was having a ball while I, on the other hand, was so terrified I was about to lose bladder control.

For the first time I saw that this was a choice—that I could give in to the fear, turn around, and charge back up that mountain, or I could relax and let God take over, which is exactly what my friend had been doing for so many years that it was now second nature to him.

St. Francis knew that moving *toward* what he feared instead of away from it was the key to liberation, that this was one of the things Jesus meant when he said, "Whoever finds his life will lose it, and whoever loses his life for my sake will find it" (Matt. 10:39). Francis knew, for example, that he had to turn his horse around and ride back toward that leper in the road, that he had to dismount and kiss the hand of somebody who filled him with a horrified revulsion. Moreover, he knew that he had to keep coming back, which he did through his visits to the lazaretto, or leper colony, until that fear had turned to love.

He taught his friars to do the same, to give over control of everything to God, to make themselves entirely vulnerable, and then to put themselves at the mercy of their fellow human beings. At times, they were cruelly mocked; other times they were beaten or dragged about the streets by their cowls. More often, their humble request for charity was simply ignored. Still, they were known far and wide for their endless good cheer and gentle peaceableness. No matter what the circumstances, they seemed remarkably confident and free.

St. Thomas described this kind of confidence (*fiducia* or *confidentia*) as a steadfast or intensified hope arising from a deep faith in the goodness of God.[16] St. Francis de Sales, speaking of those who rely on divine providence, added the following to his predecessor's description: "They are well assured that nothing can be sent, nothing permitted by this paternal and most loving heart, which will not be a source of good and profit to them. All that is required is that they should place all their confidence in Him."[17]

Such confidence in God's providence bears marvelous fruit: a childlike innocence, an exuberant joy, and a supernatural fearlessness.

Francis's most striking attribute was the simple, even childlike, way that he approached what other people would consider major problems. He refused to make anything more complicated than it already was; he confronted every situation with a trusting faith that God was ultimately in charge. Certainly, Fr. Bernard is like this in the sense that he never borrows trouble; he assumes, like Dame Julian of Norwich, that all will ultimately be well because God is love. If we wish not just to believe this but to act on it, we must relinquish fierce self-protectiveness.

Reginald Garrigou-Lagrange says, "This holy self-abandonment is not at all opposed to hope, but is child-like confidence in its holiest form united with a love becoming ever more and more purified." [18] Francis was living proof of this; the more he abandoned "security" of all kinds, the more loving he became. No human being was too poor, too unintelligent, too diseased, or too threatening; Francis embraced them all.

Aldous Huxley might have been thinking of the little poor man of Assisi when he wrote the following passage:

> Heaven cannot be entered except by those who are as little children. . . . [and] a man cannot become childlike unless he chooses to undertake the most strenuous and searching course of self-denial. In practice the command to become as little children is identical with the command to lose one's life. [19]

In other words, one must set aside one's natural tendency to protect the self at all costs.

When we do this, joy follows. In a famous anonymous autobiography from nineteenth-century Russia, *The Way of the Pilgrim*, the narrator has divested himself of everything but a small bag, the Bible, and a copy of the *Philokalia* (the collected wisdom of the Orthodox tradition). He sets off across Siberia, looking for a holy man to teach him how to pray. He is sometimes hungry, sometimes footsore, often completely alone, but somehow his journey is characterized by a deep and abiding happiness:

> Again I continued with my solitary journey and
> I experienced such great consolation that I felt
> as if a mountain had been removed from my
> shoulders . . . at times my heart burned with
> unspeakable love for Jesus so that my whole
> being was caught up in ecstasy.[20]

Such confidence, as Francis realized and as my friend Fr. Bernard has so clearly discovered, becomes at its highest level an astonishing fearlessness. Orthodox theologian Alexander Schmemann speaks about this supernatural courage, which he believes to be a natural outgrowth of the "resurrection vision":

> [T]his Easter faith has shown itself to be a
> tremendous and uninterrupted living force, by
> which men may find joy in suffering and
> death. . . . Under the Bolshevist yoke many thou-
> sands have suffered torture and death for their
> Christian faith (8,000 clergy alone); racked, some
> even torn to pieces, shot, burned, imprisoned.
> And they died cheerfully. And this persecu-
> tion . . . could not kill their Easter joy. . . . There

awoke in the hearts of these people a spirit akin to
that of primitive Christianity which had its source
in the same faith.[21]

I could not have been further from such courage. In spite
of the disciplines I was so pleased with myself for adopting—
solitude, silence, fasting—this was far harder, this business of
abandoning self-protectiveness in order to gain that promised confidence. It was not that I didn't believe that it would
work—all the great spiritual heroes have proven that it
does—but simply that I couldn't let go of my fearful hedge-
building long enough to get a taste of the reward.

A Safe Place to Be

I decided to quit brooding about my failures and to simply get on with it, the way Francis would. The first step
was just to notice *when* I felt afraid or insecure, and then
to observe my response to that—what action I automatically took. As I expected, money quickly proved that it
had the power to shake me.

Quite soon after I began this experiment, I got an
insufficient funds notice in the mail. Immediately, my
heart began to race. I could not *believe* it. I was *so careful*
with our checking account—how could this be? Worse,
how much damage had already been done? Checks could
be bouncing left and right! Creditors could be closing in!
This had to be a terrible mistake! Angrily, I charged
toward the phone to get this mess straightened out—then
realized that I hadn't even opened the envelope yet.

Carefully, I set it down on the table and went outside to sit down for a few minutes by the pond. What had just happened in there? One would think the sky had fallen or—worse yet—the stock market had collapsed. What a mountainous molehill I'd made in such record time. How silly!

Just becoming aware of these automatic reactions to perceived threats began to change things; it was almost impossible to act on pure emotion anymore without embarrassing myself. The real change came, however, when I finally figured out that I should pray instead of tremble.

The triggering event took place in my fiction-writing class when a male student I did not know well submitted a story about a bloody shooting. The victim, I was shocked to discover, was none other than I myself. Much ado ensued. The university took official action. Among other things, the student was temporarily banned from the campus. Suddenly, I was in a very vulnerable position. Our small town looked different now, far more threatening; the student could be lurking in the parking structure or waiting just around the corner. He could pop out of the library stacks or accost me in the grocery store. What if he found out where we lived?

I could feel the panic setting in, the automatic, frantic urge to throw up the barricades. For a few days, life became a nightmare—and then I noticed what I was doing and I remembered Fr. Bernard and the lion. Clearly, I was helpless in this situation—completely vulnerable, as I'd been so many years before when, too ill to drive, I'd let my Dodge Dart find the curb on its own. In that instance, a 145-pound Methodist minister, an angel with a brown beard, had rescued me. It could have been anybody who dragged me out of that front seat—I wouldn't have been able to put up a fight—but it was *him*.

I decided to give up, to surrender to the situation. What would be would be; I wasn't helping anything by becoming paranoid. Instead, and for the very first time, I said a prayer for *myself*, a special prayer that years before a minister had taught me to use when I was worried sick about one of our kids: I drew a circle in the air around the image of myself, then put the sign of the cross over it and let it go. God was all around me, but in my fear I was forgetting that.

In fact (if I could just let myself believe this), it is a "God-bathed world," as Protestant theologian Dallas Willard says in *The Divine Conspiracy*. It is a "perfectly safe place for us to be"—and the whole challenge of faith is to live as though this is so, even when we are caving in to doubt.[22] Jesus himself assures us over and over again that it is true, that our confidence in God's providence rests on firm ground. He tells us, "Ask and it will be given to you; seek and you will find; knock and the door will be opened to you" (Matt. 7:7).

Francis not only believed this, he saw the world with the joyful vision of one who had complete confidence in God's care. "Praised be my Lord God with all his creatures," he sang in his famous "The Canticle of All Creatures," "and specially our brother the sun, who brings us the day and who brings us the light; fair is he and shines with a very great splendor: O Lord, he signifies to us thee!"[23]

During his final illness, in 1226, he added a last verse to this long, thankful hymn to God's providence: "Praised be thou, O Lord, for our Sister Bodily Death, from whom no living man can escape. . . . Blessed those who have discovered thy most holy will, for to them the second death can do no harm."[24] This, I thought, was confidence at its highest level: the utter refusal to capitulate to the specter of pride, fear, or death itself.

Not surprisingly, Francis's religious life ended in the same state in which it began in the piazza of Assisi, where he had returned the packet of his clothing to his angry father and set off naked to see what God wanted of him. The moment he knew he was dying, nearly blind and suffering intense pain, he asked to be stripped and placed on the ground so that he could feel the good earth beneath his body as he was leaving it. Then he recited Psalm 142, a psalm that celebrates God's steadfast care in the midst of terrible trouble: "I cry out to you, LORD, / I say, You are my refuge, / my portion in the land of the living. / . . . / Lead me out of my prison, / that I may give thanks to your name. / Then the just shall gather around me / because you have been good to me" (Ps. 142:6, 8).

Francis proved over and over again that self-abandonment, the embracing of poverty in its deepest and most spiritual sense, is, as Thomas Merton once said, the "door to freedom . . . because finding nothing in ourselves that is a source of hope, we know there is nothing in ourselves worth defending. . . . We go out of ourselves therefore to rest in Him Who alone is our hope."[25]

CHAPTER 8

Integrity:
The Way of the Reformer

I . . . beg you in Jesus Christ not to
turn your eyes away from injustice,
but to see that, according to justice,
everybody, whether important or not,
is given his due. And be careful not to
let desire to please, or fear of anybody, prevent your doing so.[1]

St. Catherine of Siena (1347–1380)

Some years ago, when the kids were not yet teens, but
almost, I assembled them in front of our studio monitor to watch a videotape. We didn't have a "real" TV, one
with actual channels, and we didn't rent movies very
often, so this was a bit of an event, and I made sure they
knew this. Dutifully, they sprawled on the floor in front
of the monitor, still not sure what it was they were about
to see, while I somewhat dramatically hit the play button.
A grainy black-and-white image, obviously captured during television's less sophisticated years, filled the screen.
You could make out a crowd, and umbrellas, and a man

speaking in a voice as deep and rich and grainy as the televised image itself.

Moments later and to my own shock, I found myself weeping uncontrollably, face hidden in my hands. My children, who'd never seen me this way, froze in their positions on the floor, embarrassed, concerned, and completely clueless about what to do. Meanwhile, I cried on, nearly wailing, for a good three minutes. Then, still gulping for breath, I tried to reassure them. Everything was fine, Mom was not depressed or having some kind of breakdown. It was just . . . too much, being taken back to that hopeful time in American history—that long-gone age of faith in the courage and integrity of ordinary citizens.

Martin Luther King Jr., his face radiant, was continuing his address to the 200,000 people gathered in Washington that day. "I have a dream that one day on the red hills of Georgia the sons of former slaves and the sons of former slaveowners will be able to sit down together at the table of brotherhood. I have a dream that one day even the state of Mississippi . . . will be transformed into an oasis of freedom and justice."[2] The words rang out like hammer blows, sentence after sentence. Nothing in his expression acknowledged the fact that death was waiting for him just around the corner. Perhaps he was genuinely unaware, in spite of the threats piling up around him. Perhaps instead, he'd come to terms with the fact that truth telling and dying often go hand in hand.

Afterward, my kids and I talked about heroes—who they were, how they qualified, and why there were so few of them. Johnny, nine at the time, asserted in his reedy little voice that they were people who "didn't care what anyone thought of them," which seemed a fairly wise insight and entirely consistent with his own approach to life. Eleven-year-old Andrea, who was more mature and less voluble than her brother, sat mum. "And why don't they care about people's opinions of them, do you think?" I prompted her.

Silence. Then, with a soft sigh (Mom never quits, does she?), her somber blue gaze met mine. "Because they know they're right?"

"Exactly!" I was elated. Aside from my unplanned bout of hysterical tears, this hour had gone the way I hoped it would—another successful "teaching moment" in my never-ending string of them. Yet there was something woefully naïve in my self-congratulation, for I really had no idea how powerful a force I was unleashing in my children. All I wanted was for them to become decent people with fulfilling careers; it never crossed my mind that they might try to become heroes themselves.

I went through more than a little private dismay when they began to strike out riskily on their own. First, Andrea headed for Nepal, where she lived for six months with a family of rice farmers in the Kathmandu Valley. When she returned, she finished college and became a VISTA volunteer with a food bank in Portland where she taught cooking and nutrition classes to impoverished people: immigrants, refugees, the homeless, and the unemployed. Johnny spent six months studying in the Middle East, India, and Asia. After graduation, he took a job with Teach for America. He was assigned a seventh-grade class in one of the most violent neighborhoods in Newark.

Of course, I was proud of them—how could I not be?—but the price for that was uncomfortably high. When I let myself think too hard about where they were living and what they were doing, I shuddered. Personal courage is one thing, but maternal courage was another thing entirely. St. Francis didn't have kids, after all; maybe he wouldn't have been quite so fearless if he had.

Even worse than my worry, however, was my guilt over all those high-minded discussions of heroism when the kids were so young and impressionable. I hadn't been lying to them; I did love heroes. I loved the way they transcended the normal boundaries for young American adults. I loved being brought to inspired tears. Unfortunately, heroes were generally a short-lived bunch. They took their stands, they made their enemies, and they paid their prices. Never did I intend for my children to actually *put into practice* the lofty ideals I so glibly espoused.

I could talk the talk but, like hypocrites everywhere, I refused to walk the walk. I reluctantly had to admit that I had an integrity problem.

If there was one virtue at the core of a simple, unified life, the kind I so admired when I visited the Amish or made my retreats at the hermitage, I knew it had to be integrity. The word *integrity* means wholeness, or the state of being complete. Without integrity, I was living at cross-purposes, professing ideals I was more often than not afraid to uphold. I was a person at war with herself, always weighing the personal pros and cons instead of operating on principle. I was like Dostoyevsky's anonymous antihero in *Notes from the Underground:* "never a coward at heart" though "always a coward in action."[3]

Meanwhile, my own kids were putting me to shame. Somehow, I had to find a way to bring my ideals and actions into alignment. Though the words of men like Martin Luther King Jr. could make me weep, the men themselves seemed almost dauntingly courageous, another class of human being entirely. I needed to find an exemplar more like me, someone who was not quite so obviously . . . *heroic,* yet still willing to take a strong public stance. I needed a person of great integrity who was also (why did it take me so long to think of this?) a woman.

Catherine of Siena first appeared on my radar screen via a brief note in Thomas Bokenkotter's *A Concise History of the Catholic Church,* which was a book I thought I'd better at least dip into before I tried to teach medieval literature. In a section called "The Unmaking of Christendom," he describes the famous fourteenth-century kidnapping attempt of Pope Boniface VIII by King Philip IV of France, whose nationalistic ambitions took precedence over his loyalty to the church.[4] Though Philip's plot was unsuccessful, he was finally able to get a Frenchman elected pope (Clement V) and the papal headquarters transferred to Avignon in southern France, where it remained for the next seventy years.[5]

When Pope Gregory XI, the seventh and last Avignon pope, was trying to make up his mind about how and when to return the papal court to Rome, says Bokenkotter, he was "urged on" by the courageous Italian Catherine. Her arguments carried enough weight that he gave up his pre-varicating and headed south.[6] My ears pricked. This was exciting—a woman who'd not only helped change the course of history but had actually been recognized for it.

Later I was given a book called *Woman to Woman: An Anthology of Women's Spiritualities* by Phyllis Zagano in which I discovered that Catherine of Siena was one of only three women to be named Doctor of the Roman Catholic Church. In fact, she was, historically speaking, the first woman to earn this honor—this, despite the fact that she could not write until she was thirty.

At that time, I didn't follow up on my interest in Catherine of Siena. I didn't because I was too busy focus-ing on my integrity problem, which had taken a sudden turn for the worse.

The issue of my integrity arose at work, where such issues often arise. It had to do with the hierarchy of and my position within a large institution, which (as anyone knows who has ever worked in such an institution) can become *the* issues. Ironically enough, the crisis came *after* I'd been through all my soul-searching about right liveli-hood. I'd had my marvelous revelations about work-obsession as a form of idolatry. I'd declared myself free, never again to be enslaved by competition for status in the marketplace. So what was going on? Why was I sud-denly in such a tizzy? For indeed I was: I could not fathom what had just happened to me, much less what I should do about it.

For ten years, I'd taught in an English department that required its tenure-track faculty to hold a Ph.D. All I had was the master's degree that had once cost my family so dearly. I had earned that degree in the department where I now taught. I was a hometown girl, in other words. When I published my first novel, my colleagues-who-had-once-been-my-teachers were as pleased as punch—and even more so when I managed to snag a couple of respectable awards along the way.

They backed this up with some course assignments that lecturers like me almost never taught. Creative writing, Great Books, the modern novel—I was cashing in on some of the real perks of the tenure track and all without having to go to faculty meetings! This was great, and for a long time I was satisfied with my position of being a "special" lecturer. Somebody, I thought rather smugly, who continued to make her *valuable* contribution to the department for the purest of reasons, never thinking of asking for a higher salary, sabbaticals, or the other goodies that came with tenure.

Then one day, I was asked by another campus in the California State University system to become an advisory board member for a new master of fine arts program in creative writing. Five campuses had formed a consortium in order to offer this low-residency degree. Suddenly, I realized how long I'd been waiting for a similar gesture from my own school and department. It was the kind of gesture that, coming from my own faculty, would have meant I was no longer just the hometown-girl-made-good to them, an anomaly who'd somehow leapt the normal lecturer bounds.

The hard work of setting up the new consortium program distracted me awhile longer from the unsatisfactory situation in my home English department. I finally had a chance to teach graduate students, after all, to make governance and admissions decisions, and to work on a faculty team. I was getting my chance to take on an adult role in the academic world, and I thrived on it. I began to assume that when a tenure-track fiction job finally opened up on my home campus, I would be invited (thanks to all my hard work) to apply . . . Ph.D. or not.

In the course of my work with the M.F.A. program, I discovered that my own department had taken a rather hard line on this issue of academic credentials for creative-writing jobs. I also discovered that a number of other schools did it differently. I was a viable candidate elsewhere, if elsewhere I wanted to go.

When I returned to school that particular fall, I was shocked to discover that the fiction job I'd been waiting for had indeed opened up, and I hadn't been invited to submit my application. Worse, I hadn't even been informed about the opening, which, the job announcement said, most definitely required a Ph.D. At first I was furious (how could they possibly be so ungrateful?), and then profoundly hurt (how could they do this to me after all these years?).

In time, of course, I began to blame myself. Hadn't I requested a half-time teaching schedule, after all—thanks to Fr. Michael and his revolutionary oblate training? Hadn't I sent a fairly strong message that career no longer took top priority in my life? Maybe my colleagues were simply responding to my signals; maybe they were just making a reasonable assumption about where I stood. As soon as I talked myself down this road, however, I fell back into wounded anger. At the very *least,* I insisted to the bathroom mirror, they owed me the courtesy of asking. At the very *least,* after all I've done for them. On and on and on I went, becoming more entangled in my unruly emotions the longer I kept at it.

What did not occur to me, not until much later, was that, at its core, this situation had little to do with *me.* Certainly I had been personally affected by it, but the real problem was that the department was following a rule, intended to protect academic integrity, in such an inflexible way that every option but one (a writer with a Ph.D.) had been effectively blocked by it. The department had tied its own hands, and it apparently couldn't even see this.

I wasn't alone; hundreds of candidates around the country, published writers with M.F.A.s from prestigious programs, were also off the list. Why on earth had I worked so hard to develop this new system-wide graduate program when my own department would not consider hiring the students who completed the degree?

Meanwhile, I took a poll among my writer friends at other institutions. I was advised that I probably had a grievance, and possibly even a case, if I wanted to pursue it. I began to look at my options . . . and suddenly I realized that I could never do it. I could not, despite my sense that the department was committing a deep injustice to *some-body*, make my public protest. I could not walk the walk.

The very *thought* of taking official action made me tremble. It would call so much attention to my already humiliating situation; it would spark controversy; people would pass judgment on me without knowing all the facts. I could lose the respect of my colleagues and cause undeserved and embarrassing trouble for my much-loved department head and dean, who were not to blame. I could be lumped into the same category as those irritating women who cry discrimination indiscriminately—I could become a pariah. Worse, people might no longer think I was *nice.*

Ultimately, I did nothing. Moreover, I finally convinced myself that in this situation it was better to turn the other cheek—that my refusal to protest was actually more Christlike than cowardly. I dragged out the Sabbath time argument again. Maybe it was downright dangerous for me to take up arms in this case; maybe I was just operating off of the same old insatiable need to be recognized for my accomplishments, making my work into an idol again.

I rationalized my lack of courage, ignoring what might have been my real duty in that situation. I didn't consider that I might be the very best person to challenge this shortsighted and unfair departmental rule, or that creative writers in a weaker position than I was—there were several other potential candidates in my very own lecturer's pool—might need me to fight this fight. Instead, I tucked in my chin and shouldered on, working overtime to contain my anger at the personal hurt.

I failed the integrity test, but at least I could see, for the first time, where lay my own impediment to "the state of being complete." It was my need to meet social expectations, to be *approved.* Rocking the boat over what was clearly an injustice, no matter how minor, was for me the ultimate faux pas, a truly dreadful social mistake. Yet social mores were exactly what Martin Luther King took on in the South of the 1960s—social mores that declared racial equality simply "not the thing." He took on a social system so deeply entrenched that nobody had to talk about it anymore. You just knew from birth why God had created buses with back seats in them. To suggest otherwise was to fly in the face of tradition, convention, and the unquestioned opinion of the group, which was, if nothing else, incredibly *rude.*

Somewhat ironically, considering my private struggles, I happened to be teaching a class in argumentation during this time and had assigned my students King's "Letter from a Birmingham Jail." In this eloquent plea to eight Alabama ministers who had called his demonstrations "untimely and unwise," King dealt head-on with what he saw as the most frustrating impediment to social justice:

> I have almost reached the regrettable conclusion
> that the Negro's great stumbling block in the
> stride toward freedom is not the White Citizen's
> Councilor or the Ku Klux Klanner, but the
> white moderate who is more devoted to "order"
> than to justice; who prefers a negative peace
> which is the absence of tension to a positive
> peace which is the presence of justice. . . . who
> lives by the myth of time and who constantly
> advises the Negro to wait until a "more conven-
> ient season." . . . Shallow understanding from
> people of good will is more frustrating than

absolute misunderstanding from people of ill
will. Lukewarm acceptance is much more bewil-
dering than outright rejection.[7]

Over and over, King makes the point that necessary
reforms do not take place without some measure of social
upheaval. In the South of his day, this meant the disrup-
tion of a complacent but ultimately illusory faith in "law
and order." He talks about his early feeling that the deseg-
regation movement would "have the support of the white
church." Instead, "all too many . . . have been more cautious than courageous and have remained silent behind
the anesthetizing security of the stained-glass windows."
In fact, he says, he has "watched white churches stand on
the sideline and merely mouth pious irrelevancies and
sanctimonious trivialities."[8]

This, I thought admiringly, is *really* rude. How angry he
must have made them. What a truly magnificent pariah he
must have been. My eyes suddenly filled with hot tears at
the sheer beauty of his integrity—and my lack of the same.
It was time to read about that Catherine woman.

St. Catherine and the Courage of Truthfulness

Catherine of Siena and her twin sister were born on
March 25, 1347, the twenty-third and twenty-fourth
children of their parents, Iacopo di Benincasa, a cloth-
finisher, and Lapa de'Piagenti (Lapa would give birth to a
twenty-fifth and last child a year later). When Catherine
was one, the Black Death began its rampage through

Europe, ultimately killing a third of the population. Certainly, this intensely sensitive child must have felt at some very deep level the darkness and despair of her time. Catherine's later writings are permeated with a persistent sorrow over the human condition. In one of her ecstatic prayers, she says, "I see the whole world lying down in death, such a bad one that my soul faints at this sight."⁹

Her unusual spiritual gifts manifested themselves early. At age six, walking home after visiting one of her married sisters, she had a beautiful vision of Christ, dressed in pontifical robes and flanked by the apostles Peter, Paul, and John. He smiled at her kindly, then reached out and with his right hand gave her his blessing. Her immediate response was to seek retreat, like Anthony and the other Desert Fathers before her, in a small cave where she could pray alone, an eremitical stint that lasted only half a day because she knew her mother would be frantic with worry. The vision stayed with her, however, and was followed within a year by a precocious vow of lifetime virginity.

When she turned twelve, Lapa—who seems to have consistently failed to recognize her daughter's special calling—began pressuring her to dress more attractively; it was time, she said, to begin thinking about a husband. For a while, Catherine dutifully complied. Then one of her sisters died during childbirth, and the young visionary decided that this was the sign she had been waiting for: clearly, her vow to God was more important than her mother's wishes. After consulting with her spiritual advisor, she cut off her hair to show her determination never to marry. Lapa was furious. Catherine was forbidden access to her small prayer room and ordered to do all the household chores.

Catherine's response—she was fifteen at the time—was to call her enormous family together to announce that she had taken Christ as her spouse, an announcement her father saw as proof enough that she had received a genuine call to the religious life. He advised the family to leave her alone and his wife to stop pushing her toward marriage. A year later, Catherine joined the Sisters of Penance of St. Dominic, a lay branch of the Dominicans, and, without leaving her parents' house, took up a life of intense prayer in her former small room.

Four years later, she had a vivid vision of Jesus standing at the threshold of her sanctuary, asking her to come out and rejoin the world. She obeyed immediately, going to the local hospitals, where she devoted herself to nursing the sick of Siena. Despite the fact that she was still barely out of her teens and could not seem to learn to write, her reputation for holiness grew rapidly. Soon she found herself mediating disputes between individuals and warring families. A group of disciples formed around her, and eventually she was receiving letters from people in far-flung places seeking her advice; she dictated her responses (381 of these still exist) through friends.

In 1374, the Black Death swept through Italy again, and Catherine, refusing to succumb to plague-induced terror, went back to the hospitals of Siena to nurse the stricken, some of whom were her own relatives. Her reputation for sanctity increased. A year later, she received, like Francis of Assisi, the stigmata, or wounds of Christ.

During the miracle-venerating medieval era, this phenomenon would have placed her in rare company indeed and also given her enormous spiritual authority, authority she did not flinch at using.

When Pope Paul VI proclaimed her Doctor of the Church, he referred to her extensive involvement in the politics of her day, declaring that "the teaching of this singular woman politician is still meaningful and valuable."[10] During her relatively short life—she died at age thirty-three—she communicated freely with popes and kings, queens and cardinals. She dictated her letters with the confidence of the hero who, as my children put it, "didn't care what other people thought" of her "because she knew she was right." For Catherine, the issues were always the same, no matter how complex the situations themselves might appear: The power of those in positions of governance had been given to them "on loan." Their authority was not their own, but God's. In order to govern effectively, whether they be secular lords or princes of the Church, they had to first govern their own individual lives. "I do not see how we can rule anybody," she said, "unless we start by ruling ourselves."[11]

She had utter faith in the Church and its earthly mission, despite the unchecked, malignant corruption that had so weakened it in her day, and therefore many of her reforming efforts were directed at the highest-ranking men in the ecclesiastical hierarchy. For only these, she said in a letter to Pope Gregory XI, had the power to "uproot the stinking flowers, full of impurity and greed, swelling with pride"—the "bad pastors and rectors who poison the garden" of the Church "and make it putrid." Only Christ's chosen governors had the authority to "plant in this garden sweet-scented flowers: pastors and rectors who may prove true servants of Jesus Christ, with no other concern but the honour of God and the salvation of souls, and to be fathers to the poor." [12]

Always, she urged the men of the church, whether they be popes or priests, to accept their role as "Christs on earth," their obligation to continue Christ's revivifying action in the "dead" world. "Since he has given you authority, and you have accepted it," she sternly reminded Pope Gregory, "you have to make use of your privileges and power; if you are unwilling to do so, it would be better for you to renounce them, so as better to give honour to God and save your soul." [13]

Gregory did return the papacy to Rome but died shortly thereafter, throwing the Roman population into turmoil. What if another Frenchman was elected? Crowds rioted around the Vatican, threatening the cardinals debating within, and the conclave wasted no time in choosing an Italian archbishop as their next pontiff. The harshly austere Pope Urban VI—who, according to some historians, was a genuinely courageous reformer, and to others, a cruel lunatic—then became the catalyst for one of the most tumultuous periods in Catholic history: the forty-year Great Schism.

At one point during the Schism, up to three popes vied for power at the same time. Catherine did not live long enough to see this. However, she did see the first rival pope elected—by the same cardinals who had originally placed Urban VI on the pontifical throne. Once again, she saw the papacy divided between Avignon and Rome, a development she knew could only further imperil an already disintegrating Christendom.

This disunity in her beloved Church literally broke her heart: in January 1380, she suffered what appears to have been a severe myocardial infarction and for two days could not move or speak. In February, consumed by her concern for the faltering institution, she began her own personal quest to save it—each morning, she left her sickbed to walk to St. Peter's, where she spent the whole day praying and fasting. On April 29, thin and exhausted, she died. Three days later, crowds converged on the church of Santa Maria sopra Minerva to say goodbye to her. There, according to the records, many sick were healed.

Catherine, I thought glumly, was not going to make it any easier on me than Martin Luther King Jr. had.

I reread her letter to three of the cardinals who turned on Urban VI, keeping my eyes peeled for any hint of self-serving diplomacy. As I might have expected, there was none to be found:

> O blindness upon blindness, preventing you
> from seeing evil, and damage to soul and body!
> Had you seen it, you would not have so easily
> parted from truth with slavish fear, under the
> sway of your passions: pride and a habit of dis-
> posing at pleasure of human delights. You
> could not endure . . . even a harsh word of
> reproof. . . . And this is the motive for your

change. . . . In fact, before Christ-on-earth [the
duly-elected pope] began to bite you, you
acknowledged and revered him as the Vicar of
Christ that he is.[14]

Catherine, however, never "chose sides," as reformers
so often do. She dealt with everyone on an individual
basis. In fact, she could be equally tough in a completely
different way on Urban himself, who was notorious for
being inflexible. When she was trying to negotiate peace
between a rebellious Florence and Rome, she sent him an
imploring letter that was also clearly a rebuke for his failure to show love in this difficult situation:

> I beg you, and compel you in the name of
> Christ crucified, for the sake of his blood whose
> minister you are, not to delay in receiving the
> sheep that have been away from the fold. . . .
> And, suppose they are not asking for it with
> such true and perfect humility as they should,
> let your holiness supply their imperfection and
> bring it to perfection. Accept from the sick
> what they can give.[15]

In addition, she wrote to the warring kings of England
and France, addressing them both as Christian "brothers"
and admonishing them not to forget Christ's "inestimable
charity." Their violent animosity was destroying both their
people and themselves; the logic of violence is inexorable:
"One must be a blind fool not to see that with the knife

of hatred he is killing himself." She also argued vehemently for the protection of innocent women and children during this bloody and protracted war: "I wonder how you can help committing to this aim [of peace] . . . your very life . . . on considering what harm there has been to souls and bodies, and how many religious, women, girls, have been abused and persecuted because of this war. No more, for the sake of Christ crucified!" [16]

If she was unstoppable in her efforts to reconcile warring countries or factions in the church, she was even more so when it came to making peace between an individual soul and God. Hearing of a man in prison who had been sentenced to die and was furious about having to give up his life so young, she made it her business to visit him there. After long conversation, she convinced him of her own strong belief that death, no matter how frightening, is in fact the moment of union with God. Then she waited for him on the scaffold, prayed for him as he knelt, helped him to place his neck in the best position for the executioner, and sent him on his way with the joyous words, "Down, to the wedding feast, my sweet brother! Soon shall you be in everlasting life!" [17]

Like Martin Luther King Jr., she was more than willing to perish, if need be, in service of the truth: "God grant that I may always be a lover and proclaimer of truth, and that for the sake of truth I may die." [18] Her unusual personality, a combination of mystic and reformer, allowed little room for caution or expediency when truth was what was required. In fact, she was downright ruthless when it came to my own particular temptation: evading confrontation for fear of giving offense. "[W]e must avoid miserable love of self, the source of servile fear, which is so timid as to be afraid of its own shadow," she said, ". . . so that, on seeing that God and neighbour are being offended, someone will pretend not to see the offence . . . moreover, to please and avoid displeasing, he will show agreement with the same crimes that are being committed, and behave against conscience." [19]

Clearly, I stood convicted. How could I begin to more fully integrate ideals and action? How could I learn to do battle when battling was necessary? One big problem was that turning-the-other-cheek business in the New Testament, and not only because it kept me from taking uncomfortable stands. For me, it was the heart of the Gospel, the way of love, the difference between the violent world and the peaceful Eden of the hermitage, where even wild foxes felt safe on my front porch. How could the quest for justice be reconciled with the path of love?

The Integrity of Jesus and Sr. Mary Pat

Then I realized that it could be no other way. If there was any human being who had ever been whole and complete, it was Christ. If there'd ever been a human being with integrity, it was he. Therefore, everything he did—even the things I preferred to skip over in my reading, such as his wrathful diatribe against Pharisaical hypocrisy—sprang from the same unified source. Which was, as John says so firmly, nothing other than love: "God is love, and whoever remains in love remains in God and God in him" (1 John 4:16). Love and justice were bound together, part and parcel of one another. Loving and truth telling were linked. I could not ignore this basic fact and all its ramifications.

Reluctantly, I pulled out the Bible to read those passages I'd always managed to skip over, the ones in which lamb becomes lion.

There were a number of these. I'd always had problems, for example, reconciling my preferred view of Jesus-the-gentle-peacemaker with the dusty, hungry, and no doubt exhausted man who cursed an innocent fig tree for its lack of fruit—a fig tree that then "withered to its roots" (Mark 11:20). How could he be so demanding? Even his disciples were shocked. As it turns out, however, this was a teaching moment, a far more powerful and effective version of the teaching moments I used to inflict on my kids. His point was this: "Have faith in God. Amen, I say to you, whoever says to this mountain, 'Be lifted up and thrown into the sea,' and does not doubt in his heart but believes that what he says will happen, it shall be done for him" (Mark 11:22–23). He was using the situation at hand—hungry disciples, an unproductive tree—to teach in this very visceral way what it meant to wield supernatural power. I could now see that what really rose off the page was not simple irritation—an embarrassing deficiency, one would think, in the Son of God—but instead unwavering strength of purpose.

Then there was the cleansing of the temple, a scene that, frankly, made me cringe. How did he expect to win people over with such in-your-face tactics? I could just see him barreling into the crowded temple area, attracting all sorts of negative attention—even, possibly, murderous rage, which one would think he'd be trying to avoid at this point—as he began literally to drive out of the temple those selling and buying there. Even worse was yet to come. Like the low-grade hero of a contemporary action movie, he then turned physical, pushing over the tables of the money changers and the seats of those who were selling doves. It was high drama all the way, calculated to raise emotions and cause contro-versy. Why? Couldn't he have taken a more civilized approach, employed a little diplomacy?

Possibly; but would the crowd have absorbed the les-son if their hearts had not been racing so? While they still huddled together, aghast, he stood before them and said, "Is it not written: / 'My house shall be called a house of prayer for all peoples'? / But you have made it a den of thieves" (Mark 11:17). Chances are, they never again for-got that ancient injunction against commercializing what is holy. In order to make it stick, he had to take a signifi-cant risk, one for which his enemies were waiting. In fact, "The chief priests and the scribes came to hear of it and were seeking a way to put him to death, yet they feared him because the whole crowd was astonished at his teach-ing" (Mark 11:18). This was the interesting part: they *feared* him. Once again, this was a deliberate show of power on his part, and not for ego's sake.

Besides all this, my gentle Jesus was also quite the truth teller, sometimes almost brutally so. In his last hours with the disciples, for example, he waited until everybody was reclined around the table and then announced, "'Amen, I say to you, one of you will betray me, one who is eating with me.' They began to be distressed and to say to him, one by one, 'Surely it is not I?' He then said to them, 'One of the Twelve, the one who dips with me into the dish. For the Son of Man indeed goes, as it is written of him, but woe to that man by whom the Son of Man is betrayed. It would be better for that man if he had never been born'" (Mark 14:18–21).

Later the same evening, when he'd given them more bad news—they would all have their faith shaken by the events that were to come—Peter insisted that even if everybody else ran off and hid, he would remain loyal. Jesus, without any attempt to cushion the truth, simply replied, "Amen, I say to you, this very night before the cock crows twice you will deny me three times" (Mark 14:30). It was crucial for their later survival that they be able to look back on that evening and understand that he knew it all in advance, that they were not dealing with utter chaos, but the unfolding of a divine destiny. At the time, of course, Peter must have been devastated by his beloved Master's apparent lack of faith in him.

I found that these moments occur all through the Gospels—Jesus telling it like it is, often very bluntly, often through the use of upsetting imagery. He *intended* to shake things up: "Do not think that I have come to bring peace upon the earth. I have come to bring not peace but the sword" (Matt. 10:34). He knew that people who actually heard what he was saying and allowed themselves to be transformed by it could never again relax into complacency or a timid dependence on social approval. He understood, centuries before Martin Luther King Jr., that evil is not overcome without a certain amount of upheaval, that tension accompanies growth.

I thought about a friend of mine, and her quiet but persistent efforts over the years to force me out of my artificial pacifism. I thought about Sr. Mary Pat, diminutive warrior for social justice, a woman, I suddenly realized, with a good dose of the integrity I lacked.

I first met Sr. Mary Pat when she was hired as codirector of the Newman Center on my campus. I liked her— how could you not, with those deerlike eyes, that smile?—but could tell we were on different paths entirely. I'd spent most of my adult life competing in the world; she'd spent her first twenty years as a nun in a strictly enclosed cloister. I had just discovered silence and solitude; she seemed completely absorbed in social-justice issues. I wanted nothing but a cessation of stress and anxiety in my life; she seemed to thrive on controversy. This persistent little nun, I thought, is going to sidetrack me if I let her. She's going to sweep me onto committees and lure me into worthy projects. I can't do those and simplify at the same time.

I dragged my feet a bit when she invited me to attend my first Newman forum. First of all, she was simply naive if she really believed that a visiting priest—even the Maryknoll founder of School of the Americas Watch, Fr. Roy Bourgeois—could fill up that huge campus auditorium. Students didn't give up homework time, much less beer and pizza time, to listen to priests. Second, she seemed to want me to become personally involved in this—to sit beside this Fr. Roy on a local talk-radio show—at the very time I was trying to keep from taking on new obligations in my life.

It was not that her request made no sense; I'd spent three years researching and writing a novel about some of the same problems Fr. Roy had spent a decade trying to solve. I knew all about the School of the Americas and the tax-sponsored destruction it was wreaking in Central and South America. I'd seen some of that damage with my own eyes. I just didn't want to be involved with Mary Pat's social-justice agenda, regardless of how much I liked her, regardless of how worthy her causes were. I knew that there would be no end to it. I was trying to walk the simple path, and I needed some peace and quiet. Period. At least this was how I explained my reluctance to sign on.

I finally did capitulate, mostly because I couldn't figure out a good enough excuse to stay away. I'd meet Fr. Roy at the radio station for the show, and I'd be there for the on-campus speech that evening. But that was it; no Newman Center Mass the following day—too busy— and no Mass at my own parish the following evening. Lots of grading, Mary Pat, I said. You know how it is. She did know, she said, and thanked me in her warm way for helping however I could.

Imagine my shock, then, when Fr. Roy finally arrived and I found myself behaving like a starstruck groupie, tagging along as he moved from event to event, and hanging onto his every word. I was not the only person affected in this way; the campus auditorium was filled to standing-room-only capacity, and our usually jaded students were utterly riveted. There was power in Fr. Roy, the kind of power that blows through the Gospels—and this despite his gentle, self-deprecating humor and the patches on his pants. After he finally left us, I stammered my thank-yous to Sr. Mary Pat for making sure I'd had some conversation time with him out of the public spotlight. "What an incredible human being!" I said, my eyes swimming with inspired tears. "Good Lord—what a hero! It was like . . . like having dinner with Martin Luther King Jr.! I'm so glad you let me be part of this!"

She could have said a lot of things right then. She could have mentioned that it had taken some serious arm-twisting to get me to even show up. Instead, she gave me one of her signature smiles and leaned forward, patting my hand. "I just know," she said, "how much you're going to love our next speaker. Have you ever heard of Sr. Helen Prejean? The nun in *Dead Man Walking*?"

Much as I liked and admired her, if Mary Pat had confined her efforts to event organizing, I might have been able to give her my blessing and send her on her way. She and I are completely different people, I told myself; we have different callings and different lives to lead. She's something to behold, but she can't be my role model. I'm looking for a hermit instead.

I might have successfully pushed her off my radar screen if she hadn't kept *following through* on the events she organized, if she hadn't kept taking things to the next level, putting herself on the line. The year after Fr. Roy's visit, she went to Fort Benning, Georgia, for the annual School of the Americas Watch demonstration. There, along with thousands of other protesters against United States support of brutal Latin American regimes, she risked arrest and imprisonment for trespassing on military grounds. Less than a year after September 11, she traveled to Afghanistan with an interfaith peace delegation to interview children who'd been maimed in the bombing. Upon her return, she hit the speaker's trail as an advocate for the shattered Afghan nation during a time when war rhetoric—this time against Iraq—was at its most vociferous. Most recently, in protest against that same war, she crossed the line at Vandenberg Air Force Base, knowing as she did so that her case would be heard under the terms of the new Patriot Act.

I shuddered at her rudeness, but admired it, too. Rude, rude, *rude*. Good for you, Mary Pat.

She and all the other brave souls—my own kids, for example—who willingly place themselves in danger for the sake of those less powerful have convinced me of one thing, at least: I'm full of hot air when it comes to genuine heroism.

I have come to see that standing up for truth and justice, on however small a scale, is my responsibility, too. Even though I'll never change the world in any big way, by living with integrity, I am ultimately helping to simplify life for myself and everyone around me. It is falsehood and injustice that are complex and confusing; as Jesus once said, the devil is the "father of lies" (John 8:44). Truth can cut like a knife, but the pain is ultimately clarifying. The struggle for justice, even if this is confined to a struggle for what is right and good in marriage or between friends, causes tension and upheaval but leads to a new order and a new peace.

In my nonheroic life, this has meant trying to deal with bad or unhealthy situations instead of explaining them away or rationalizing my own passivity. It has meant, for example, some painful decisions about a wayward and increasingly disturbed relative who has been enabled by our family for years. It has meant taking a tough stand with tenants who were also friends—a stand that led to their abandoning the friendship. It has meant setting some clear-cut boundaries for a fellow oblate who was beginning to mistake spiritual compatibility for romantic destiny.

In a simpler and more daily way, integrity has required a commitment to veracity in small things: to being more careful with my words; to resisting the old habit of assuring others that all is well when sometimes it really isn't. It has meant bearing some ongoing tension for the sake of the truth. I have learned that a false peace that denies the reality of evil in a given situation only compounds an already nasty state of affairs, one that then feeds on itself and grows.

I learned this the hard way when, trying to avoid conflict at all costs, I refused to raise my protest at work. The wound from being denied the opportunity to apply for that job stayed open far longer than it should have; my buried anger no doubt contaminated my individual relationships with people in my department. I found that, in the end, false peace blocks genuine forgiveness.

On the other hand, when we strap on the armor without first being sure of our motives, we can do terrible harm. Fr. Roy Bourgeois expressed this well in his closing remarks to the six hundred students who came to hear him that night. "Many of you," he said, "are hearing about the School of the Americas for the first time. And what you've heard has outraged you, and you want to come help us close this place down. That's great. We'd love to have you join us. But just remember one thing if you do." He leaned forward over the podium, gazing out at the audience. There was the sound of restless rustling; they had no idea of what he was about to say next. He smiled at them, a gentle smile, full of light. "Find somewhere to leave your anger when you come," he said. "Because *this* movement is about love."

Most of us are not heroes, but we can all try to live with integrity. Our days are literally filled with choices about what we'll do next—what we will say; how we will respond; what we will protest; what we will continue to bear; how we will behave when nobody is watching; what we will uphold and what we will deny; who we will reach out to and what we will cut free. We are in constant mental and physical motion. In the long run, to be able to live our lives in an "unbroken" way requires that all this activity, as insignificant as most of it may seem, must pour from the same undiluted source.

The genuinely heroic author of the letter of James, who was stoned to death under the high priest Ananus II in A.D. 62, directs us to this source—the Word of God—and shows us the way to a life of integrity:

> Be doers of the word and not hearers only,
> deluding yourselves. For if anyone is a hearer of
> the word and not a doer, he is like a man who

looks at his own face in a mirror. He sees himself, then goes off and promptly forgets what he looks like. But the one who peers into the perfect law of freedom and perseveres, and is not a hearer who forgets but a doer who acts, such a one shall be blessed in what he does (James 1:22–25).

St. Catherine of Siena would have agreed. Her most famous work, the *Dialogue,* which records a years-long revelation from God, ends in a hymn of praise to her divine teacher. In it, she reveals the secret of her undivided strength, the source of her courageous truth telling, and the impetus for her struggle to reform the unjust practices of her beloved Church: "In the light of faith I am strong, constant and persevering; in the light of faith I hope: it does not allow me to fail on my way. This light shows me the way: without it I should walk in darkness." [20]

PART V

RETURNING TO THE WORLD

The Desert Fathers understood that we might battle our demons for many years—chances are good, right up to the moment of death. The dying words of the saints are interesting in this regard, for often they confess in real anguish to sins nobody else can see in them. They know exactly how close the dark fears lie, how easy it would be to fall backwards off the mountain. The work never ends; instead, it gradually becomes less absorbing. It stops taking every ounce of our time and attention, for even while we are in the midst of it, we are slowly reawakened to the world in a whole new way.

Simplification is ultimately a method, not the goal. It is the path, not the endpoint; the field, and not the treasure. It is meant to free us up from all needless anxiety and distraction, to clear away the clutter of ambition and envy and insecurity, so that we might come as close to God as we can in this life. When we do, we experience love at a depth we never suspected was possible.

Once we know how much we are loved, we cannot help but turn back to the hostile, anguished, and confused place we once inhabited. We cannot help but pour ourselves forth in compassion, either through direct service or through a life of contemplative prayer. Most of the great saints have managed to do both: to pray without ceasing while serving with both hands. For those of us just arriving at this stage, it is enough to heed the call to reconnect. This is a time to resist the impulse to jealously guard our hard-won peace. It is time to open up to whatever awaits us next.

The following two chapters, "Generosity: The Way of the Servant" and "Tranquility: The Way of the Contemplative," deal with this part of the journey. St. Ignatius of Loyola (1491–1556) founded the Society of Jesus in order to reach the spiritually hungry who had no access to a formal theological education. He began as a street preacher harassed by the Inquisition and went on to send Jesuit teachers to every corner of the globe. Bede Griffiths (1906–1993) was a Benedictine monk from England who established a "Christian ashram" in southern India long before many Westerners knew anything about Hinduism. He believed that the West had as much to learn from the East—particularly in the area of contemplative prayer or meditation—as the East did from the West.

CHAPTER 9

Generosity:
The Way of the Servant

In dealing with the neighbor pray
every day especially with the intention
that God give you the grace of
discretion, so that you will build up
and not tear down.[1]

[L]ove ought to be put more in deeds
than in words.[2]

St. Ignatius of Loyola (1491–1556)

Late June, and the weather was unseasonably golden for this usually overcast month. It was fruit-picking time. I kept noticing the bright air outside—such a rare gift for coast dwellers—as I steamed around doing critical, last-minute tasks. The intensive summer residency for the system-wide M.F.A. began the next day, and I was the coordinator. I was not only coordinator but an instructor for one of the classes. How had I gotten myself in this position? I didn't want to think about it. I had made the commitment four years earlier, sometime before I'd fallen in love with unscheduled summers. I couldn't get out of it now.

I was sad about the simple joys I'd miss out on this year. Setting up the residency had taken most of spring quarter; I'd been stuck on campus till late in the evenings completing everything. My garden, which should have been flourishing by now, was pretty much a wreck—choked with weeds and ravaged by gophers. I was tired, resentful, and stressed-out, and the program hadn't even begun yet. I was also dreading the class itself. Because I'd taught in the M.F.A. before, I knew exactly how grueling it was going to be, both for me and for the students: three hours a day, five days a week, for three weeks straight. Some of the students would not make it. Maybe *you* won't either, whispered an ominous little voice in my head.

Rooting through my desk for a quotation I remembered stashing somewhere—a potential intro to my first-day lecture—I glanced out the second-story window. Down below, the great red galleon of a barn sailed a sea of clover and vetch. A pair of bluebirds flashed back and forth between birdhouse and garden. Suddenly it was clear that I was overdue for a good long cry, yet I didn't even have time to do *that*. When was I ever going to arrive, to claim as my own that life of solitude and silence I'd been seeking for so long? My flirtation with holy simplicity was beginning to seem like a whimsical little experiment, doomed before it began. Its only lasting effect, it appeared, was purely negative; it had taken away my ability to cope with the world at all. I was stranded in a no man's land, unable to go back to my former life but blocked from proceeding any further down the path.

Naturally, this made me even crankier.

I slammed the desk drawer—no quotation, damn it—and started leafing through my coordinator's binder, making sure for the fifty-third time that I really did have the caterer's weekend cell-phone number. Then I heard the familiar *ah-oo-gah* of Valerie's 1965 orange VW bug. *No, not now,* I thought, not when I had so incredibly much to finish before I went to bed that night; not when my mind was cluttered with ten thousand details I hadn't even begun to sort through yet. But there she was, with the top down, pulling into our driveway; and she was not alone. Chris and their son, the four-month-old, irrepressible, inimitable Baby Jack, our honorary grandchild, were also with her. Jack knew where he was—you could tell by the joyful circles he was so vigorously air-drawing with his chubby fists. Beloved friends, one and all—and the last people on earth I wanted to see at this moment.

They were here, of course, to make jam. Jam! I'd brought this on myself when the week before in Valerie's kitchen I'd moaned about the fact that this was going to be the first year in I didn't know how many that I would not be able to preserve my usual batch of ollalieberries, apricots, and plums. Picking time was almost over, and I still hadn't been able to get to it.

Valerie, a slender, dark-haired beauty of thirty-three, gave my shoulder a little pat. "Don't worry, Paula," she said. "We'll make the jam for you. You just tell us what to do."

This had thrown me into a fast backpedal. "Oh, that's okay—really," I told her. "Thanks, but everyone'll live. Maybe they'll even appreciate it more from now on, right?"

"No, honestly," she said firmly. "We'd love to. You know how long I've been trying to get you to teach us."

So here they now were, full of innocent enthusiasm about the long day of work ahead of them. And long it was, indeed. They picked, they washed, they crushed, they boiled. They filled hot jars—innumerable hot jars—with lovely, translucent preserves. "What fun!" they kept saying. "And think of all the years we've been trying to get you to do this!" When I fell into bed late that night, flat-out exhausted, I'd had absolutely no time to stew and fret in front of the computer screen. The syllabus for the M.F.A. course lay accusingly on the desk, only half revised. Who knew what was still missing from my coordinator's binder?

In the end, of course, it all worked out. The M.F.A. students came and went, I taught the class, and that summer's jam, thanks to my hardworking apprentices, was made after all. It took a whole year, however, for me to figure out the real lesson here, a year during which our friends were transferred to another state. One morning, Valerie called from their new house in Arizona. "I can't remember," she said, "which recipe we used for the apricots."

"The apricots?"

"Yes—I made sure to buy the same kind of pectin, but for some reason I can't remember which recipe."

"Valerie," I said, astonished, "are you by any chance . . . making jam?"

She was. I rang off, glowing. Another generation of jam makers, successfully launched; the baton passed. Then I recalled my urge to hide on the day they'd come for their lesson. I remembered that silent struggle between my "duty" (the M.F.A.) and my longing to escape to the garden where I could cry in peace. Now I saw something else, something I'd completely missed at the time: teaching my friends how to make jam might have been the most important thing I could have been doing at that moment, no matter how it conflicted with my personal agenda.

Pilgrims in Need of Reengagement

The path of holy simplicity leads inexorably to a paradox. We withdraw, we reassess almost everything we've ever believed in, we go through painful kinds of renunciation. We strip down our lives, we grapple with our hidden bog creatures, we taste the sweetness of silence and tranquility. Then, when we can finally see it, just down the road a bit and around a bend, our imagined Eden evaporates. We realize to our shock that the path is looping back on itself, that we cannot get to that place we are longing for—Aelred's "homeland of our hope"—unless we are willing to help others do the same. We are, in fact, being called to reenter the world.

This can be a frightening thought, one that we resist. After all, there's still so much to work out in our own lives. We've learned to avoid the things that activate our demons—we've given up the news because it triggers our rage or anxiety; we've set aside ambitious striving because it keeps us wired and stressed-out; we've learned to avoid socializing because it reanimates our need to be the life of the party. All this takes vigilance, doesn't it? Reentering the world means opening up to all that again. Aren't we still too weak? Too liable to succumb? Can we even be trusted to help anybody else? Look what a hash of things we made in the past.

It is all true.

Yet, how do people even start unless others are willing to show them the way? The life of holy simplicity is a life lived against the natural flow of things, a deliberate departure from business as usual. Its wisdom cannot be tapped into via the normal channels. Robert Inchausti, in his book *Thomas Merton's American Prophecy*, suggests why this is so:

> In the old world . . . stupidity was simple igno-
> rance, illiteracy; one didn't know anything, but
> one could learn. In the modern world, stupidity
> has evolved into a new more virulent form: the
> nonthought of received ideas. There is just as
> much ignorance today as ever, but individuals
> hide it behind phrases acquired through superfi-
> cial contact with the mass media, opinion mak-
> ers, and the schools.[3]

Our society has been programmed to accept certain "givens." Many of the received ideas Inchausti refers to are not only superficial but also antithetical to the values embodied by a life of holy simplicity. To change, people must first rid themselves of the false and/or destructive notions they've come to see as truth. As Thomas Merton says in his *Conjectures of a Guilty Bystander:*

> The greatest need of our time is to clean out the
> enormous mass of mental and emotional rub-
> bish that clutters our minds and makes of all
> political and social life a mass illness. Without
> this housecleaning we cannot begin to see.
> Unless we see, we cannot think.[4]

How do people know what to take to the landfill if they can't recognize the problem? How can they grasp the nature of their ignorance if their ignorance has blinded them?

They can do so in one of two ways, according to the Christian tradition. The first is to hear, believe, and act upon the promise God makes in Isa. 42:16: "I will lead the blind on their journey; / by paths unknown I will guide them. / I will turn darkness into light before them / and make crooked ways straight. / These things I do for them, / and I will not forsake them." When seekers have nothing to go on but an inarticulate urge to find a better life, God assures them that he himself will help them on their way. Like Moses in the desert, they can pray for vision, for hearing, and for understanding, and he will send them their own personal column of fire.

They can also pray for a teacher, a God-energized human being who can lead them through this new and unfamiliar landscape. In the desert tradition, these would be the old men or abbas—those venerable, holy hermits, the very mouthpieces of God. It was they and their female counterparts, the ammas, who trained the next generation. First, however, the next generation had to roust them from their caves and cells by making the dangerous journey, as Cassian did, into one of the harshest zones on the planet.

In nineteenth-century Russia, the same impetus sent pilgrims out into the steppes and Siberian forests seeking *startsi* who would "give them a word." The anonymous seeker in *The Way of a Pilgrim* describes his several-thousand-mile trek in the general direction of Kiev, birthplace of Russian Orthodoxy and home of the renowned Lavra of the Caves, in hopes of finding a spiritual master who would show him what came next.

In the more formal Latin monastic tradition that developed out of the sixth-century Rule of Benedict, novice masters literally "formed" young would-be monks and nuns into new kinds of human beings—people who could let go the pleasures of the world while embracing for the rest of their lives a tightly interwoven, highly interdependent community. Elders oversaw the ongoing development of all, even those steeped for years in the discipline.

Pilgrims in Need of Leaders

In our times, people who have heard the call to a simpler, holier life but do not know how to begin can certainly turn to books, many of which were not available in the past. They can go to the library and put their hands on good translations of the Desert Fathers, the Russian *startsi,* and the Doctors of the Church. Books can take them a long way. What books cannot provide, however, is the face-to-face human interaction that has always been an integral part of this particular process.

If pilgrims are determined, however, they can go even further; they can find a flesh-and-blood abba, or at least a contemporary version of one. Nowadays, would-be spiritual directors can take courses for university credit, pass exams, and receive degrees. As "professionals," they can then counsel seekers on the spiritual path. The seekers themselves are no longer required to hike across Siberia to ferret out a hermit who might (or might not) give them "a word." This is a more convenient situation for everyone involved, certainly.

With all these resources available today, some of them quite good, why then do so many people still struggle alone with spiritual impulses they cannot identify? Why do they waste so much energy fighting the very transformation they unconsciously long to make? Why do they finally give up, defeated and even bitter about the project that never got off the ground?

This may be, in part, because of that special burden unique to our age: what Merton refers to as the "enormous mass of mental and emotional rubbish" we've absorbed, thanks to the media and our commercialized culture, that is so difficult to see beyond, especially at the beginning. Perhaps it is also because academic credentials do not a starets make—sometimes the "professional" knows *about* things he doesn't actually know in the lived-through sense. Perhaps it is because the most valuable books do not reveal their wisdom to the inexperienced.

My own struggles on the path have convinced me that what beginners need most is not a teacher or director in the official sense of these words. They need instead someone who is simply wiser, more holy, and further along the trail than they are. They need a friend who is also a servant—someone who will give them that which they must have at the moment they are crying out for it, even when they don't have a clue what it might be.

In other words, they need the company of those of us who have been at this for a while.

St. Ignatius and the Long Road to Generosity

St. Ignatius of Loyola had the same intuition five hundred years ago, at the dawn of a new era in Western culture, one that feels closer to our own than anything that preceded it. The rarely questioned modern belief that human potential is probably unlimited had its roots in his time, as did the companion notion that the quest for knowledge should never be restricted. It would take several hundred years for the clash between the medieval worldview and the one that was just beginning to emerge in Ignatius's day to be resolved—and by the time it was, Western culture would have changed almost beyond recognition.

In the meantime, however, Christians in Ignatius's era were facing enormous new challenges. The great church, which had stood battered but undivided for so many centuries, had finally begun to splinter. From Lutheranism in Germany and Calvinism in Switzerland, to a myriad of other new sects in various parts of Europe, the Reformation was everywhere calling into question the undisputed authority of the pope. More and more, believers were turning inward, to their own particular relationship with God. This was in many ways a whole new landscape, frightening but exhilarating at the same time.

I first became interested in Ignatius when Mark, a friend who (probably without knowing it) served as one of my early mentors, mentioned almost in passing that he'd gone through the Ignatian Spiritual Exercises. My ears pricked up. I'd already learned that Mark was someone to be watched, that his little spiritual experiments could act like painted arrows on a winding road. "How were they?" I asked him, trying not to sound too curious. He was a bit like a cat, Mark was; enthusiasm could spook him off.

"Good," he shrugged—which, from a man as habitually quiet as a hermit, was saying a lot. I knew that if I wanted to glean more on the subject, I'd need to read up on my own. I went to the university library and checked out two books: *The Autobiography of St. Ignatius of Loyola* (not "confessions," as in Augustine, I noted, but the more modern "autobiography") and a sampling from the massive collection of letters that this first Father General of the Society of Jesus wrote to his troops around the world.

The autobiography, I discovered, was written reluctantly, under pressure from his brothers in the Society— so reluctantly that he refused to tell it in the first person and referred to himself throughout as "he." Ignatius dictated the story in three short installments over a period of two years to a young Portuguese Jesuit named Luis Gonçalves da Camara. It does not cover Ignatius's entire life, only the portion he deemed to be of most use to his brothers—the seventeen years between his great conversion experience and his arrival in Rome with a small band of compatriots, ready to serve.

He was born Iñigo Lopez de Loyola in 1491, the youngest of thirteen children, to noble Basque parents in the old kingdom of Castile. Much like Augustine, the youthful Iñigo showed few signs of incipient sainthood; rather, he enthusiastically pursued the life of caballero, courtier, and soldier in the service of the king of Spain. In 1521, when he was about thirty, his garrison was stationed in the citadel of Pampeluna (Pamplona), which came under attack by the French. Ignatius admits in the opening lines of his autobiography that it was he himself who "gave so many reasons to the commander that he persuaded him at last to defend it," even though the Spanish were clearly doomed. This was because, as Ignatius puts it, he himself had a "great and vain desire to win fame."[5]

The bombardment began, and during the course of the battle, a five-pound cannon ball passed between his legs, shattering his right shin and tearing open his left calf. The victorious French treated him courteously; they ordered their doctors to set the fractured bones and sent him on a litter to his own home for convalescence. There, new doctors advised that the legs, which were healing badly, should be rebroken and reset—naturally, without anesthesia of any kind. Afterward, when he failed to improve and in fact was declared as good as dead, he made his final confession, and almost immediately began to recover.

Unfortunately, one leg turned out to be considerably shorter than the other, with a large protrusion below the knee. He asked if this could be sawed away, since it would be difficult to squeeze into his boot. After this third anesthesialess surgery, he voluntarily placed the leg for many days on a kind of rack, hoping to stretch it—an agonizing enterprise that was not, in the long run, very successful.

During this enforced downtime, the young soldier read. Though he preferred books of chivalry, none of these could be found. Instead, he was given a copy of the *Life of Christ* and a Spanish edition of the lives of the saints. The saints set a new and exciting standard for him, that of goodness, and in his brash, competitive way, he thought to himself, "St. Dominic did this, therefore, I have to do it. St. Francis did this, therefore, I have to do it."[6]

The chivalrous ideal of the brave knight still had the power to move him deeply, and for some time he bounced back and forth between opposing fantasies:

> Yet there was this difference. When he was
> thinking about the things of the world, he took
> much delight in them, but when he was tired
> and put them aside, he found that he was dry
> and discontented. But when he thought of
> going to Jerusalem, barefoot and eating nothing
> but herbs and undergoing all the other rigors
> that he saw the saints had endured, not only
> was he consoled when he had these thoughts,
> but even after putting them aside, he remained
> content and happy.[7]

Little by little, he tells us, "he came to recognize the difference between the spirits that agitated him, one from the demon, the one from God."[8]

This long internal struggle to discern what it was he should do next in life provided the primitive foundation for his *Spiritual Exercises*. Though, as he fully admits, he was still too "blind" to "dwell on any interior thing, nor did he know what humility was or charity or patience or discretion to regulate and measure these virtues," he sincerely desired to "please and placate God."[9] This, apparently, was enough to get him through his lengthy, bumbling, and ultimately unsuccessful attempt to live a simple life in the holy city of Jerusalem, where he thought he could "help souls" by teaching other people to do the same.

"God," he says, "treated him at this time just as a schoolmaster treats a child whom he is teaching. Whether this was on account of his coarseness or his dense intelligence or because he had no one to teach him . . . he clearly believed and has always believed that God treated him this way."[10] He offers as evidence of God's "schoolmasterly" methods a series of visions over a period of several years—one of the Trinity, one of the creation of the world, one of the humanity of Christ. The most important insight, however, and one that most scholars see as a pivotal moment in his life, took place on the bank of a river near Manresa:

> While he was seated there, the eyes of his
> understanding began to be opened; though he
> did not see any vision, he understood and knew
> many things, both spiritual things and matters
> of faith and learning, and this was with so great
> an enlightenment that everything seemed new
> to him.[11]

Raised a Lutheran, I found this passage positively fascinating. Here was a devout Catholic, a man who would found a powerful new company of "spiritual soldiers" who took their orders directly from the pope. Here was a major figure of the Counter-Reformation, a man who would lead the effort to reclaim spiritual territory lost in Germany, Switzerland, and France, yet I might have been reading the ecstatic words of George Fox, the Quaker, or Jonathan Edwards, the Puritan. However the Reformers might have interpreted his claim, Ignatius is describing a very *personal* and unmediated revelation, God speaking directly to an ordinary man.

At a time when Protestantism loomed so threateningly, this sort of spiritual individualism was bound to get him in trouble, and it did. Between 1526 and 1528, during his first years of formal study, he was investigated no less than four times by the Inquisition, twice serving lengthy jail time before being cleared. The issue was invariably the same: he was still a relatively uneducated man—initially, he was so far behind that he had to study Latin with young boys—and he had taken no formal religious vows, yet he was presuming to teach the people about God. How did he know that he was not inadvertently spreading heresy?

Asked by one investigator to describe what he and his small group of comrades preached, he replied that they did not preach at all. Instead, he said, "we do speak famil-iarly with some people about the things of God." Pressed further, he said, "We speak . . . sometimes about one virtue, sometimes about another, praising it; sometimes about one vice, sometimes about another, condemning it." This, he was told, was a dangerous practice, for "no one can speak about these except in two ways: either through education or through the Holy Spirit."[12] The implication being, of course, that he had no credibility from either source.

The judges of Salamanca ordered him to stop defining the difference between venial and moral sin until he had studied for four more years. He complied but continued to feel the powerful urge to "help souls" become holy and simple, which led to his decision to go to Paris for university studies. Arriving penniless and on foot, he found once again that he was so deficient in the fundamentals that he had to begin at the beginning. In spite of all the setbacks, including chronic stomach problems, he managed to complete his bachelor's and master's degrees, and part of a doctoral program, before being advised by doctors to return to the air of his native Spain if he wanted to be healthy again.

Meanwhile, he continued to give out his exercises to fellow students, some of whom had profound conversion experiences after going through them. On August 15, 1534, six of these student-companions and Ignatius took a vow to make a pilgrimage together to Jerusalem—or if this proved impossible because of the wars raging everywhere, to go to Rome and offer their services to the pope. In primitive and as-yet unofficial form, the Jesuits were born.

Nearly five hundred years later, I found out, thanks to Mark, that people are still making retreats based on the Spiritual Exercises of St. Ignatius. In fact, there have been 450 translations of them in the past 480 years. Millions have had their lives profoundly shaped by the spiritual acuity of this Basque soldier with a limp who had to struggle so hard to learn Latin.[13] The most common version of the silent Ignatian retreat lasts eight days, but there is also a thirty-day version for those willing to completely immerse themselves in the mysterious realm of spiritual psychodynamics. Traditionally, a spiritual director oversees each retreatant during the process.

A recent book by poet, professor, and biographer Paul Mariani describes the life-changing experience of a thirty-day retreat at the Gonzaga Eastern Point Retreat House east of Gloucester, Massachusetts. As Ignatius once did, Mariani painstakingly tracks his own internal responses to the passages he has been assigned:

> There's very little of the personal in any of this
> at first. Even the Scripture passages seem iso-
> lated and discrete, though sooner or later they
> begin forming patterns for reflection. Usually
> one of them turns out to speak to something
> deep within you as you come back to it in
> prayer. Scripture reading at this level is unusu-
> ally dynamic, resonating more and more as you
> allow it to work on you.[14]

Ultimately, retreatants who stay the course find themselves turned inside out—scoured clean, then filled with "what is necessary for our spiritual health." As Mariani says in his afterword, "[T]he thirty-day retreat . . . was not the end but only the beginning of a healing, which has turned out to have ongoing implications, both in its desolations as well as in its deeper consolations."[15]

Ignatius still speaks to the modern mind, primarily because he lived in a world caught in the tide wash between the ancient and the new. Though he never left the traditional Christian cosmos, he must have foreseen a world in which human beings would become far more dependent on their own internal resources than they'd ever had to be in the past; a confusing world; a world in which self-exploration, self-control, and personal commitment would be crucial if one were not to be irrevocably lost; a world in which (no matter how he himself strove to uphold the authority of the undivided Church) people would be forced, to a large degree, to seek and find on their own.

To this end, Ignatius studied himself like a scientist, recording his most minute reactions to the spiritual winds that swept him. Then he passed on what he had learned to anyone who asked, anyone who needed food for the journey.

Gifts of Good Teachers

When I thought about it, I realized how blessed I'd been. Great teachers have always appeared when I most needed them, people who saw what was really going on with me while I myself was still awash in the shallows. In fourth grade, for example, I was a broody little girl, beset by younger siblings as by devils, with a heart that cried out for silence, beauty, and peace. Everything at home seemed too much—too many people, too much noise, too much *stuff* everywhere. I couldn't think straight. Instead, I lay in bed making up long conversations between people who didn't exist. This imaginary world was both richer and more satisfying than the one in which I actually lived.

My teacher that year was Mrs. Gold. She must have been all of twenty-eight at the time, though she seemed the most sophisticated, elegant creature who'd ever lived. Somehow, she figured out what was going on with me. Somehow, she knew I was an incipient writer who needed to be encouraged. One day, she asked me directly if I ever "worked on anything" after school. I didn't get it. "Stories," she said. "Do you ever write stories or poems at home, things that aren't homework?" Shyly (I was so in love with the elegance of Mrs. Gold), I nodded. "Would you show some of them to me?" she asked.

Thus began our private, weekly creative-writing session on Thursday afternoons when the other kids had gone home. I brought my poems and stories; she critiqued them—critiqued as though I were a small adult, halfway through a prestigious M.F.A. program. There was no condescension in Mrs. Gold, nothing remotely patronizing. She truly cared that I wrote; she wanted me to continue; she thought that I was "meant to be a writer."

I still remember the first poem I brought to her, a poem that, seen from the perspective of forty years, clearly reveals her discreet improvements here and there: "I have a little puppy / He's very round and fat / He's growing bigger, day by day / I'm very sure of that . . . ," and on and on and *on* (Mrs. Gold was nothing if not patient). Without her, however, I don't know when (or if) I would have learned that fantasies aren't enough and that art requires time, care, great discipline, and most of all, an astute critic. She helped me see that my need for peace and order and beauty was real and that artists required such an atmosphere to be able to create. Most of all, she showed me that I should take my gift, no matter how embryonic a stage it was in, completely seriously.

By the time I was thirty-six, my noisy, sibling-filled childhood had started to look calm in comparison to the life I was leading. Mike and I were in the early stages of our marriage and doing our ineffectual best to deal with a disintegrating custody situation. It seemed that our only recourse, if we wanted simply to maintain the existing visitation arrangement, was to go back to court on a regular basis. This was having a profoundly detrimental effect on my stepdaughters' desire to be with us at all, which was completely understandable.

Between the stress of dealing with lawyers, judges, and court-appointed psychologists, and the anxiety I felt over the tremendous outflow of money all this required, I was a nervous wreck; not just a nervous wreck, but an angry one. This is not what I had planned on; this was not how I wanted to be living my life. It was in this frame of mind that I went back to school to finally complete my B.A. degree. I wound up in an ethics class that eventually pointed me in a whole new direction.

The professor was a fine classroom teacher. I learned that ethics, which I'd assumed would be a crashing bore, had the power to keep me riveted. A good class, however, was not enough to hold my attention at this point in my life—I was too upset, too distracted by the ongoing familial stress. The course made such an impression on me because of the teacher himself, who was willing to go beyond the boundaries of the class text, who was able to see me as Mrs. Gold once had and to open my mind to another way of looking at things.

What the professor did was allow me to tag along to his office after his lecture each day. On this walk, which took us through the twists and turns of the campus, he listened patiently while I attacked whatever philosopher he'd been discussing that afternoon. He was quite patient, considering I had neither critical-thinking skills nor a shred of training in a subject he'd been teaching for years. At the end of my daily diatribe, which usually ended just about the time we reached his office door, he'd sigh, smile, shake his head, and then drop a question that stopped me cold—a question that revealed, without his having to say another word, what utter confusion abided in me.

Years later when both he and his wife had become dear friends of mine, he told me that I'd been one of the angriest women he'd ever met. This meant that it was not my untapped potential in philosophy that he first spotted (there was none), but, instead, the simmering fury that was keeping me from any sort of growth. He could recognize this anger because he'd had a few dealings with his own over the years.

If he'd kept this personal information private, however, I might have remained trapped for a long time to come. Instead, when I'd finally become worn out with my diatribes and become open to a discussion of the *real* problem, he told me stories, his own stories. Because they sounded so hauntingly familiar to me—anger has a peculiar tone to it—I listened intently to the rest of what he had to say. I gained courage along the way to begin the painful process of transformation.

Only later did I realize how generous he'd been. He was a respected and popular professor who could have just lectured me about morality from a book; instead, he took the time to listen to my questions and shared with me stories from his own storehouse of dark memories. He was a true friend to me, someone astute enough to understand the real source of my anger (I'd heard the call to a simpler, holier life yet couldn't seem to fight my way to the starting place) and compassionate enough to give me the time I needed to figure this out for myself. "Without cost you have received," says Jesus, the greatest of teachers; "without cost you are to give" (Matt. 10:8).

With those tumultuous years of anger long over, I now had the lesson of Valerie and the jam to mull over, particularly my ungenerous response. Something in the way Mike and I lived—and who knew what this was?—had filled this young woman full of questions. Because I was so mentally focused on the M.F.A. syllabus lying on my desk that day, I'd completely missed her real purpose in coming, which was probably not jam at all. As I worried about teaching, I'd missed out on a chance to teach.

How many other times had I disappointed would-be students this way, seekers like I'd once been who didn't yet know what it was they were seeking? I found a clue in the *Spiritual Exercises:*

> The captain and the leader of an army on cam-
> paign sets up his camp, studies the strength and
> structure of a fortress, and then attacks at its
> weakest point. In the same way, the enemy of
> human nature prowls around and from every
> side probes all our theological, cardinal, and
> moral virtues. Then at the point where he finds
> us weakest and most in need in regard to our
> eternal salvation, there he attacks and tries to
> take us.[16]

Though written in the language of the 1500s, it made
sense to me, particularly the part about our virtues mask-
ing our weakest spots. The fact was, up until now, I'd
always prided myself on my teaching ability. In a classroom situation, I was diligent and thorough, well prepared and organized, interesting (I thought modestly),
even *intelligent*. What more could a student ask for? Yet,
herein lay the problem.

For pride and true generosity make incompatible bed-
fellows. It suddenly appeared that my teaching, both in
and out of the classroom, sprang from more complicated
motives than I'd ever admitted to myself: the unconscious
expectation of gratitude; the smug sense that I knew more
than the average human being; the secret desire to be wise
and important—to leave my mark on other people's lives.

Nothing brought me to a boil faster than someone who
didn't seem to "get" how much effort and attention I had
lavished on him. Someone who took up my valuable time

with his questions, who nagged me into reading two chapters of his not-very-good manuscript, and then was miffed when I suggested his starting premise was probably off. The ungrateful wretch! I never stopped to think that maybe the "teaching" he'd been after was something he couldn't even articulate. That the manuscript was an excuse—and that I'd missed the point.

What about the young creative-writing student who dared to believe he knew more than I did, who'd been writing alternative lyrics to Bob Dylan tunes since he was fourteen, and who dismissed me on day one as a hopeless anachronism? Here was a student who actually yawned when I was lecturing. These brash young artists showed up nearly every quarter, and how had I treated them? With the most withering scorn; I had used my superior position and the wit I'd never completely relinquished, and I'd taken those kids apart in front of the class. This, of course, fixed *their* wagons . . . and made the rest of the group snap to besides.

What kind of student evaluations had the power to leave me preening my feathers? The kind that declared, "She changed my life," that extolled my supposed virtues (so prepared, so open, so knowledgeable), and that vowed to live up to the example. I thrived on the evaluations that validated my need to be a very big cheese in other people's lives.

This was generosity? I hung my head, abashed; nowhere near generosity, it looked like. I'd mistaken a good performance, energized by self-centered expectations of reward, for genuine love. No wonder I'd been so devastated by my department's failure to step up and applaud. At the deepest level, my teaching was hopelessly enmeshed in ego.

In a recent book called *Benedict's Dharma: Buddhists Reflect on the Rule of Saint Benedict,* I found a passage by Joseph Goldstein that describes real teaching, that which is not performance art but servanthood: "We understand that our spiritual practice is done not for ourselves alone but for the awakening and liberation of all." [17] Our personal striving—our efforts to be virtuous, to gain knowledge and wisdom, to move closer to God—should not and cannot be private enterprises. We are meant to be "one" (John 17:22), as Jesus prays to his Father—"that the love with which you loved me may be in them and I in them" (John 17:26). In the Buddhist tradition, this notion of walking our own spiritual path for the sake of others is called *Bodhichitta.* For Ignatius, it is our way to "help souls" to a simpler and more holy life.

Seen in this light, the teacher is simply a vehicle; he neither owns his knowledge, nor is it his business to judge who is worthy to receive it. The individual person is far too mysterious and complex to be read—and dismissed—so easily. Besides, Christ has assured us that God will take care of those judgments. The generous teacher simply remains open and alert so as not to miss (as I no doubt did with Valerie) the real questions being asked. Ego—the demand for gratitude, respect, or adulation—kills our ability to see (or teach) much at all.

In the kind of society that Inchausti describes in his book on Merton, a society based on ignorant self-interest, generous mentors are absolutely crucial. Yet as Peter

Faber, one of Ignatius's companions, once pointed out in a letter meant to clarify the Jesuit position on missionary work, good teachers must first of all be good people.

> Be you vigilant therefore, and with as much
> effort occupy yourself now in teaching the
> Christian people by the example of living as
> heretofore you exerted in defense of the faith
> and the church's teaching. For how do we
> believe the good God will preserve the truth of
> holy faith in us, if we flee from virtue itself? It
> must be feared that the principal cause of errors
> of doctrine comes from errors of life, which
> unless they be corrected, the doctrinal errors
> will not be cleared from the way.[18]

Spoken at a time of such enormous upheaval in the Church, a time when Protestants clashed with Catholics, and Catholics imprisoned, tortured, and burned their own because of suspected heresy, these were bold words indeed. However, the message was completely consistent with Ignatius's generosity, his lifelong efforts—often systematically impeded—to give everyone, regardless of rank or education, the tools he or she needed to make the journey to God.

In one of the most important passages in the *Exercises,* the "Contemplation to Attain Love," Ignatius suggests an imaginative interlude meant to lead toward greater generosity. Standing before God and his saints, the retreatant is to ask for an "interior knowledge of all the great good I have received, that, stirred to profound gratitude, I might be able to love and serve the Divine Majesty in all things." [19]

For Ignatius, then, the root of what the Buddhists call "kingly giving," or the highest level of generosity, is an overflowing thankfulness. Like the psalmist, we ask, "How can I repay the LORD / for all the good done for me?"(Ps. 116:12) How, indeed, do we even begin to adequately thank this God of ours, "whose love endures forever" (Ps. 118:1)?

Christ the exemplar shows us how. He shows us in the humblest yet most profound way he possibly could, by taking a towel and tying it around his waist, getting down on his knees, and washing his disciples' feet. When he is finished, he says to his still-uncomprehending students,

> Do you realize what I have done for you? You
> call me "teacher" and "master," and rightly so, for
> indeed I am. If I, therefore, the master and
> teacher, have washed your feet, you ought to
> wash one another's feet. I have given you a model
> to follow, so that as I have done for you, you
> should also do. . . . If you understand this,
> blessed are you if you do it. (John 13:12–15, 17)

Recently, I came to a turning point in regard to my own dilemma about teaching. I came to see that, much as I loved the classroom, it was time to give up my lecturer position at the university. Despite my fond illusions, I was not, after all, strong enough to resist the temptations of the academic world. I saw that I would never be able to disentangle ego and teaching as long as the system itself required me to self-promote on such a regular basis. For a person like me, the continual focus on evaluations and merit increases and awards and promotions and newsletters filled with faculty accomplishments was death to the kind of teaching Christ calls us to do. I decided that I'd better quit while there was still time to learn a different way to share.

Shortly after my early retirement, I happened to be at the hermitage for Sunday Mass. Afterward, at lunch in the refectory, I spotted Br. Emmanuel, driver of bulldozers and healer of generators. Br. Emmanuel is close to, if not past, seventy by now and has had his aches and pains for years, though they never seem to keep him from his work. Thus, I was shocked to see how thin and pale he'd suddenly become. I slipped by the table where he was sitting to ask him if he was all right. "Sure," he said, this man of few words. "Knee replacement. It hurts for a while, and you don't eat much."

"That's good," I said. "I was worried."

As I started to pass on by, he said. "Heard you quit teaching."

This was surprising—who'd told him?—and then embarrassment descended. Maybe a hard worker like him disapproved of people giving up their careers before they had to. "I did," I said. "It still feels strange to be this young and not have a 'real' job, but I'm getting used to it."

He bobbed his head and took a sip of water, then gave me a penetrating look that seemed to go on for longer than it probably really did. "I get it," he said. "You quit so you can heal the sick, feed the hungry, and raise the dead, right?"

"What?" I started to laugh, then saw he was serious. That it *was* serious. Whatever I did in this new, officially unemployed life of mine, it had better be done as a servant, or I had missed the whole point.

"God bless you," he said then, and went back to picking at his food.

CHAPTER 10

Tranquility:
The Way of the
Contemplative

Stillness within one individual can
affect society beyond measure.[1]

Bede Griffiths (1906–1993)

Within a single year, I lost two people I loved—my oldest friend, Andrew, first, by his own hand, and then my father, who died in a warm patch of afternoon sun while drinking a cup of tea. This was before I'd found my way back to God, and both deaths made me angry and despairing. What was the point of loving, if people just . . . disappeared like that? Neither was I comforted by their funeral services—what did it matter, really, what was said?— nor by the rituals of ash scattering (Andrew) or burial (Dad). For a long time, the double loss represented a single disaster for me, their deaths indistinguishable one from another.

This black-hole time went on for nearly a year. Then one day, I realized that whenever I dreamt of Andrew, the bright-haired childhood comrade who'd committed suicide on the eve of his fortieth birthday, I woke up trembling and agitated. Some combination of rage and sorrow was brought on by his nightmarish visitations; I wished he'd stay away if he were just going to stir things up like that.

Whenever I dreamt of my father, in contrast, I awoke serene, as though I'd just been blessed. It was as though I'd had a chance to join him in those sunlit last moments, those moments of tea and laughter with my mother, right before his heart gave out. I'd open my eyes, wistful but smiling, feeling grateful to have had the glimpse, no matter how poignant. Slowly, I began to see that when we die, we leave behind us something much like music, faint but unmistakable, which lingers on in the air for many years to come. We continue to affect the living, whether for good or for ill. We bequeath our final state of soul to the people who love us most.

Andrew had been my first real friend, a brilliant little boy (he told me once, and I believed him, that his I.Q. had tested out at 165) who had to get the highest grades in class or the world came to an end. He grew into a handsome teenager, tall and graceful, who could not begin to compete in sports and refused to even try. Eventually, he became a young gay man in Hollywood, a novice screenwriter determined to validate his existence by becoming rich and famous. If I'd first met him as an adult, I doubt we'd have even bothered to carry on a conversation—we did not have much in common by then— but our relationship went far deeper than that, though I still can't put into words what this meant, exactly.

Perhaps the bond was something like "absolute loyalty." That would explain why I continued to listen for all those years to his increasingly irrational explosions over incompetent service people, malicious fellow employees, stupid socialites, money-mad studio executives, and ego-maniacal movie stars. The world was a dark and unjust place according to my chronically depressed friend, and there was no sanctuary this side of death. Rages, remorseful tears, terrors in the night, twisted love affairs: he lived alone in an open boat on a storm-tossed sea; his final act of self-destruction must have seemed like a strictly logical one to him, given the chaos of his life.

In contrast, my father was like an island of peace. I do not remember him ever raising his voice to me, a voice that was one of his distinguishing features: gentle, self-deprecating, gracious. At his retirement dinner—he was sixty-seven and would be dead within two years—his clients extolled his virtues, calling him a "true gentleman, one of the last." The image that came to me most often after he was gone was of dogs—dogs of all breeds and sizes and at every level of maturity, right down to the most surly and skittish.

I can see him, frail and tentative with congestive heart failure, in his green sweater and tweed cap, out for his morning stroll. He stops in front of the chain-link fence of an auto yard, then squats and clicks his fingers for the guard dogs, two snarling Dobermans who race toward him in a mindless, barking fury. My father holds his palms flat against the fence, and the dogs whuff closer, stiff-legged, picking up his scent. Then—amazingly—they let him put two fingers through the wire to scratch behind their ears.

Soon, in fact, they have given up their frenzy entirely and are thrusting their shark mouths against the backs of his wrists. I can see them kissing him.

In a certain way, my father was a naturally tranquil man: quiet, gentle, and slow to anger. The word *tranquil* comes from the Latin word *tranquillus,* which means "quiet," and somehow—when it came to wrath, for example—he did seem to live in a quiet, peaceful world beyond normal human parameters. Andrew, on the other hand, had such a narrowly defined comfort zone that he was rarely able to function without intense agitation. My father's friendship with the world transcended most moral categories (he had a remarkable blindness in regard to the "bad" in other people), while Andrew seemed constantly conflicted, even when he should have been happiest.

Ultimately, my father's tranquility allowed him to live a simple, open, and integrated life despite all the responsibilities of raising five children. Andrew, though single till he died, lived in convoluted secrecy, compartmentalizing every relationship to such an extent that most of his closest friends did not meet until the night before his funeral; only then did we discover that each of us had known a different man.

Once I'd thought hard about the way they lived, I understood why Andrew sent me nightmares and my father sent nocturnal blessings. I had more difficulty discerning which one *I* inhabited: my father's peaceful world or Andrew's hell. Drawn as I was to my father's serenity, it was that other, darker territory that felt more like my natural home—this, sadly, after years of trying to become a calmer, simpler, and more centered human being.

What was I to do? One clue, I thought, might lie in a practice I'd always managed to avoid—contemplative prayer, or meditation. Certainly, meditators often claimed that the discipline had made them more peaceable (the Buddha's serenity being the most famous case in point). Christianity had its accomplished meditators, too, all of whom seemed to believe that contemplative practice reduced anger and increased one's capacity for love: the Desert Fathers, who "guarded the heart" by assiduously watching their thoughts; the hesychasts, or "silent ones" of the Orthodox tradition; the contemporary practitioners of centering prayer. I'd read about these people for years, always fascinated by the subject of meditation, but never quite finding time to try it myself.

By way of excuse, I told myself that *serious* meditators had to be genuine spiritual athletes, the elite corps of the religious world, not your average Catholic or Lutheran or Presbyterian or Baptist. Not me, either, I was pretty well convinced. When I did think about meditation, I automatically visualized a zendo with its rows of practitioners on round zafus, sternly facing a blank wall, hour after unblinking hour. It was a strangely beautiful scene—but I'd never gone beyond an admiring appreciation of the picture. Quite frankly, they intimidated me.

My pathetic efforts at the hermitage only reinforced this spiritual inferiority complex. Every time I made a retreat there, I dutifully joined the monks and other guests for their silent half hour in the rotunda after vespers. However, I could never figure out exactly what I was supposed to be doing with this time. I'd get myself arranged on the little rug they provided, take some big breaths and blow them out so as to give the impression that I knew what was what, then spend the next thirty minutes willing myself not to swallow every four seconds; or worrying that my stomach was going to begin caterwauling for dinner; or fidgeting, list making, fantasizing, and yawning till my jaws cracked.

When I surreptitiously peered around the rotunda to see if anyone else were having these problems, I invariably had it confirmed that I was the only meditative loser in the group. Even Fr. Bernard at seventy-four could outlast me; hood drawn over his white hair, he'd rustle himself into a kneeling position and hold that during the whole, interminable session.

To try to drag this unsatisfying procedure into my everyday life seemed beyond my capabilities. Besides, if I couldn't get anything out of it in the company of my favorite people, then how was I going to find nirvana all by myself? Still, the arrows kept pointing toward meditation as a deeper and more profound discipline than any I'd tried before. It seemed to be the next, necessary step on the path to a less complicated, more tranquil life.

A cluttered and overburdened mental space can be one of the biggest—perhaps, when it comes down to it, *the* biggest—obstacles to simple living. Psychiatrist and brain researcher Roger Walsh describes his own first attempts to meditate, and what they revealed to him about our illusory sense of control over our own mental processes:

> I was forced to recognize that what I had formerly believed to be my rational mind . . . actually comprised a frantic torrent of forceful,

demanding, loud, and often unrelated thoughts
and fantasies which filled an unbelievable proportion of consciousness even during purposeful
behavior. The incredible proportion of consciousness which this fantasy world occupied,
my powerlessness to remove it for more than a
few seconds, and my former state of mindless-
ness or ignorance of its existence, staggered me.[2]

I thought that perhaps Walsh was really talking about
our inability to see straight because our minds are so occupied with egoistic blather. I thought of Jesus' mysterious
reference to the "eye," or the organ of perception, and what
happens to us when this is in some way clouded by the
tumultuous fantasies—whether angry, anxious, or otherwise—that Walsh refers to: "The lamp of the body is the
eye. . . . if your eye is bad, your whole body will be in darkness. And if the light in you is darkness, how great will the
darkness be" (Matt. 6:22–23).

St. Augustine believed that one of our most important
tasks as human beings is to clean that lamp so that our
perceptions are as clear as they can possibly be this side
of heaven. In their book *Purity of Heart in Early Ascetic
and Monastic Literature,* Harriet A. Luckman and Linda
Kulzer talk about what he meant. For Augustine, they
say, love of one's neighbor "purifies the mind to an
incredible degree." They quote his own words on the
subject: "When he [the seeker of tranquility] arrives at
the love of his enemy he ascends to the sixth step where
he cleanses the eye through which God may be seen in so

far as he can be seen by those who die to the world as much as they are able." [3]

Augustine, however, believed that to truly see clearly we must go quite a bit further: We must actually embrace a paradox, then try to live in the company of two antithetical notions. According to Luckman and Kulzer, he tells us that to see well, we must stop judging our neighbor and ourselves "in the light of the truth." How can we know anything if we stop judging? Isn't it our ability to discriminate that allows us to become wise? Augustine goes on to say, "On this step he so cleanses the eye of his heart that he neither prefers his neighbor to the Truth nor compares him with it." "This state," Luckman and Kulzer add, "brings about peace and tranquility." [4]

I had to admit that Augustine's theory, however difficult to grasp, did sound familiar. As Jesus so famously enjoined, "Stop judging, that you may not be judged. For as you judge, so will you be judged, and the measure with which you measure will be measured out to you" (Matt. 7:1–2). This is not merely a restatement of the Golden Rule; apparently, our vision is seriously distorted by our habit of passing judgment. We tend to exaggerate the bad in other people and minimize it in ourselves, a practice of which Jesus seems to have been fully aware: "You hypocrite, remove the wooden beam from your eye first; then you will see clearly to remove the splinter from your brother's eye" (Matt. 7:5).

Though I could not fathom how one stopped judging—we evaluate everything and everybody a hundred times a day, after all—there seemed to be a rock-bottom truth buried here somewhere. Whether my father's serenity had been linked in some way to nonjudgmentalism, I didn't know. I only knew that he rarely judged out loud and that this seemed to have something to do with the peaceful effect he had on other people. Jesus' injunction made more sense in the case of Andrew, who never seemed to take a break from his irascible weighing and measuring. Caught in his buzzing cloud of negative judgments, he suffered so much in the company of other humans that his life finally became unbearable.

These were small clues at best, and I could not pretend that I understood exactly what Christ meant. Of more urgent interest to me was whether, in the final analysis, it was really possible to become more like my father when I'd been born more like my beloved but aggravating friend, Andrew. So far, meditation seemed to be the only discipline that focused specifically on the development of a tranquil nature. However, I could not seem to settle into it, to find my path into the forest. For years, I left it aside as something I would get to "when the time was right."

Bede Griffiths and the Path of Christian Meditation

Then, I had the opportunity to take that round-the-world trip, a trip that included India. Shortly before I left, my friend Tom suggested I read something by Bede Griffiths, an English monk, eventually Camaldolese, who lived for twenty-five years in South India in a Christian ashram called Shantivanam. "I think you'll like him," he said. "You probably ought to start with his autobiography—it's called *The Golden String.*"

The name sounded familiar, and I realized that I'd seen it before in a small collection of aphorisms about the spiritual life. In fact, Bede Griffiths had a lot to say about meditation, some of which I'd copied down and promptly buried in a drawer: "Meditation consists in learning to focus and to control the mind. When the mind is stilled, then the light of the intellect begins to shine. The mind is ordinarily scattered and dissipated, but gather the mind into one and then the pure light shines in the mirror which is oneself."[5] I decided that I should take a second look.

The next time I was in the hermitage bookstore, I hunted down *The Golden String,* discovering to my surprise that Griffiths's many books took up a couple of shelves of their own. How had I managed to miss them for so long? Perhaps it was the New Agey photograph on the cover of his *A New Vision of Reality: Western Science, Eastern Mysticism, and Christian Faith.* There he sat in his tangerine-colored robe, a white-bearded ascetic who looked more like a Hindu sannyasi than a Desert Father. Perhaps it was the controversial titles he seemed to prefer—*Christ in India,* for example, or *The Cosmic Revelation.* Now that I'd caught a glimpse, however, I was hooked. I bought three books and settled down for a long read.

Alan Richard Griffiths, who eventually became Fr. Bede, was born in 1906 at Walton-on-Thames in Britain. He was the youngest of the four children of Walter and Lilian Griffiths. Before he was old enough to start school, his kindly father was hoodwinked out of his job and money by an unscrupulous business partner. From then on the impoverished family struggled to make ends meet on his mother's tiny private income. After his father's setback, they moved to a small village called New Milton, which was close to both the New Forest and the ocean. Here, the child Alan enjoyed a "wild, open-air life" in spite of the hardships suffered by his parents.[6] Because they could not afford a servant, he also learned to cook and clean house, skills not normally mastered by young men of his class and era. Later, these skills would allow him to make some serious experiments in simple living.

He was raised in the normal English way—as a faithful Anglican—and his mother, in particular, was extremely devout. Yet his religious life, like that of most people of his day, was limited to Sunday church attendance and a strict adherence to conventional moral standards. As in the preceding Victorian era, people did not discuss, even in the privacy of their own homes, matters that might lead to controversy. Politics, sex, and religion topped the list of banned topics, and as he grew older, this stricture felt increasingly stifling to the intellectually curious young Alan.

At thirteen, he entered Christ's Hospital, a charity school for boys from poor families. There, his teachers were strict disciplinarians who regularly caned their students for the smallest infractions, including missing answers in class. At least once a year, some unlucky boy was actually flogged by an ex-military officer before the assembled student body. In addition, rationing was still in effect in spite of the recent armistice that had ended

World War I, and the boys slept on extremely thin mattresses and were "permanently so cold that they all got chilblains."[7] Griffiths later said about this period of his life, "You lived in fear the whole time."[8]

Fortunately, the reign of terror ended before Alan began his second year, when the authoritarian schoolmaster was replaced by W. H. Fyfe, the first administrator in the history of Christ's Hospital who was not also an ordained clergyman. A classical scholar and a Christian humanist, he quickly spotted the talented young Alan and began a friendship that lasted until Fyfe's death in 1965. Later, Bede claimed that it was Fyfe who taught him to "think for himself and encouraged his interest in literature and art."[9] The progressive new schoolmaster immediately enlarged the library so that the boys had access to all the classics, and reading soon became Alan's primary passion.

In this way he was introduced to the great Russian novelists Dostoyevsky and Tolstoy and was in fact so influenced by Tolstoy's discussion of the Beatitudes that he and his friends declared themselves pacifists and refused to join the school army corps. He was also introduced to the British Romantics—including Wordsworth, Shelley, and Keats—who a hundred years before had shocked British society with what many saw as their "pagan" nature worship. Inspired by Wordsworth's majestic odes ("And I have felt / a presence that disturbs me with the joy / of elevated thoughts; a sense sublime / of something far more deeply interfused"),[10] young Alan had his first real spiritual experience while walking near the school playing fields one lovely summer evening:

> A lark rose suddenly from the ground beside the
> tree where I was standing and poured out its
> song above my head, and then sank still singing
> to rest. Everything then grew still as the sunset
> faded and the veil of dusk began to cover the
> earth. I remember now the feeling of awe which
> came over me. I felt inclined to kneel on the
> ground, as though I had been standing in the
> presence of an angel.[11]

By this time, conventional Christianity had lost all appeal for him, but this experience was different from ordinary religion; this was a sudden, electric, and intensely personal encounter with something that transcended the individual self. "I hardly dared to look on the face of the sky," he said later, "because it seemed as though it was but a veil before the face of God."[12] The experience was a pivotal one for him, and he spent the next few years determining how to escape what he deemed to be a soul-destroying, industrialized society.

Meanwhile, he was accepted at Oxford, where he found that his tutor was the young and still atheist C. S. Lewis. The two became fast friends, eventually rediscovering together many of the classics of Christianity that were no longer in fashion. Though irreconcilable theological differences would finally divide them years later, Bede never stopped being grateful for the immense influence Lewis had on his spiritual development.

Meanwhile, he and his best friends at Oxford, Hugh Waterman and Martyn Skinner, spent increasing amounts of time away from town, trying their best to recapture a lost connection with nature and with a simple, rustic life. Once they camped for many days on the west coast of Ireland, "on a cliff in West Kerry, a few yards from the Atlantic with nothing between ourselves and America."[13] Other times, looking for an antidote to the smoky, industrialized clamor that had overtaken much of England, they sought out Cotswold villages or studied the stained glass in the great medieval cathedrals of York. "Here," he says in his autobiography, "we seemed to be in the presence of an unfallen world, where men were possessed by a sense of beauty which had been suddenly and calamitously lost."[14]

Eventually, the three of them decided to put their convictions about the evils of modernism to the test. In April 1930, they bought a cottage of Cotswold stone—a four-roomed cottage with no running water, drainage, or lighting—in the small village of Eastington, population twenty. "It was a plain little village," he says, "at the bottom of a valley with a small stream running through it, but it had the simple beauty of everything which is in harmony with nature."[15] Here, in hopes of becoming self-sufficient, they taught themselves to milk cows and grow vegetables.

Their cottage was kept as "bare and simple" as they could make it. They used no curtains or coverlets or cushions, and very little furniture. Though they started out with an oil lamp, they soon realized that they could pay a local blacksmith to make them an iron candelabrum. Even better, they discovered a source for tallow dips, which they burned as candles:

> We found, moreover, that the four candles gave
> a perfect light for reading; and we learned from
> this one of the great lessons of our life. Our
> purpose in using the tallow dips had been sim-
> ply to do without the products of industrialism,
> but we found that the light of these candles
> reflected on the bare white walls and against the
> dark oak rafters, created an atmosphere of inde-
> scribable beauty. Thus we were able to prove in
> our own lives that when the simple, natural
> means are used for any natural end, however
> humble, they will inevitably produce an effect
> of beauty.[16]

Perhaps the most important rule they adopted was that only books from the sixteenth or seventeenth century or earlier were allowed inside the cottage—and these were primarily in their original languages. In this way, they were able to immerse themselves in a long-vanished, preindustrialized world—a world, they were increasingly forced to admit, whose beauty and coherence were directly attributable to the reign (long since ended) of Christianity.

Sometime before the experiment was abandoned less than a year later, Alan began reading the Gospels. He was startled at how real they seemed. The human Christ, he found, "had all the roughness and unexpectedness which one finds in a character from life as opposed to the smoothness and conventionality of legend and the ideal portrait. But . . . there was another element, that of the supernatural, which was no less evident than the first."[17]

In addition, and to his surprise, the first three Gospels seemed to complement one another perfectly even though they described the same people and events from somewhat different perspectives.

The book of John, however, was another story and did not so easily fit into the picture. The poetic style and haunting tone, the mystical theme, the description of events not recorded elsewhere: all of this at first gave him pause. Finally, however, he decided to judge this Gospel in what we would call a holistic way, paying closer attention to the overall impression it made on him than on whether or not it matched up, fact for fact, with the first three books of the New Testament:

> Modern criticism had been engaged in tearing
> the Gospels to pieces to discover the truth
> behind them, but might it not be that their
> true meaning could only be seen as a living
> whole . . . ? In judging a work of art, it was by
> one's sense of the whole, of an integral organic
> structure, that one was able to see the signifi-
> cance of the parts. Might there not be a sense
> of the whole, a spiritual perception, by which
> the inner meaning of the Gospel would be
> revealed?[18]

This early impulse to look at things organically or holis-tically rather than analytically was to lead, years later, to Bede Griffiths's pioneering attempt to create a "marriage of East and West," or to mark out the common ground between the great religions of Asia and Europe. Before that, however, he would grapple alone for years with his seemingly eccentric spiritual impulses, not understanding that the way of life he so craved was actually available to him, even in the modern age. He would go to ascetic extremes, fasting until he became weak and ill, and praying on his knees for hours on end. He would withdraw entirely from family, friends, and society, putting his very sanity at risk. Finally, he would become a Catholic, then a Benedictine monk of Prinknash Abbey in England, and then, after several assignments that took him farther and farther north, he would discover his real life's work . . . in India.

I had to admit that I was completely captivated by this twentieth-century man who had so firmly opted out of the modern world. As a young intellectual and atheist, he seemed marked out for all the torments suffered by the dark geniuses I taught in my modern literature courses: Hemingway, Faulkner, Joyce. In Griffiths's youthful preconversion days, he reminded me a bit of my dead friend Andrew, at least in terms of his complicated psychology, his passion, and his sense of living in a state of unrelieved alienation.

He also seemed to have understood in his very bones how conventionalized and stagnant, how hypocritical and thoroughly dead much Christian practice had become by the early 1900s. Somehow, and in spite of the open scorn toward religion so prevalent within his intellectual community, he managed to both hear and respond to God's call. Where did this lead him? He found a simple, austere, and ancient way of living, a radically holy simplicity that was twice as astonishing because he was able to achieve it in an age of such hair-tearing complexity.

Bede Griffiths also became one of the first Christians in history to look with deep respect and genuine spiritual curiosity at the great religions of the East, particularly Hinduism. As a 1960s teenager, I half believed in the notion that all mainstream American religions had become hopelessly moribund—worse, that they were narrow-minded, uptight, and intolerant. If any significant improvements were to be made in the culture, I thought, they probably weren't going to be initiated by the churches.

The spiritual urge was still strong in me, whether or not I could identify it as such. Looking for some kind of answer, I read, watched, listened, and fantasized about the mysterious pilgrimages made by my youthful compatriots to "the East": Kathmandu, Varanasi, Allahabad. Where were they all going? What was *there* that was so clearly *not here?* Something, I thought, that had to do with unity instead of dogmatic wrangling. Something that might bring peace to our chaotic planet.

When the idealism of the 1960s began to unravel, I became disillusioned with the whole quest, redirecting my spiritual energy into self-fulfillment, which meant getting an education and developing a career. The natural conclusion, after the habit of religion had faded away completely, was that I must be an atheist after all.

Now, in 1998 as I read Griffiths for the first time, I wondered, What if I'd found *The Golden String* in, say, 1980, the year it was republished with a photograph of Bede Griffiths on the back, seated in his loincloth amongst the cattle and the palms of Shantivanam? Perhaps I'd have been tempted to take a second look at my so-called atheism. Perhaps I'd have thought twice about discarding "outdated" Christianity.

Maybe Griffiths still had something to teach me about contemplative living in a complicated context—about tranquility. My father's version, I'd finally, sadly, con-cluded, seemed to have been a special gift requiring a cer-tain temperament that I just did not have. Still, didn't Christ promise peace to all of us, regardless of who we were? "Peace I leave with you," he says to his disciples at the last supper; "my peace I give to you. Not as the world gives do I give it to you. Do not let your hearts be troubled or afraid" (John 14:27).

The ability to first accept, then live within this space of peace seems available in some measure to us all, regardless of natural inclination: "For my yoke is easy," he assures us, "and my burden light" (Matt. 11:30). Even for the passionate? Yea and verily, Christ seems to be saying: even for the half-mad.

As I reread *The Golden String*, I began to understand that the "half-mad" category might include Bede Griffiths himself. Like so many gifted people—Andrew, for example—he seemed to have been his own biggest chal-lenge. Biographer Shirley du Boulay highlights this lifetime struggle in *Beyond the Darkness*. Though Griffiths was forty-nine before he actually arrived in India, he spent the following thirty-eight years there, first in Kerala with a community called Kurisumala, then in Tamil Nadu at Shantivanam, or Saccidananda Ashram. From the moment he set foot on the subcontinent, he felt that he'd arrived home. Perhaps this was because India seemed to mirror his own passionate nature. As he wrote to a friend:

> In the West life has been confined within certain limits—it is civilized and rationalized. Here it is still unconfined—beneath the surface of civilization the world of nature, primeval, elastic, violent, evil, but also sacred, holy, passionate, pure and lovely is always present. It is in many ways a terrifying experience—you feel that you cannot trust anyone or anything, everything is unstable.[19]

This exciting and turbulent culture produced turbulent people, ultimately transforming even the foreigners who settled there, and at times Griffiths was overwhelmed by this. At a certain point, for example, he found himself completely unable to continue working at Kurisumala with his first prior, Fr. Francis; the tension of trying to share leadership in such a context with someone as strong-willed as himself was manifesting itself in a gastric ulcer. Later, when a young monk named Stephen turned against him at Shantivanam, he wrote, "Indians are very emotional by temperament and seem incapable of dealing rationally with any problem. . . . I am too emotional myself and the strain of it [has] made me ill."[20]

When in 1968 he was made prior of Saccidananda Ashram and was finally able to give freer rein to his creative impulses, he still found himself in conflict. As he wrote to Hugh Waterman two years into the experiment, "The life at the ashram here is not going too well, and I sometimes wonder whether I can cope with it. I don't seem to be able to keep people together and enable them to live at peace." Admitting that he was suffering from insomnia and nervous exhaustion, even in a place he utterly loved, he added, "Probably it is largely due to my temperament which you found at Eastington. I don't seem able to change myself." [21]

Even in old age, when he had become internationally famous and thousands of pilgrims had made their way to Tamil Nadu to meet him, he still struggled with an anxious irritability he'd never quite been able to conquer. Says du Boulay:

> It was usually sparked by the smallest things, for instance if he was unable to fold his shawl properly, or if, in the chapel, a cushion, a prayer book, or a lamp was not in the right position. He would indicate his irritation with a gesture and a 'Tss.' He was infuriated if the dogs barked during the office, saying, "Christudas, please get a gun and shoot them all," though one can imagine his remorse if Christudas had obeyed him. [22]

Bede Griffiths was no saint, if by saintliness one means perfect tranquility. I wondered, however, what he might have been like without his fifty years of highly disciplined spiritual life. What might he have been like without his daily meditation, a form of which (*lectio divina,* or "chewing" on the Scripture) he practiced even in his early Prinknash Abbey days back in England? Would he have ever channeled his surging passions into such useful endeavors or harnessed his boundless creative energy for serious and sustained work?

Baby Boomer Meets a Calmer Way

I had my doubts that he would have—primarily because of my years of working with talented but emotionally undisciplined young writers, but also because I'd struggled enough times in that river myself. I knew from personal experience that I could not accomplish much when everything was focused on that "frantic torrent of forceful, demanding, loud, and often unrelated thoughts" that Walsh so accurately describes. I knew how hard it was to think of others when I was caught up in my own mental drama.

I decided to finally get serious about meditating, whether I enjoyed it or not. I decided to stick with it for a long enough period—a couple of years, at least—that I could see some effects, or, perhaps, see none at all. Either way, at least I would have given it a real try.

I began by looking for a good spot in which to sit—not that easy to find, actually, in spite of the fact that the house was finally kidless. Mike is a busy man, moving purposefully from barn to garden to house, and I never knew when he might come striding in upon me without meaning to. At this early stage, for whatever reason, I was as shy about being surprised in the act of meditating as I'd once been about being caught in the bathtub.

It seemed such an . . . *exotic* sort of thing to be playing at. Not just exotic, but pretentious. I was still cowed by that image of the Zen practitioners doing zazen, that old notion of the spiritual elites.

I tried out an unused upstairs bedroom for a while, but Mike noises, whether real or imagined, kept startling me at critical moments. Then I decided to get up extremely early—at 4:00 A.M., while he was still peacefully slumbering—and set up shop on the living-room floor. This worked well for about three days, until I became so sleep deprived that my eyelids drooped the moment I sat down on the floor . . . and soon I was snoring away in a heap.

I thought of my bench beneath the jack pine, but it was too narrow to support me in the cross-legged position, and, in general, outdoors seemed too stimulating for me. Birdsong, for example, or a light breeze against my face would distract me, and pretty soon I'd be admiring nature instead of meditating. Finally, however, I thought of our old camper, parked in the back of the property under some trees and pretty much ignored until we took a trip, which didn't happen often. I unscrewed the dining table, lay the support aside, and rested my new platform on top of the facing seats. This gave me a flat, raised area plenty large enough for crossed legs.

I fashioned a pillow out of some blankets, set up a little crucifix as my focal point, and hunkered down for some serious contemplative prayer. I did not last long, however, because ten minutes into the exercise my lower back began to cramp, then call out in serious distress. My stack of blankets, though comfortable, did not begin to provide the stability I needed for a sustained sit of thirty minutes. As soon as my back began to hurt, I once again lost focus.

My sister Tina, a longtime practitioner of transcendental meditation (TM), urged me to purchase a sturdy zafu. So I went to the local health-food store, where I found a pillow, one stiff with barley husks and covered in thick material. This made all the difference, and much of my fidgeting faded away once my hips and back were tilted at the proper angle.

Something was still off, however. I knew I was supposed to be breathing in a certain way, or at least that breathing was important, but nothing felt right to me. Then, while I was on retreat at the hermitage, I met Donna, a woman who had studied meditation with a Sikh mentor for fifteen years before becoming a Camaldolese oblate. She taught me how to "belly breathe"—to fill my lungs by thrusting my abdomen out instead of pulling it in, and to empty them by pushing up against them with my diaphragm. This, she told me, should be practiced to a slow, regular count of four. Although at first it felt uncomfortable and unnatural, this technique soon began to make a difference, perhaps because I had to really focus to sustain it.

My bodily position was still a problem—despite my lovely zafu, I couldn't quite mold myself into the "rock" I needed to become for sustained sits. *The Beginner's Guide to Zen Buddhism* by Jean Smith was a great help to me; it contains a step-by-step set of instructions for achieving a good, stable posture during zazen. Among the several leg positions possible (full lotus, half lotus, the Burmese position, kneeling on a seiza bench, the horse), I found the half lotus, in which the right foot rests on the left thigh, to be most natural for me.

Whatever leg position is chosen, I discovered, the straightness of the spine is key. It helps, as Smith points out, to imagine the back of your head suspended from the ceiling by an invisible string. I found that the Zen method of holding the eyes open while keeping the gaze on the floor about two or three feet in front of me kept me awake and alert, but not distracted. I also appreciated Smith's advice for swallowers: "Place your tongue against the roof of your mouth, just where your teeth and your gums meet. This position helps prevent excessive salivation."[23]

Perhaps the most helpful tidbit, however, was her description of the hand position, known in the tradition as the *cosmic mudra.* "Your active hand . . . palm up, cradles your passive hand, and your thumbs meet about an inch below your navel, forming an oval in front of the part of your abdomen known as the hara."[24] I found that there was no quicker way to realize I'd once again galloped away on the backs of my thoughts than the collapse of my thumbs into my palms.

Traditionally, people have used mantras, or a single silently repeated word or phrase, to keep the mind at its task. Smith says that novice meditators often spend their first year or so of daily practice simply counting to ten over and over. If you find yourself at sixteen, goes the theory, you know you've been distracted. I tried this for a while, but found that the numbers themselves took too much of my attention.

Griffiths himself used a mantra, in his case the very ancient Jesus Prayer, known among the Orthodox as the "Prayer of the Heart." Much has been written on the subject, including a whole volume entitled *Writings from the Philokalia on Prayer of the Heart.* I found that there are several versions of the actual phrase, but the most basic is "Lord Jesus Christ, have mercy on me." This is the same prayer described in *The Way of the Pilgrim,* which comes out of the later hesychast (solitaries who practiced silent contemplation) tradition of Eastern Orthodoxy. Countless generations of Christian contemplatives have made use of it.

Griffiths, who meditated for two hours each day, preferred "Lord Jesus Christ, Son of the Living God, have mercy on me, a sinner." As he said in response to an inquiry, "I find that the words of the Jesus Prayer normally repeat themselves. Sometimes it goes on rather mechanically, the mind wanders; sometimes it seems to gather strength and one prays in a concentrated manner."[25] He also recommended the books of two different Cistercians, Basil Pennington and Thomas Keating, both teachers of centering prayer. The meditation teacher he admired most, however, was fellow Benedictine Fr. John Main.

According to Laurence Freeman, it was John Main who in the 1950s first recognized the similarity between Hindu meditative practices and those of the Desert Fathers. At the time, he had been trained in Hindu techniques by a teacher in the East but had been advised by his Benedictine novice master not to continue this method of prayer, which was not considered Christian. While Main was studying John Cassian's *Conferences* 9 and 10, however, he came upon a description of an imageless method of prayer that anchors itself on a repeated phrase—Cassian called this a "formula" rather than a mantra—both during specific times of meditation and throughout the day.

Cassian used the words, "God, come to my assistance. Lord, make haste to help me," words that were meant to become "part" of the monk and to lead to "prayer without ceasing." Main realized that Cassian was here talking about a practice long forgotten by the twentieth-century Western Church.[26] After his discovery, he felt called to resume the meditative discipline that had brought him to the Benedictines in the first place, ultimately becoming one of the founders of a new international Christian meditation movement. The mantra he recommended was "maranatha," which is an ancient Aramaic phrase meaning "Come Our Lord." Laurence Freeman has continued his work through the World Community of Christian Meditation.

I found that a combination of the Jesus Prayer and *maranatha* worked best for me. I began my sessions with the longer phrase, which I mentally repeated until my mind began to pay attention. Then I shifted to the far more soothing *maranatha,* which, I found, can put you to sleep if you are not careful. At times, spontaneously, this phrase would transform itself into the words "Come Lord Jesus."

Bitter Gifts

Slowly, it was becoming not exactly *easier* but definitely more natural to meditate. I found that when I had to skip a session or cut it short, I felt weirdly disjointed that day. It became increasingly important to have a permanent place, a little sanctuary set aside specifically for these prayer sessions. We figured out that we could probably move—with a crane—an old treehouse Mike had built for the kids years before. One morning Louie-the-crane-guy and six reluctant neighborhood volunteers unlashed the 8' x 10' hut from its moorings in a eucalyptus grove and swung it through the air to its new berth above the turtle pond. I swept it out, bought a Russian-looking red rug for the floor, and hung an icon of Christ over one of the windows.

Cistercian Andre Louf tells us in his classic *Teach Us to Pray* that once meditative prayer has taken root in the heart, "nothing, no one, can stem this flood inside you":

> It used to be normal for you to find that the
> time for praying was limited; because after all
> you were far too busy, despite your sincere
> desire to spend more time in prayer. Now
> prayer itself has taken all your spare time in
> tow. It is like an irresistible force, seeping
> through here, there and everywhere into your
> daily routine.[27]

In spite of my new meditation hut, this certainly had not happened to me. After yet another distracted session, I had little faith that it ever would. However, it was good to know, from the experience of people like Bede Griffiths who'd made a lifetime practice of meditation, that sometimes it actually did. That gave me hope, and by then I had begun to believe that hope might be the would-be meditator's best friend.

This was because there is a downside to contemplative prayer, though it took me a long time to figure out the link between my strange, new spiritual symptom and the fact that I was now sitting on my cushion everyday. What I began to notice was that the more time I spent in the half-lotus position under that icon of Christ, the glummer I became. The more time I spent contemplating things not of this world, the more this world with all its darkness and evil and suffering was making its presence felt. This occurred at the point when it seemed I'd most fully withdrawn from "all that." What was going on here?

Worse, the darkness began intruding at random times during the day, times when I was working away at some absorbing project or sharing a cup of coffee with Mike or lying in bed, exhausted and wanting to sleep. Suddenly the chill would descend upon me, the utterly horrifying conviction that we as a species are both too fragile and too dangerous to be loose on this earth. I would find myself literally quivering in the face of this dark truth. Strangely enough, not much of this seemed personal in the way it would if I were, say, suffering from depression. Instead, it felt more like being chained, ankle and wrist, to a mass of writhing humanity, all of us helpless and sinking beneath gray waves.

This was not good. Something had clearly gone awry with this meditation business. I made an appointment to go see my spiritual director, Fr. Isaiah.

We sat face to face in the tiny chapel just off the nave. I'd been in this room a number of times over the years—for confessions, for chatting with Fr. Bernard on nights when it was too rainy for our walk, and, on one memorable occasion, for sitting in the presence of a mystic in full trance. As Fr. Isaiah sat across from me, it was he who now looked like one of the Fathers: long beard, deep-set eyes, translucent skin—the very face of charity. I told him about my darkness problem, and (nodding and stroking the underside of his beard) he listened.

"And certain things make it worse," I added.

"Like?"

"Like having to go to L.A., for example."

"You mean the metastasized parking lot?"

I gave him a morose smile. "But it's not depression," I reminded him for the third time. "Something that feels more universal than that."

"Hmm . . . *hmm*." He was gazing up at the far corner of the room. Both elbows rested on the arms of his chair, and he'd made a little tent out of his fingers—a thinking tent. Then he dropped his hands and leaned forward. "This might sound weird," he said, "but it seems to me that what you're experiencing is a kind of gift. A *bitter* gift, for sure, but still a gift. If you can see that, it might help some."

"A gift in the sense . . . ?"

"Your hyperacute awareness of the suffering of the world. That's a gift. The alternative is more common. Blindness or denial or naiveté. But for some reason your eyes have been opened to it, and what a great thing that is."

"It doesn't *feel* so great."

"Of course it doesn't. You might try—hmm—you might try reading Isa. 35? And there's a prayer that helps. You just cross your arms and rest your palms against your shoulders, then pray that you might be crucified to the darkness with Christ and rise with him in the light. See?" He proceeded to demonstrate the hand position.

The prayer helped, as did Isa. 35; as did the person who'd gotten me started on this meditation stuff in the first place, Bede Griffiths.

The most interesting thing about this experience of universal darkness and sorrow was that strange sensation of being chained, not by choice, to the sinking mob of people. People in general had been giving me grief for a long time, but that was because I found them so . . . *disappointing*. I'd come to the reluctant but firm conclusion that most people on this planet were, in the moral and spiritual sense, a pack of sorry losers. Either they just didn't get it or they refused to care; either way, genuine goodness was such a rare commodity out there that it could make me weep when I came across it.

I longed to find good people, but it seemed that they were in lamentably short supply. Even though I wasn't such a shining example myself, at least I knew what was missing, which, I'd concluded, put me in a class pretty much by myself. The result of my self-imposed exile from the human race was a sour puckering of the soul. I had a growing conviction that, despite the handful of folks I loved to the point of distraction, I did not know a thing about Christ's kind of love.

Griffiths's answer to this terrible dilemma, the dilemma of being awakened to the beauty of holy simplicity and, at the same disappointing moment, to the reality of its absence in this world—was ultimately *advaita,* or nondual consciousness. The word itself comes from the Hindu Vedas, but he believed that there could be a Christian version in which God and creature are "not two." As he wrote to a friend:

> All meditation should lead into silence, into the world of "non-duality," when all the differences—and conflicts—in this world are transcended—not that they are simply annulled, but that they are taken up into a deeper unity of being in which all conflicts are resolved—rather like colours being absorbed into pure white light, which contains all the colours but resolves their differences.[28]

This way of seeing things is neither logical (he calls it a "mystery") nor conventional within the Christian tradition—yet to me it seemed to strike in the same zone as Jesus' strange and paradoxical statements about judgment, anger, and nonresistance to evil. I could not begin to "think" in a nondual way, as Griffiths describes it, for we are trained from birth to draw distinctions between things, to separate one thing from another, to analyze parts in order to understand the whole. Neither could I get a sense of the moral ramifications of this—how can we decide what is right and what is wrong in a nondual fashion, for example? The only place, in fact, that I could get a glimpse about what Griffiths might mean was during meditation—particularly meditation that followed one of those painful and involuntary immersions in the general suffering of the world.

Says Griffiths, "We become more ourselves as we enter more deeply into relationship with others. We do not lose ourselves but we lose our sense of separation and division."[29] It seemed to me that this sat at the heart of Griffiths's version of *advaita:* a way of seeing one another that leaps over the usual chasm that separates us. What creates that chasm? More often than not, the creators of this chasm are disappointed anger and all its cousins: irritation, resentment, fear, disgust, contempt, cold rejection.

Hesychius of Jerusalem, a practitioner of the Jesus Prayer, said of this most powerful passion:

> For the nature of anger is to be destructive. If it is moved against evil thoughts, it destroys and exterminates them; but if it is moved against men, it destroys in us good thoughts toward them. . . . For [anger] is given us by God as a shield and a bow and is such if it does not deviate from its function. But if it begins to act contrary to its function, it becomes destructive. I have seen a dog, at times a brave fighter of wolves, attack and rend sheep.[30]

Here it was in a nutshell: before I began the practice of meditation, I'd been a frequent render of sheep. Something about meditation, however, put me back where I belonged: right in the middle of the flock. Who had ever made *me* the sheepdog, anyway? Where had I gotten the notion I was somehow in a class by myself; separate and above; able, from my Olympic perch, to pass divine judgment on the entire race of man?

I began to understand that seeing the world from the nondual perspective does not mean we no longer judge, only that we naturally include ourselves in every judgment we make because we never lose sight of our essential oneness. In this shared sense of sin, failure, and anguish over our lost Eden, we can finally look at one another with genuine compassion instead of purse-lipped judgmentalism. It was this kind of snake-eyed judgmentalism, I was pretty sure, that drove Andrew to suicide. Instead, Griffiths says, "[t]hrough meditation we discover and uncover our links with the whole creation. We put ourselves into harmony with the universe and integrate ourselves with all humanity." [31]

For the first time I had a sense of how my tranquil father must have experienced those furious, imprisoned dogs—and why their anger did not frighten him. For the first time, I could fathom his secret: somehow, he'd seen himself as *one* with them.

Fr. Isaiah had been trying to clue me in on this when he called my chilling experiences of the darkness a "bitter gift." Without this sense of our mutual lostness, we cannot begin to grasp what Christ went through for the sake of love. Griffiths, who was so deeply committed to contemplative prayer, thought in his last days of nothing *but* love: "[H]e spoke only of love, love was his entire universe, the central experience of his consciousness." [32] Like St. Paul, who had also experienced the heights of meditative ecstasy, he had learned what it meant to be "called in one body" (Col. 3:15).

Because Griffiths had learned this, he could then see beyond the darkness to the light. There are no shortcuts to the transfigured vision; the way leads directly through the valley of the shadow of death. The slow and laborious practice of training the mind away from its usual pursuits opens us up to this journey. When we are discouraged, we can turn once again to St. Paul, knowing that he tracked the way before us: "For you were once darkness, but now you are light in the Lord. Live as children of light" (Eph. 5:8).

CHAPTER 11

Beginning

Empty yourself completely and sit
waiting, content with the grace of
God, like the chick who tastes nothing
and eats nothing but what his mother
brings to him.[1]

from the Brief Rule of St. Romuald (952–1027)

The Apennines are particularly lovely in mid-September. Rain blows through in the afternoon, soaking the steep green meadows, and then sunlight once again spills over the tops of the clouds. Wildflowers abound—tiny pink cyclamen, miniature snapdragon, Queen Anne's lace. The boars and the butterflies are out. In the damp earth under the beeches and firs, aggressive snouts have rooted out the truffles and porcinis; purple wings flash and dart above the carnage.

Italians love their forests, and trimmed branches lie in neat piles beneath the chestnut trees, ready to be taken away. You can stand here on a section of cobblestone Roman road, peering through a galaxy of wet black trunks at a herd of deer a quarter mile away. You can turn and put your hand against the stone wall of a five-hundred-year-old shrine, still tended: Our Lady of the Snow.

Up the road a bit, and set beside a cold and rushing stream, is a second shrine, far older. This one is dedicated to St. Romuald, accidental founder of the Camaldolese. Accidental because he never intended to found anything, did not particularly want to lead, wanted only to live a simple, contemplative, and solitary life here in these mountains where St. Francis would also someday retreat. Yet Romuald's vision, that the eremitical life of St. Anthony and the cenobitic life of St. Benedict could be happily combined, turned out to be a gift to his era. The living church, he thought, was slowly being crushed beneath the weight of pomp and circumstance. It was time to go back to the simplicity of earlier times.

I was hiking up the mountain to one of Romuald's last cells, at the Holy Hermitage of Camaldoli in Tuscany. I wanted to see it for myself because I knew it would teach me something I couldn't read about. Up ahead were a couple of oblates from Connecticut; behind me, Fr. Andrew (Andrea, in Italian), who was returning "home" this morning, back to the place he'd come thirty-some years before to be formed as a Camaldolese monk.

"It was *cold* here," he said. "I thought I would die, getting up in the dark for vigils in the winter. So much snow, and no heat in that church." I turned and looked back at him. He was shaking his head. Then came his marvelous grin. "I loved it," he said, shrugging. "The first year I thought I wasn't going to make it. But then we got a new superior. A holy man, very kind. Probably like Romuald,

I think. Then it was so beautiful, so peaceful. Still very hard, but full of love."

At thirty-five hundred feet, past the three wooden crosses that used to bar the way, the hermitage came into view: a wooden gate, a small square, a church, and a wrought-iron fence behind which twenty stone huts nestled in a walled green bowl. Our little group split apart; we all went off to sit by ourselves and think about things. Romuald's cell was not behind the iron fence, but stood open to a rose garden and darting swallows.

I went inside.

His cell consisted of a vestibule, large enough for walking when the weather was too severe to go out, and three small rooms, all smelling of dark and ancient wood; a platform bed, covered with a straw mat, built into the wall; a hatch that opened to the outside so that the daily bread and vegetables could be put through; a few shelves; and a tiny chapel with candles, flowers, an altar. I stood there, breathing in the must of ages, trying to get a feel for what it must have been like—the very simplest of simple lives.

He had no wife, no children, no career. He had no possessions of his own, and no home. He was a wandering hermit who often settled in one place no longer than it took to establish a small community of fellow hermits under the Rule. "He was a charismatic, free person who trusted in Divine Providence for all decisions," says Peter-Damian Belisle, who has written about the history of the Camaldolese. He was a "sensitive and humble" man, "living in a prophetic manner radiating holiness to others."[2] Somehow, in this cell at the Holy Hermitage and others like it scattered across Italy and Dalmatia, he found his treasure in the field.

Later that morning, after Mass with the thirteen monks who still live here (the organist, a powerful man with a fierce dark beard, I'd seen earlier splitting logs with an ax), I went into a side chapel to admire the marvelous glazed terra-cotta haut relief by Andrea della Robbia in which Romuald stands beside Mary and her baby son. Here was a face—thin, tonsured, bearded—with deep-set eyes looking off to the side at something beyond my vision. What was it?

I was suddenly filled with a thirsty curiosity I'd felt before in the presence of profoundly simple, holy people: at the Raj Ghat, for example, Gandhi's memorial tomb; before the bones of St. Francis; once, in the presence of an ancient Hopi elder. What did they see? Maybe the real question should be: How did they see? What did this complicated, frustrating, mixed-up world look like to *them?*

I didn't know, but I was certain that what they saw was critically linked to how they lived. Intellectual knowledge is never enough; wisdom at this level comes from putting one's feet on a certain kind of ground, from *physically living out* what one professes to believe.

Everything in contemporary culture mediates against this kind of "incarnated" wisdom. First, in this economic and political system, it is not really necessary to hold our own beliefs at all; it is enough to have blind faith that everything will continue to function as it should and that we will be taken care of as promised. Instead of truly living our lives, we are encouraged to exist vicariously, to lounge on comfortable sofas and fantasize while others—more beautiful, more talented, more powerful than us—act out on the screen or in magazines or books the lives we'll never even attempt to lead.

Sadly enough, this is often just as true in the church world as it is in the secular one. We now have "Christian celebrities" who sing better than we do, who preach to millions via satellite, who build enormous cathedrals of glass and found universities in their own names. We can sign up for expensive "Christian cruises" that allow us to overeat beside tropical waters while listening to famous experts on the spiritual life. We can let these people—far smarter than we are, no doubt—direct us through radio, Internet, or a dozen different TV channels.

Who are we to set forth on our own small and simple paths when it so clearly seems to be the institutions—ecclesiastical, governmental, or corporate—that really determine how life goes for us?

Dostoyevsky saw this crisis coming 140 years ago. "We are all divorced from life," he said. "We are all cripples, everyone of us, more or less. . . . Why, we have come almost to looking upon real life as an effort, almost as hard labor, and we are all privately agreed that it is better in books." Take away our books, he prophesied, and we "shall not know what to join on to, what to cling to, what to love and what to hate, what to respect and what to despise. We are oppressed at being men—men with a real individual flesh and blood."[3] Take away our DVD players, our big-screen TVs, our Internet access, our Epcot Centers, and what is left of us? How can we—actual flawed human beings—compete with the powerful, the beautiful, and the computer enhanced?

How can we begin to set our small selves against the mighty and inexorable flow?

Holy Simplicity: A Drastic Step of Faith

This was the question that stopped me cold for a long time. My conviction that something was seriously wrong with what is considered to be normal life made me restless and unhappy, but that's as far as it went. Solutions? There didn't seem to be any. I brooded help-lessly, not understanding that deep psychological unease is often the harbinger of a spiritual transformation wait-ing in the wings.

Taking those first tentative steps outside the norm—seeking out solitude, learning to keep silent—was thus exhilarating and terrifying at the same time. Sort of like, I once told a friend, floating away from a spaceship with-out a line attached to my suit. The mysterious world of deep space (the spiritual path with all its unknowns) was compelling, but I kept looking back over my shoulder to see who might still be watching for me through the port-hole. I dreaded the moment when everyone lost interest and went back to life as usual.

This was a particularly awful possibility in regard to my immediate family: my husband and companion, Mike; my stalwart kids, Andrea and Johnny; my long-suffering stepdaughters, Kelly and Greta. Though all of them were remarkably patient with me, my choices were not theirs, and at various times they let me know this. You go ahead, Mom, they'd sigh as I packed up for yet another drive to the hermitage in Big Sur. You probably need a rest from us, right?

Well, yes and no. That didn't quite sum up what it was like to be overcome by the irresistible urge to be completely alone, completely silent, and far away from the people I most loved. I couldn't really explain that. I'm sure, at times, it hurt each of them in different ways.

I'm sure it hurt Mike, especially, a man who had worked out, through years of public-school teaching, an ethical system and a way of being in the world that did good for lots of people—kids, especially. Religion? He'd quietly given that up long ago; he couldn't see that it helped much, especially the kind that pitted people against one another, as it had in our very own extended family. Though he agreed with the general notion of simplicity—he was a direct descendent of the frugal Scots, after all—my inept attempts to explain ancient ascetical practices (especially chastity) resulted in raised eyebrows and a kindly pat on the knee. "It's okay," he told me. "You've always been a thinker—you'll get it all figured it out," as though I was suffering from some kind of mental illness, I thought ruefully, and maybe I am.

Way down deep, however, I wondered: How far can I travel on this path without losing him? Without losing our easy camaraderie, our happy partnership? How far can I go without driving the kids away? Then I'd stumble, once again, across Jesus' words in Luke, "No one who sets a hand to the plow and looks to what was left behind is fit for the kingdom of God" (Luke 9:62), and I'd feel chilled with the enormity of what I was putting into motion.

Eventually, however, and all on his own, Mike redis-covered religion, this time through a new lens. In time, he set off on the path himself. Now, thanks perhaps to his natural-born Scottish bent for simple living, he's far ahead of where I'll ever be. In many ways, he's become my teacher.

This is true, also, for the kids. Each in his or her own way is discovering that we don't have to accept the status quo; we do have choices. Somehow, they survived my try-ing to turn our house into a hermitage, my nauseatingly cheerful little printed reminders stuck in every nook and cranny (Peace and blessings, kids. Please don't forget to wash your own dishes when you are done eating. Many thanks and have a good day.). Somehow, everyone sur-vived: my siblings adjusted, my friends either accepted my new path or disappeared, and my life—tipped upside down and right side up again—held together after all.

Of course, this is easier to say in retrospect. Perhaps my situation was easier than most people's. Perhaps my friends and relatives were more understanding than theirs could ever be.

Setting out in this direction is always an act of faith, however, no matter what the circumstances. It's an act of faith because stripping ourselves down this way makes us naked and vulnerable, far more open to the realities of life (the ephemeral nature of relationships, the inexorable aging process, inevitable death) without any guarantees that we'll be "happier" for doing so. We open ourselves, unshielded by a fortress of possessions or an array of awards on the wall, to the common and bittersweet fate of all human beings everywhere. We spiritually join hands with the poorest of the poor.

We do so because we've voluntarily withdrawn our faith in material wealth and social status. We no longer believe that these will or can protect us from life's most searing wounds. I know, for example, that my own circumstances could change in a moment: Mike could die, our house could burn down, terrorists could attack. My only hope is that I would still be able to find God in the midst of the wreckage; that I would wake up from the shock with my eyes still fixed on that treasure in the field; and that the hard-won lessons of the simple path might help sustain me as I struggled to rebuild.

How to Begin a Better Life

Interestingly enough, taking the first step toward holy simplicity may be the most difficult part of the process. Somehow, we sense that once we make that first move, nothing will ever be the same; and if we start, we won't be going back again. This thought can be unnerving—so unnerving that we quietly give up on the whole idea. A nice fantasy, we tell ourselves, but I'm not Buddha, after all. I'm no saint. I'd better get back to real life and forget about it.

If I were to meet someone like me at the beginning of all this, some tense and semiguilty seeker looking for what he or she could not yet identify, I would suggest the following:

Accept this cross. Figure out what to do with it. Don't deny it or fight it. It is a great gift, and (if you survive) your life will be more joyful.

Look for models. Look in books, look in movies, but most of all, look around in real life and see who else is quietly and purposefully living against the grain. Take heart: others have been this way before you.

Rediscover ancient wisdom, especially the wisdom of the Desert Fathers. Nowadays, that material is once again readily available. Think about their lives. Listen to their advice. Let their example begin to sink into you.

As Romuald once said, never leave the Psalms. "Eat" the Bible every day. Don't study, chew. Learn about *lectio divina,* the ancient meditative way of listening to the Scriptures. Nourish yourself on the Good News.

Pray, pray, pray. Pray without ceasing.

Make one change at a time. Don't rush yourself. Don't compete with anyone. Don't worry about your progress. Just keep at it. Start small and build on that: fifteen minutes of silence every morning for a year, for example, before you add the next fifteen. Understand that habits are broken slowly and new ones created over time. Don't be discouraged when you lose momentum temporarily. Just start up again.

Understand that the path of holy simplicity has a certain sweep to it. Stages must be moved through. We crawl before we walk. Keep praying for ears to hear and eyes to see. Anxiety prevents that. You'll know when it's time for the next thing. How? If you are going slowly, prayerfully, without anxiety, you'll "hear" the call when it comes.

Remember that others are affected by your trajectory. Don't let that stop you, but have compassion. Love them even when they make you angry. If they love you back, they'll stick around to see what happens. If they respect what they see, they might try it themselves.

Understand that there are dark times; times of self-doubt and discouragement; stages that feel cold; demons in the night. Remember that the simple path involves stripping. We lose social identity. We lose consoling fantasies about ourselves. We give up certain comforts and conveniences. When darkness overwhelms, read Isaiah 35 and pray to rise with Christ in the morning light.

Don't forget about the quicksand: Pride lurks. We can give up some bad habits, then fall into the worst of all: condemnation of others. Remember that love is the method and the goal. When pride catches you, go to confession, go to Mass, look for the face of Christ in the boy with the spiked hair and earrings.

Find a spiritual director, somebody who has lived the path. Credentials are irrelevant. If your ears are starting to hear and your eyes to see, you'll know when this person crosses your path.

Understand that you yourself will one day teach others. You are in training for some serious work in the world. Whatever you are doing now will be transformed into something else you can't predict. Do not be afraid. And pray without ceasing.

> In the beginning was the Word,
> and the Word was with God,

and the Word was God.
He was in the beginning with God.
All things came to be through him,
    and without him nothing came to be.
What came to be through him was life,
    and this life was the light of the human
        race;
the light shines in the darkness,
    and the darkness has not overcome it.
    (John 1:1–5)

Or, in the words of Christ himself: "I came so that they might have life and have it more abundantly" (John 10:10). Stretch out your hand and take the gift. Live.

Notes

Introduction

1. Paul Evdokimov, *Ages of the Spiritual Life,* 158.

2. Quoted in Peter-Damian Belisle, ed., *The Privilege of Love: Camaldolese Benedictine Spirituality,* 87.

3. Paul Evdokimov, op. cit., 75.

4. Ibid., 75.

5. Ibid., 189.

6. Ibid., 102.

Chapter 1
Solitude: The Way of the Hermit

1. Benedicta Ward, *The Sayings of the Desert Fathers: The Alphabetical Collection,* 3.

2. Information about St. Anthony's life is taken from Henri Queffélec, *Saint Anthony of the Desert,* 13–65, and Peter F. Anson, *The Call of the Desert: The Solitary Life in the Christian Church,* 13–15.

Chapter 2
Silence: The Way of the Cenobite

1. Armand Veilleux, trans., *Pachomian Chronicles and Rules,* 156, 160.

2. From the *Bohairic Life of Pachomius.* Quoted in Armand Veilleux, trans., *The Life of Saint Pachomius and His Disciples,* 146.

3. Ibid., 25.

4. Ibid., 27.

5. Ibid., 27.

6. Ibid., 28.

7. Ibid., 28–29.

8. From the *First Sahidic Life of Pachomius.* Quoted in Armand Veilleux, trans., *The Life of Saint Pachomius and His Disciples,* 432.

9. Armand Veilleux, trans., *The Life of Saint Pachomius and His Disciples,* xx.

10. Ibid., 146.

11. Ibid., 150.

12. Ibid., 156.

13. Ibid., 156.

14. Ambrose Wathen, *Silence: The Meaning of Silence in the Rule of St. Benedict,* ix–x.

15. Morton Kelsey, *The Other Side of Silence: A Guide to Christian Meditation,* 94.

16. Ibid., 100.

17. Ambrose Wathen, *Silence,* xii.

18. Matt. 11:15; 13:9; 13:43; Mark 4:9; Luke 8:8; 14:35.

19. Armand Veilleux, *Life of Saint Pachomius,* 147.

20. Ambrose Wathen, *Silence,* xii.

21. Ibid., 13–17.

22. E. Kadloubovsky and G. E. H. Palmer, *Writings from the Philokalia on Prayer of the Heart,* 186.

23. Ibid., 58.

Chapter 3
Awareness: The Way of the Ascetic

1. John Cassian, *The Monastic Institutes, Consisting of "On the Training of a Monk" and "The Eight Deadly Sins" (in Twelve books)*, 108.

2. Ibid., 76.

3. Columba Stewart, *Cassian the Monk*, 42.

4. Ibid., 42.

5. Information about Cassian's life is taken primarily from Columba Stewart, *Cassian the Monk*, 3–26.

6. Armand Veilleux, *The Life of Saint Pachomius and His Disciples*, 30.

7. Jacques Lacarriere, *Men Possessed by God: The Story of the Desert Monks of Ancient Christendom*, 210.

8. Adalbert de Vogüé, *To Love Fasting: The Monastic Experience*, 8–9.

9. Ibid., 10.

10. John Cassian, *The Monastic Institutes*, 83.

11. Adalbert de Vogüé, *To Love Fasting*, 10.

12. Ibid., 10.

13. Ibid., 26.

14. John Cassian, *The Monastic Institutes*, 73.

15. Plato, *Republic*, 6.

16. John Cassian, *The Monastic Institutes*, 83.

17. Ibid., 109–110.

18. E. F. Schumacher, *Small Is Beautiful: Economics As If People Mattered*, 32.

19. Ibid., 32.

20. Laurence Freeman, "Purity of Heart: Discovering What You Really Want," in *Purity of Heart and Contemplation,* ed. Bruno Barnhart and Joseph Wong, 247.

21. Duane Elgin, *Voluntary Simplicity: Toward a Way of Life That Is Outwardly Simple, Inwardly Rich,* 137.

22. Ibid., 137.

23. Columba Stewart, *Cassian the Monk,* 46.

24. David Fagerberg, "Time in the Desert Fathers," *ABR* 50:2, 195.

25. Columba Stewart, *Cassian the Monk,* 41.

26. E. Kadloubovsky and G. E. H. Palmer, *Writings from the Philokalia on Prayer of the Heart,* 59.

Chapter 4
Purity: The Way of the Celibate

1. St. Augustine, *Enchiridian of Faith, Hope and Love,* 139.

2. St. Augustine, *The Confessions,* 67.

3. Ibid., 70.

4. Ibid., 65.

5. Ibid., 77.

6. Ibid., 150.

7. Ibid., 150.

8. Ibid., 154.

9. Ibid., 193.

10. Ibid., 194.

11. Ibid., 202.

12. Romans 13:13–14. Quoted in St. Augustine, *The Confessions,* 202.

13. St. Augustine, *The Confessions,* 202.

14. Iris Murdoch, "The Sovereignty of Good over Other Concepts," in *Existentialists and Mystics: Writings on Philogophy and Literature,* 384.

15. Ibid., 384.

16. St. Augustine, *The Confessions,* 43.

17. St. Augustine, *Treatises on Various Subjects,* 213.

18. Ibid., 202.

19. St. Augustine, *The Confessions,* 256.

20. St. Augustine, *Treatises on Various Subjects,* 189.

21. Laurence Freeman, "Purity of Heart: Discovering What You Really Want," in *Purity of Heart,* 253.

22. St. Augustine, *Treatises on Various Subjects,* 208.

23. St. Augustine, *The Confessions,* 254.

24. St. Augustine, *The Enchiridion of Faith, Hope and Love,* 140.

25. Laurence Freeman, "Purity of Heart," 258

26. Ibid., 258.

27. Bede Healey, "On the Recreating of Desire and Purity of Heart," in *Purity of Heart,* 265.

28. Ibid.

29. Benedicta Ward, *Harlots of the Desert: A Study of Repentance in Early Monastic Sources,* 59.

30. St. Augustine, *The Enchiridion of Faith, Hope and Love,* 139.

Chapter 5
Devtion: The Way of the Psalm Singer

1. Timothy Fry, ed., *The Rule of St. Benedict,* 28.

2. *American Heritage Dictionary,* 2nd college ed., s.v. "devotee."

3. Alasdair MacIntyre, *After Virtue: A Study in Moral Theory,* 263.

4. Information about St. Benedict's life is taken chiefly from Theodore Maynard, *Saint Benedict and His Monks*, and Dom Hubert Van Zeller, *The Benedictine Idea*.

5. From St. Gregory the Great, *Dialogues*. Quoted in *St. Benedict and His Order: A Brief History*, www.christdesert.org/noframes/scholar/benedict/benedict_history.html.

6. Hubert Van Zeller, *The Benedictine Idea*, 3.

7. *St. Benedict and His Order*.

8. Paul Delatte, commentary on *The Rule of St. Benedict*, 170.

9. Adalbert de Vogüé, *The Rule of Saint Benedict: A Doctrinal and Spiritual Commentary*, 132.

10. Ibid., 133.

11. Anne M. Field, ed., *The Monastic Hours: Directory for the Celebration of the Work of God and Directive Norms for the Celebration of the Monastic Liturgy of the Hours*, 26.

12. Adalbert de Vogüé, *The Rule of Saint Benedict*, 134.

13. Anne M. Field, ed., *The Monastic Hours*, 25.

14. Ibid., 44.

15. Ibid., 33.

16. E. Kadloubovsky and G. E. H. Palmer, eds., *Writings from the Philokalia*, 244.

17. Fyodor Dostoyevsky, *The Idiot*, 368.

18. Josef A. Jungmann, *The Early Liturgy to the Time of Gregory the Great*, 16–17.

19. Paul Delatte, *Commentary*, 131.

20. Ibid., 129. Taken almost verbatim from Cassian's *Institutes IV*, xxxix.

21. Bruno Barnhart, "Christian Self-Understanding in the Light of the East," in *Purity of Heart*, 300.

22. Ibid., 301.

23. Timothy Fry, ed., *The Rule of Saint Benedict,* 28.

24. Donald Corcoran, "Benedictine Humility and Confucian 'Sincerity,'" in *Purity of Heart,* 238.

25. Gregory the Great, *Life and Miracles of St. Benedict, Book Two of the Dialogues.* Quoted in Donald Corcoran, op. cit., 238.

Chapter 6
Right Livelihood: The Way of the Laborer

1. Aelred Squire, *Aelred of Rievaulx: A Study,* 56.

2. Henry Adams, *Mont-Saint Michel and Chartres,* 8.

3. Louis J. Lekai, *The White Monks: A History of the Cistercian Order,* 11.

4. Ibid., 9.

5. Thomas Merton, *The Seven Storey Mountain,* 392.

6. Ibid., 393.

7. Information about Aelred's life is taken primarily from Amedee Hallier, *The Monastic Theology of Aelred of Rievaulx: An Experiential Theology,* and Aelred Squire, *Aelred of Rievaulx: A Study.*

8. Amedee Hallier, *The Monastic Theology,* 35.

9. Ibid., 35.

10. Aelred Squire, *Aelred,* 126.

11. Amedee Hallier, *The Monastic Theology,* 13.

12. Ibid., 36.

13. Ibid., 44.

14. Aelred Squire, *Aelred,* 68.

15. Amedee Hallier, *The Monastic Theology,* 109.

16. Glyn Coppack and Peter Fergusson, *Rievaulx Abbey,* 9.

17. Amedee Hallier, *The Monastic Theology,* 50.

18. Aelred Squire, *Aelred,* 2.

19. Ibid., 136.

20. Ibid., 59.

21. Francis Kline, *Lovers of the Place: Monasticism Loose in the Church,* 97.

22. Ibid., 96.

23. Thomas Merton, *The Seven Storey Mountain,* 316.

24. Aelred Squire, *Aelred,* 126.

25. Amedee Hallier, *The Monastic Theology,* 36.

Chapter 7
Confidence: The Way of the Mendicant

1. Paschal Robinson, trans., *The Writings of Saint Francis of Assisi,* 42.

2. Gerard Straub, *The Sun and Moon over Assisi: A Personal Encounter with Francis and Clare,* 40.

3. Ibid., 302.

4. Paul Sabatier, *The Life of St. Francis of Assisi,* 33.

5. Ibid., 31.

6. Quoted in Paul Sabatier, *The Life of St. Francis,* 16.

7. Ibid., 52.

8. Paul Sabatier, *The Life of St. Francis,* 55.

9. Ibid., 61.

10. Paschal Robinson, *The Writings of Saint Francis of Assisi,* 32.

11. Ibid., 33.

12. Ibid., 40.

13. Ibid., 42.

14. Ibid., 41.

15. Ibid., 43.

16. Quoted in Reginald Garrigou-Lagrange, *Providence*, 234.

17. Ibid., 236.

18. Ibid., 235.

19. Aldous Huxley, *The Perennial Philosophy*, 107.

20. Helen Bacovcin, trans., *The Way of the Pilgrim and the Pilgrim Continues His Way*, 57.

21. Nicholas Arseniev, *Mysticism and the Eastern Church*, 42–43.

22. Dallas Willard, *The Divine Conspiracy: Rediscovering Our Hidden Life in God*, 66.

23. Paul Sabatier, *The Life of St. Francis*, 305.

24. Gerard Straub, *The Sun and Moon*, 288.

25. Quoted in Gerard Straub, *The Sun and Moon*, 336.

Chapter 8
Integrity: The Way of the Reformer

1. Quoted in Giuliana Cavallini, *Catherine of Siena*, 113.

2. Quoted in Annette T. Rottenberg, *Elements of Argument: A Text and Reader*, 710.

3. Brian Wilkie and James Hurt, eds., *Literature of the Western World*, 1032.

4. Thomas Bokenkotter, *A Concise History of the Catholic Church*, 160–161.

5. Ibid., 161.

6. Ibid., 164.

7. Annette T. Rottenberg, *Elements of Argument*, 699.

8. Ibid., 703.

9. Cavallini, *Catherine of Siena*, 80.

10. Ibid., 108.

11. Ibid., 114.

12. Ibid., 100.

13. Ibid., 101.

14. Ibid., 11.

15. Ibid., 127.

16. Ibid., 122.

17. Ibid., 13.

18. Ibid., 22.

19. Ibid., 129.

20. Ibid., 153.

Chapter 9
Generosity: The Way of the Servant

1. William J. Young, trans., *Letters of St. Ignatius of Loyola*, 158.

2. "Contemplation to Gain Love," *The Spiritual Exercises of St. Ignatius of Loyola*, www.ccel.org/i/ignatius/exercises/exercises1.0. html.

3. Robert Inchausti, *Thomas Merton's American Prophecy*, 147.

4. Ibid., 64.

5. Saint Ignacio de Loyola, *The Autobiography of St. Ignatius Loyola, with Related Documents*, 21.

6. Ibid., 23.

7. Ibid., 24.

8. Ibid., 24.

9. Ibid., 30.

10. Ibid., 37.

11. Ibid., 39.

12. Ibid., 67.

13. Paul Mariani, *Thirty Days: On Retreat With the Exercises of St. Ignatius,* 5.

14. Ibid., 10.

15. Ibid., 281.

16. Ibid., 82–83.

17. Patrick Henry, ed., *Benedict's Dharma: Buddhists Reflect on the Rule of Saint Benedict,* 23.

18. Saint Ignacio de Loyola, *The Autobiography,* 105.

19. "Contemplation to Gain Love."

Chapter 10
Tranquility: The Way of the Contemplative

1. Peter Spink, ed., *Bede Griffiths: Selections from His Writings,* 59.

2. Quoted in Duane Elgin, *Voluntary Simplicity,* 126.

3. Harriet A. Luckman and Linda Kulzer, *Purity of Heart in Early Ascetic and Monastic Literature: Essays in Honor of Juana Raasch, O.S.B.,* 186.

4. Ibid., 187.

5. Peter Spink, *Bede Griffiths,* 42

6. Shirley du Boulay, *Beyond the Darkness: A Biography of Bede Griffiths,* 4.

7. Ibid., 10.

8. Ibid., 11.

9. Ibid., 13.

10. William Wordsworth, "Lines Composed a Few Miles Above Tintern Abbey on Revisiting the Banks of the Wye During a Tour, July 13, 1798," Brian Wilkie and James Hurt, *Literature of the Western World,* 627.

11. Bede Griffiths, *The Golden String: An Autobiography,* 9.

12. Ibid., 9.

13. Ibid., 40.

14. Ibid., 39.

15. Ibid., 66.

16. Ibid., 69.

17. Ibid., 83.

18. Ibid., 97.

19. Shirley du Boulay, *Beyond the Darkness,* 142.

20. Ibid., 151.

21. Ibid., 150.

22. Ibid., 195.

23. Jean Smith, *The Beginner's Guide to Zen Buddhism,* 17.

24. Ibid., 17.

25. Shirley du Bouley, *Beyond the Darkness,* 173.

26. "Christian Meditation with Laurence Freeman," in Lawrence G. Muller, *Wisdom Roads: Conversations with Remarkable Meditation Masters,* 18.

27. Andre Louf, *Teach Us to Pray,* 105.

28. Shirley du Boulay, *Beyond the Darkness,* 175.

29. Peter Spink, *Bede Griffiths,* 33.

30. E. Kadloubovsky and G. E. H. Palmer, *Writings from the Philokalia on Prayer of the Heart,* 285.

31. Peter Spink, *Bede Griffiths,* 27.

32. Shirley du Boulay, *Beyond the Darkness,* 262.

Chapter 11
Beginning

1. Quoted in Peter-Damian Belisle, ed., *The Privilege of Love: Camaldolese Benedictine Spirituality,* 87.

2. Peter-Damian Belisle, "Overview of Camaldolese History and Spirituality," in *The Privilege of Love,* 7.

3. Fyodor Dostoyevsky, *Notes from the Underground,* in Brian Wilkie and James Hurt, *Literature of the Western World,* 1077.

Bibliography

Adams, Henry. *Mont-Saint Michel and Chartres*. Boston: Houghton Mifflin, 1963.

Aelred of Rievaulx. *The Mirror of Charity*. Translated by Elizabeth Connor, O.C.S.O. Kalamazoo, Mich.: Cistercian Publications, 1990.

Anson, Peter F. *The Call of the Desert: The Solitary Life in the Christian Church*. London: S.P.C.K., 1964.

Arseniev, Nicholas. *Mysticism and the Eastern Church*. Translated by Arthur Chambers. Crestwood, N.Y.: St. Vladimir's Seminary Press, 1979.

Augustine, St. *The Confessions of St. Augustine*. Translated by John K. Ryan. New York: Image Books, 1960.

———. *Enchiridian of Faith, Hope and Love*. Edited by Henry Paolucci. Washington, D.C.: Regnery Gateway, 1961.

———. *Treatises on Various Subjects*. Vol. 14, *The Fathers of the Church*. Editorial director, Roy Joseph Defarrari. Washington, D.C.: The Catholic University of America Press, 1952.

Bacovcin, Helen, trans. *The Way of a Pilgrim and The Pilgrim Continues His Way*. New York: Doubleday, 1978.

Barnhart, Bruno, and Joseph Wong, eds. *Purity of Heart and Contemplation: A Monastic Dialogue between Christian and Asian Traditions*. New York: Continuum, 2001.

Belisle, Peter-Damian, O.S.B.Cam., ed. *The Privilege of Love: Camaldolese Benedictine Spirituality.* Collegeville, Minn.: The Liturgical Press, 2002.

Bokenkotter, Thomas. *A Concise History of the Catholic Church.* Revised ed. New York: Doubleday, 1990.

Burton-Christie, Douglas. *The Word in the Desert: Scripture and the Quest for Holiness in Early Christian Monasticism.* New York: Oxford University Press, 1993.

Cavallini, Giuliana, O.P. *Catherine of Siena.* London: Geoffrey Chapman, 1998.

Cassian, John, Abbot of Marseilles. *The Monastic Institutes Consisting of "On the Training of a Monk" and "The Eight Deadly Sins" (in Twelve Books).* Translated by Fr. Jerome Bertram of the Oxford Oratory. London: Saint Austin Press, 1999.

Chadwick, Owen. *The Making of the Benedictine Ideal.* Washington, D.C.: St. Anselm's Abbey, 1981.

Chitty, Derwas, trans. *The Letters of St. Anthony the Great.* Oxford: SLG Press, n.d.

Clément, Olivier. *Conversations with Ecumenical Patriarch Bartholomew I.* Translated by Paul Meyendorff. Crestwood, N.Y.: St. Vladimir's Seminary Press, 1997.

———. *On Human Being: A Spiritual Anthropology.* Translated by Jeremy Hummerstone. New York: New City Press, 2000.

Coppack, Glyn, and Peter Fergusson. *Rievaulx Abbey.* Swindon, England: English Heritage Publications, 1994, 1997, 2000.

Dean, Eric. *Saint Benedict for the Laity.* Collegeville, Minn.: The Liturgical Press, 1989.

Delatte, Dom Paul, O.S.B., Abbot of Solesmes and Superior-General of the Congregation of Benedictines in France. *The Rule of Saint Benedict.* Translated by Dom Justin McCann. Latrobe, Penn.: The Archabbey Press, 1921 and 1959.

De Vogüé, Adalbert, Monk of La Pierre-qui-vire. *To Love Fasting: The Monastic Experience.* Translated by Jean Baptist Hasbrouck, O.C.S.O. Petersham, Mass.: Saint Bede's Publications, 1989.

———. *The Rule of Saint Benedict: A Doctrinal and Spiritual Commentary.* Translated by Jean Baptist Hasbrouck, Monk of Our Lady of Guadalupe Abbey. Cistercian Studies Series, 54. Kalamazoo, Mich.: Cistercian Publications, 1983.

De Waal, Esther. *The Way of Simplicity: The Cistercian Tradition.* Traditions of Christian Spirituality Series. Series editor Philip Sheldrake. New York: Orbis Books, 1998.

Dostoyevsky, Fyodor. *The Idiot.* New York: Bantam, n.d.

Du Boulay, Shirley. *Beyond the Darkness: A Biography of Bede Griffiths.* New York: Doubleday, 1998.

Elgin, Duane. *Voluntary Simplicity: Toward a Way of Life That Is Outwardly Simple, Inwardly Rich.* New York: Quill, 1993.

Englebert, Omer. *Saint Francis of Assisi: A Biography.* 2nd English ed. Chicago: Franciscan Herald Press, n.d.

Evdokimov, Paul. *Ages of the Spiritual Life.* Translated by Michael Plekon and Alexis Vinogradov. Crestwood, N.Y.: St. Vladimir's Seminary Press, 1998.

Fagerberg, David. "Time in the Desert Fathers." *ABR* 50:2, June 1999, 180–202.

Field, Anne M., O.S.B, ed. *The Monastic Hours: Directory for the Celebration of the Work of God and Directive Norms for the Celebration of the Monastic Liturgy of the Hours.* 2nd ed. Collegeville, Minn.: The Liturgical Press, 1981 and 2000.

Fry, Timothy, O.S.B., ed. *The Rule of St. Benedict.* New York: Vintage, 1981.

Garrigou-Lagrange, The Rev. Reginald, O.P. *Providence.* St. Louis: B. Herder Book Co., 1953.

Griffiths, Bede. *The Golden String: An Autobiography.* Springfield, Ill.: Templegate Publishers, 1954 and 1980.

———. *A New Vision of Reality: Western Science, Eastern Mysticism, and Christian Faith.* Edited by Felicity Edwards. Springfield, Ill.: Templegate Publishers, 1989.

Griffiths, Bede. *Christ in India: Essays Towards a Hindu-Christian Dialogue.* Springfield, Ill.: Templegate Publishers, 1966, 1984.

Hallier, Amedee, O.C.S.O. *The Monastic Theology of Aelred of Rievaulx: An Experiential Theology.* Translated by Columban Heaney, O.C.S.O. Translations of Aelred's works by Hugh McCaffery, O.C.S.O. Shannon, Ireland: Irish University Press, 1969.

Halligan, Frederica R., and John J. Shea. *The Fires of Desire: Erotic Energies and the Spiritual Quest.* New York: Crossroads, 1992.

Harton, F. P. *The Elements of the Spiritual life: A Study in Ascetical Theology.* London: S.P.C.K, 1957.

Henry, Patrick, ed. *Benedict's Dharma: Buddhists Reflect on the Rule of Saint Benedict.* New York: Riverhead Books, 2001.

Huxley, Aldous. *The Perennial Philosophy.* New York: Harper and Row, 1944.

Inchausti, Robert L. *Thomas Merton's American Prophecy.* New York: SUNY Press, 1998.

"Introduction to the Rule for Camaldolese Benedictine Oblates." Adapted from the *Camaldolese Constitutions.*

Jung, Carl. *Modern Man in Search of a Soul.* New York: Harcourt Brace, 1933.

Jungman, Josef A. *The Early Liturgy to the Time of Gregory the Great.* Translated by Francis A. Brunner, C.S.S.R. *Liturgical Studies.* Notre Dame, Ind.: University of Notre Dame Press, 1959.

Kadloubovsky, E., and G. E. H. Palmer, trans. *Writings from the Philokalia on Prayer of the Heart.* London: Faber and Faber, 1952, 1992.

Kelsey, Morton T. *Companions on the Inner Way: The Art of Spiritual Guidance.* New York: Crossroad, 1996.

———. *God, Dreams, and Revelation: A Christian Interpretation of Dreams.* Revised ed. Minneapolis, Minn.: Augsburg, 1991.

———. *The Other Side of Silence: A Guide to Christian Meditation.* New York: Paulist Press, 1976.

Kline, Francis, O.C.S.O. *Lovers of the Place: Monasticism Loose in the Church.* Collegeville, Minn.: The Liturgical Press, 1989.

Lacarriere, Jacques. *Men Possessed by God: The Story of the Desert Monks of Ancient Christendom.* Translated by Roy Monkcom. Garden City, N.Y.: Doubleday, 1964.

Lawrence of the Resurrection, Brother. *The Practice of the Presence of God.* Translated by Donald Attwater. Springfield, Ill.: Templegate, 1974.

Lea, Henry Charles, L.L.D., S.T.D. *History of Sacerdotal Celibacy in the Christian Church.* Vol. 2. 3rd ed., rev. New York: MacMillan, 1907.

Lekai, Louis J., Ph.D., S.O. Cist. *The White Monks: A History of the Cistercian Order.* Okauchee, Wis.: Cistercian Fathers, 1953.

Louf, Andre. *Teach Us to Pray.* Translated by Hubert Hoskins. Cambridge: Cowley Publications, 1992.

Loyola, Saint Ignacio. *The Autobiography of St. Ignatius Loyola, with Related Documents.* Translated by Joseph F. O'Callaghan and edited by John C. Olin. New York: Harper and Row, 1974.

Luckman, Harriet A., and Linda Kulzer, O.S.B., eds. *Purity of Heart in Early Ascetic and Monastic Literature: Essays in Honor of Juana Raasch, O.S.B.* Collegeville, Minn.: The Liturgical Press, 1999.

MacIntyre, Alasdair. *After Virtue: A Study in Moral Theory.* 2nd ed. Notre Dame, Ind.: University of Notre Dame Press, 1997.

Magnificat 4:8 (October 2002).

Mariani, Paul. *Thirty Days: On Retreat with the Exercises of St. Ignatius.* New York: Viking Compass, 2002.

Maynard, Theodore. *Saint Benedict and His Monks.* London: Staples Press Limited, 1956.

Merton, Thomas. *The Seven Storey Mountain.* New York: Harcourt Brace, 1948.

Mitchell, Leonel L. *The Meaning of Ritual.* New York: Paulist Press, 1977.

Muller, Lawrence G. *Wisdom Roads: Conversations with Remarkable Meditation Masters.* New York: Continuum, 2000.

Murdoch, Iris. "The Sovereignty of Good over Other Concepts." *Existentialists and Mystics: Writings on Philosophy and Literature.* London: Allen Lane, The Penguin Press, 1998.

Plato. *The Republic.* Translated by Robin Waterfield. Oxford: Oxford University Press, 1994.

Queffélec, Henri. *Saint Anthony of the Desert.* Translated by James Whitall. New York: Dutton, 1954.

Robinson, Fr. Paschal, trans. *The Writings of Saint Francis of Assisi.* Philadelphia: The Dolphin Press, 1951.

Rolheiser, Ronald. *The Holy Longing: The Search for a Christian Spirituality.* New York: Doubleday, 1999.

Rottenberg, Annette T. *Elements of Argument: A Text and Reader.* 5th ed. Boston: Bedford Books, 1997.

Russell, Norman, trans. *The Lives of the Desert Fathers: The Historia Monachorum in Aegypto.* Cistercian Studies Series, 34. Kalamazoo, Mich.: Cistercian Publications, 1980.

Sabatier, Paul. *The Life of St. Francis of Assisi.* Translated by Louis Seymour Houghton. New York: Charles Scribner's Sons, 1928.

Schmemann, Alexander. *Church, World, Mission: Reflections on Orthodoxy in the West.* Crestwood, N.Y.: St. Vladimir's Seminary Press, 1979.

Schumacher, E. F. *Small Is Beautiful: Economics As If People Mattered.* New York: Perennial Library, 1989.

Smith, Jean. *The Beginner's Guide to Zen Buddhism.* New York: Bell Tower, 2000.

Sophrony, Archimandrite. *His Life Is Mine.* Translated by Rosemary Edmonds. Crestwood, N.Y.: St. Vladimir's Seminary Press, 1977.

Spink, Peter, ed. *Bede Griffiths: Selections from His Writings.* The Modern Spirituality Series. Springfield, Ill.: Templegate Publishers, 1992.

Squire, Aelred, O.P. *Aelred of Rievaulx: A Study.* London: S.P.C.K., 1981.

Straub, Gerard Thomas. *The Sun and Moon over Assisi: A Personal Encounter with Francis and Clare.* Cincinnati: St. Anthony Messenger Press, 2000.

Stewart, Columba. *Cassian the Monk.* Oxford Studies in Historical Theology. New York: Oxford University Press, 1998.

Taylor, Charles. *Sources of the Self: The Making of the Modern Identity.* Cambridge: Cambridge University Press, 1989.

Van Zeller, Dom Hubert. *The Benedictine Idea.* Springfield, Ill.: Templegate, 1959.

Veilleux, Armand, Monk of Mistassini, trans. *The Life of Saint Pachomius and His Disciples.* Vol. 1, *Pachomian Koinonia.* Cistercian Studies Series, 45. Kalamazoo, Mich.: Cistercian Publications, 1980.

———, trans. *Pachomian Chronicles and Rules.* Vol. 2 of *Pachomian Koinonia.* Cistercian Studies Series, 46. Kalamazoo, Mich.: Cistercian Publications, 1981.

Wathen, Ambrose G., O.S.B. *Silence: The Meaning of Silence in the Rule of St. Benedict.* Washington, D.C.: Cistercian Publications, 1973.

Ward, Benedicta, S.L.G. *Harlots of the Desert: A Study of Repentence in Early Monastic Sources.* Kalamazoo, Mich.: Cistercian Publications, 1987.

———. *The Sayings of the Desert Fathers: The Alphabetical Collection.* Cistercian Studies Series. Kalamazoo, Mich.: Cistercian Publications, 1975.

Ware, Bishop Kallistos. *The Inner Kingdom.* Vol. 1, *The Collected Works.* Crestwood, N.Y.: St. Vladimir's Seminary Press, 2000.

Weil, Simone. *Waiting for God.* Translated by Emma Craufurd. New York: Harper and Row (G.P. Putnam's Sons), 1951.

Wilkie, Brian, and James Hurt, eds. *Literature of the Western World.* Vol. 2. 4th ed. Upper Saddle River, N.J.: Prentice Hall, 1997.

Willard, Dallas. *The Divine Conspiracy: Rediscovering Our Hidden Life in God.* San Francisco: HarperSanFrancisco, 1998.

Young, William J., S.J. *Letters of St. Ignatius of Loyola.* Chicago: Loyola University Press, 1959.

Zagano, Phyllis. *Woman to Woman: An Anthology of Women's Spiritualities.* Collegeville, Minn.: The Liturgical Press, 1993.

Index